3rd Workshop on Knowledge Extraction and Integration for Deep Learning Architectures (DeeLIO 2022)

Deep Learning Inside Out

Dublin, Ireland
27 May 2022

ISBN: 978-1-7138-6733-3

Printed from e-media with permission by:

Curran Associates, Inc.
57 Morehouse Lane
Red Hook, NY 12571

Some format issues inherent in the e-media version may also appear in this print version.

Association for Computational Linguistics
209 N. Eighth Street
Stroudsburg, Pennsylvania 18360

Phone: 1-570-476-8006
Fax: 1-570-476-0860

acl@aclweb.org

Additional copies of this publication are available from:

Curran Associates, Inc.
57 Morehouse Lane
Red Hook, NY 12571 USA
Phone: 845-758-0400
Fax: 845-758-2633
Email: curran@proceedings.com
Web: www.proceedings.com

DeeLIO 2022

Deep Learning Inside Out (DeeLIO 2022): The 3rd Workshop on Knowledge Extraction and Integration for Deep Learning Architectures

Proceedings of the Workshop

May 27, 2022

Preface

Welcome to the Third Workshop on Knowledge Extraction and Integration for Deep Learning Architectures! Following the previous two successful editions of the workshop at EMNLP 2020 and NAACL-HLT 2021, DeeLIO 2022 continues to bring together the knowledge interpretation, extraction and integration lines of research in deep learning, and to cover the area in between. Now in its third year, DeeLIO is an established forum for the exchange of ideas on these topics, fostering collaboration within these research fields.

The year 2022 has introduced the first hybrid edition of the workshop after two fully virtual events. Following the changes in *ACL Conference organization, DeeLIO 2022 has undergone some other core changes as well, including the full transfer of the reviewing process to the OpenReview platform, and the opportunity to commit papers previously evaluated through the ACL Rolling Review process.

This volume includes the 10 papers presented at the workshop as posters. We received a batch of high-quality research papers, and decided to finally accept 7 out of 14 fully reviewed submissions, and 3 out of 7 committed submissions. DeeLIO 2022 was co-located with the 60th Annual Meeting of the Association for Computational Linguistics (ACL 2022) and was held on May 27, 2022 as a hybrid workshop.

It is again great to see that the accepted papers cover both thematic axes of DeeLIO: the extraction of linguistic knowledge from deep neural models as well as the integration of knowledge from external resources into the models, and all this for different languages and applications. All papers were presented as posters during on-site and virtual poster sessions with live interactions and Q&A sessions.

We take this opportunity to thank the DeeLIO program committee for their help and thorough reviews. We also thank the authors who presented their work at DeeLIO, and the workshop participants for the valuable feedback and discussions. Encouraged by the great research presented at the workshop and all the positive feedback received, we hope to continue with the DeeLIO organization in the years to come. Finally, we are deeply honored to have three excellent talks from our invited speakers Yejin Choi, Allyson Ettinger, and Tal Linzen.

The DeeLIO workshop organizers,

Eneko Agirre, Marianna Apidianaki, and Ivan Vulić

Organizing Committee

Workshop Chairs

Eneko Agirre, University of the Basque Country
Marianna Apidianaki, University of Pennsylvania
Ivan Vulić, University of Cambridge & PolyAI

Invited Speakers

Yejin Choi, AI2 and University of Washington
Allyson Ettinger, University of Chicago
Tal Linzen, New York University

Program Committee

Program Committee

Abdellah Fourtassi, Aix-Marseille University
Aina Garí Soler, Télécom-Paris
Aishwarya Kamath, New York University
Aitor Soroa, University of the Basque Country
Alessio Miaschi, University of Pisa
Anne Cocos, Iggy
Anne Lauscher, Bocconi University
Carolin Lawrence, NEC Labs
Davide Buscaldi, Université Paris 13
Deyi Xiong, Tianjin University
Fangyu Liu, University of Cambridge
Ilias Chalkidis, University of Copenhagen
Jonas Pfeiffer, New York University
Leonardo F.R. Ribeiro, TU Darmstadt
Linzi Xing, University of British Columbia
Maria Becker, University of Heidelberg
Prodromos Malakasiotis, Institute of Informatics & Telecommunications, NCSR Demokritos
Qianchu Liu, University of Cambridge
Roi Reichart, Technion, IIT
Simone Paolo Ponzetto, University of Mannheim
Steven Schockaert, University of Cardiff
Vered Shwartz, University of British Columbia

Table of Contents

Program

Friday, May 27, 2022

09:20 - 09:30 *Opening Remarks*

09:30 - 10:30 *Invited Talk 1: Tal Linzen*

10:30 - 11:00 *Coffee Break*

11:00 - 12:30 *On-Site Poster Session*

Cross-lingual Semantic Role Labelling with the ValPaL Database Knowledge
Chinmay Choudhary and Colm O'Riordan

How Do Transformer-Architecture Models Address Polysemy of Korean Adverbial Postpositions?
Seongmin Mun and Guillaume Desagulier

Trans-KBLSTM: An External Knowledge Enhanced Transformer BiLSTM Model for Tabular Reasoning
Yerram Varun, Aayush Sharma and Vivek Gupta

On Masked Language Models for Contextual Link Prediction
Angus Brayne, Maciej Wiatrak and Dane Corneil

12:30 - 14:00 *Lunch*

14:00 - 15:00 *Virtual Poster Session*

Cross-lingual Semantic Role Labelling with the ValPaL Database Knowledge
Chinmay Choudhary and Colm O'Riordan

How Do Transformer-Architecture Models Address Polysemy of Korean Adverbial Postpositions?
Seongmin Mun and Guillaume Desagulier

Query Generation with External Knowledge for Dense Retrieval
Sukmin Cho, Soyeong Jeong, Wonsuk Yang and Jong C. Park

Uncovering Values: Detecting Latent Moral Content from Natural Language with Explainable and Non-Trained Methods
Luigi Asprino, Luana Bulla, Stefano De Giorgis, Aldo Gangemi, Ludovica Marinucci and Misael Mongiovi

Jointly Identifying and Fixing Inconsistent Readings from Information Extraction Systems
Ankur Padia, Francis Ferraro and Tim Finin

KIQA: Knowledge-Infused Question Answering Model for Financial Table-Text Data
Rungsiman Nararatwong, Natthawut Kertkeidkachorn and Ryutaro Ichise

Trans-KBLSTM: An External Knowledge Enhanced Transformer BiLSTM Model for Tabular Reasoning
Yerram Varun, Aayush Sharma and Vivek Gupta

Fast Few-shot Debugging for NLU Test Suites
Christopher Malon, Kai Li and Erik Kruus

On Masked Language Models for Contextual Link Prediction
Angus Brayne, Maciej Wiatrak and Dane Corneil

What Makes Good In-Context Examples for GPT-3?
Jiachang Liu, Dinghan Shen, Yizhe Zhang, Bill Dolan, Lawrence Carin and Weizhu Chen

15:00 - 15:30 *Coffee Break*

15:30 - 16:30 *Invited Talk 2: Yejin Choi*

16:30 - 16:40 *Short Break*

16:40 - 17:40 *Invited Talk 3: Allyson Ettinger*

17:40 - 17:50 *Closing Remarks*

Cross-lingual Semantic Role Labelling with the Valpal database knowledge

Chinmay Choudhary
National University of Ireland
Galway
c.choudhary1@nuigalway.ie

Colm O'Riordan
National University of Ireland
Galway
colm.oriordan@nuigalway.ie

Abstract

Cross-lingual Transfer Learning typically involves training a model on a high-resource source language and applying it to a low-resource target language. In this work we introduce a lexical database called **Valency Patterns Leipzig (ValPal)** which provides the argument pattern information about various verb-forms in multiple languages including low-resource languages. We also provide a framework to integrate the ValPal database knowledge into the state-of-the-art LSTM based model for cross-lingual semantic role labelling. Experimental results show that integrating such knowledge resulted in am improvement in performance of the model on all the target languages on which it is evaluated.

1 Introduction

Semantic role labeling (SRL) is the task of identifying various semantic arguments such as Agent, Patient, Instrument, etc. for each of the target verb (predicate) within an input sentence. SRL is useful as an intermediate step in numerous high level NLP tasks, such as information extraction (Christensen et al., 2011; Bastianelli et al., 2013), automatic document categorization (Persson et al., 2009), text-summarization (Khan et al., 2015) question-answering (Shen and Lapata, 2007) etc. State of the art approaches to SRL such as (Zhou and Xu, 2015; He et al., 2017a,b; Wang et al., 2021) are supervised approaches which require a large annotated dataset to be trained on, thus limiting their utility to only high-resorce languages. This issue of data-sparsity (in low-resource languages) has been effectively addressed with numerous cross-lingual approaches to SRL including *Annotation Projection* approaches (Padó and Lapata, 2009; Kozhevnikov and Titov, 2013; Akbik et al., 2015; Aminian et al., 2019a), *Model Transfer approaches* (McDonald and Nivre, 2013; Swayamdipta et al., 2016; Daza and Frank, 2019; Cai and Lapata, 2020a) and *Machine Translation* approaches (Fei et al., 2020).

In this work, we use the **Valency Patterns Leipzig (ValPal) online database**[1] (Hartmann et al., 2013) which is a multilingual lexical database, originally created by the linguistic research community to study the similarities and differences in verb-patterns for various world languages. Furthermore, we provide a framework to utilise the knowledge available in **Valpal** database to improve the performance of the state-of-the-art cross-lingual approach to SRL task.

2 ValPal Database

Valency Patterns Leipzig (ValPal) is a comprehensive multilingual lexical database which provides semantic and syntactic information about different verb-forms in various languages including many low-resource languages. The ValPal database provides values for the following features for each verb-form:

1. *Valency:* the total number of arguments that a base verb-form can take.
2. *Argument-pattern*: the type and order of arguments taken by a base verb-form in its most common usage.
3. *Alterations:* the alternate *argument-patterns* that can be taken by either the base verb-form or any of its morphological variant.

Table 1 depicts the information about three lexical units namely ***cook***, ***kochen*** and ***cuocere*** as provided in the ValPal database. Please note that Table 1 lists only a few of all the alterations provided for these verb-forms in ValPal database due to space constraints. Lexical units ***cook***, ***kochen*** and ***cuocere*** are *English*, *German* and *Italian* words representing base verb-form for verb activity COOKING.

[1] http://ValPal.info/

Proceedings of Deep Learning Inside Out (DeeLIO 2022): The 3rd Workshop on Knowledge Extraction and Integration for Deep Learning Architectures, pages 1 - 10
May 27, 2022 ©2022 Association for Computational Linguistics

2.1 Coding of Argument-patterns

In ValPal database each argument-pattern (including alteration) is coded with a unique coding-frame. For example, in Table 1, the argument-pattern of English base verb-form ***cook***, is coded as follows

$$1 - nom > V.subj[1] > 2 - acc$$

The code indicates that the base verb-form ***cook*** takes 2 arguments in its most common usage (valency of 2). The first argument is *cooker* (indicated as *1-nom*) and the second one is *Cooked-food* (indicated as *2-acc*). $V.subj[1]$ indicates the verb with the first argument as its agent. The order of arguments are **cooker–V–cooked_food** (eg: She is cooking the fish.).

Verb-form ***cook*** also has an *alteration* called **Causative-Inchoative** with the derived argument-pattern as follows.

$$2 - acc > V.subj[1]$$

This argument pattern indicates that verb-form can also have order of arguments as **cooked_food–V** with *Agent* argument missing from the sentence (eg: The fish is cooking).

2.2 Coding-sets

ValPal provides a unique coding-set for each language. The codes in these coding sets indicate various argument-types including modifier argument-types. For example, codes NP-Nom, NP-acc and LOC-NP indicate the AGENT (Arg0), PATIENT (Arg1) and modifier LOCATION (ArgM-LOC) arguments respectively in the coding-sets of all languages. The codes with+NP and mit+NP-dat indicate INSTRUMENT argument in English and German coding-sets. Similarly, codes UTT-NP indicate the argument TEMPORAL in most coding-sets. In these codes, the *NP* indicates the index of valency occupied the respective argument within the argument pattern (eg: code $2-acc$ in argument pattern $2 - acc > V.subj[1]$ indicates argument-type PATIENT with the valency-index of 2).

2.3 Alteration Types

As already explained, the ValPal database also provides a list of alternate argument-patterns (called alterations) for each verb-form. Some of these alterations are *morpho-independent* as they can be taken by the respective base-verb in any morphological form, whereas others are *morpho-dependent* as they can be taken by the respective verb only in a specific morphological form.

For example, both the *Reflexive-Passive* and *Impersonal Passive* alterations of the italian base verb-form *cuocere*, outlined in Table 1 are morpho-dependent alterations as these alterations are observed only when the verb-form possesses morpheme si.

The ValPal database is originally created by the linguistic research community, typically to study the similarities and differences in verb-patterns for various world languages. However this knowledge can also be used by NLP research community for building the models for data-sparse languages.

2.4 FrameNet to aid ValPal

One shortcoming of the Valpal database is that its vocabulary is limited for many languages. If we encounter a verb in the training-set that is missing in ValPal, we utilised the *FrameNet* database to extract the desired *argument-pattern* and *alterations* of it from ValPal itself.

To extract this knowledge about the missing verb, firstly we extracted the frame of the missing verb from the respective *FrameNet* database. Subsequently we extracted a replacement-verb that belongs to the same frame (as that of the missing verb) and is available in ValPal database. Finally, we assigned the argument-pattern and alterations of this replacement-verb to the missing verb. For example, the verb **barbecue** is missing from ValPal database. Yet, the verb **barbecue** belongs to frame **COOKING-45.1** in *English FrameNet* (Barkley). Another verb-form called **cook** belong to the same frame (**COOKING-45.1**) and is available in ValPal database. Thus we use argument-patters provided in ValPal for verb-form **cook** as the argument-patterns for **barbecue**.

3 FOL rules from ValPal

To inject the entire ValPal database knowledge about any low-resource target-language l in a Cross-lingual Neural Network model, we represented this knowledge as a set of First-order-logic (FOL) rules F_l. The process of generating this set of FOL rules involves two steps namely *Translating ValPal Argument-patterns to Propbank label orders* and *Writing Propbank-label order as FOL rule* described in Sections 3.1 and 3.2.

In ValPal database, the argument-pattern for verb-

Verb-form	Lang	Argument-pattern	Alterations (Alteration-name:Arg-pattern (example))
cook	English	$1 - nom > V.subj[1] > 2 - acc$	***Understood Omitted Object***:$1 - nom > V.subj[1] > 2 - acc$ (She walked in while I was cooking.) ***Causative-Inchoative*** : $2 - acc > V.subj[1]$ (The soup is still cooking.)
kochen	German	$1 - nom > V.subj[1] > 2 - acc$	***Benefactive Alternation***:$1 - nom > V' > subj[1] > 3 - dat > 2 - acc$ (Ich koche meiner Mutter eine Suppe.) ***be-Alternation***:$1 - nom > beV'.subj[1] > 4 - acc > mit + 2 - dat$ (Die Großmutter bekocht die Kranke mit Suppe.) ***Ambitransitive Alternation***:$2 - nom > V'.subj[2]$ (Das Wasser kocht.)
cuocere	Italian	$1 > V.subj[1] > 2$	***Reflexive-Passive***:$2 > siV'.subj[2] > daParteDi + 1$ (La carne si cuoce con attenzione.) ***Impersonal Passive***:$siPassV' > da + 1$ (Quando si è (stati) cotti dal sole si diventa di color rosso intenso.)

Table 1: Sample verb-form knowledge in Valpal database

form ***tie*** is outlined as equation 1 (as Q). We use this as an example to demonstrate the process of converting an argument-pattern to a FOL rule.

$$Q = 1 - nom > V.subj[1] > 2 - acc > LOC - 3(> with + 4) \quad (1)$$

3.1 Translate argument-patters to Propbank Order

In this step, we translate all the Valpal's argument-patterns (including alterations) for all lexical verb-forms in the target-language l, to the Propbank Orders. The entire process of translating a ValPal argument-pattern P of any language l into a *Propbank Label-order* involves two simple text-processing sub-steps described as sections 3.1.1 and 3.2.

3.1.1 Replace modifier argument-types

As already explained in section 2.2, the Valpal database provides a unique coding-set for each language. In this subset, we examined the entire coding-set for language l to identify the codes that refer to a modifier argument-type (eg: LOC-NP and UTT-NP etc. in English coding-set for LOCATION and TEMPORAL modifier-arguments), and created a mapping table that maps these modifier-argument codes to the corresponding Propbank annotations (eg: LOC-NP mapped to ARGM-LOC; UTT-NP mapped to ARGM-TMP etc.). The coding-set of any language in the ValPal database is small thus making it feasible to manually create such mapping table.

Subsequently, we used this mapping table to replace all modifier argument-patterns (if any) in the argument-pattern P being translated, with corresponding Propbank label.

After replacing the modifier argument-types we reduce the valency-index of all the arguments following the replaced modifier argument, in the argument-pattern being translated, by one.

$$Q = 1 - nom > V.subj[1] > 2 - acc > ARGM - LOC(> with + 3) \quad (2)$$

For example, the argument-pattern outlined in equation 1 comprises only one modifier argument-type namely LOC3. We replaced this with the corresponding Propbank label namely ARGM-LOC and reduced the valency-index of all argument-types following this replaced argument-pattern by 1 (thus $(with + 4)$ is re-written as $(with + 3)$). Hence the argument-pattern in Equation 1 would be re-written as equation 2.

3.1.2 Rewrite all non-modifier argument types

After replacing all modifier argument-types in the argument-patterns by the process described in section 3.1.1, we simply replace all left over arguments in the ValPal argument-pattern P by string as 'ARGx' where x is $valencyIndex - 1$. Hence argument $1 - nom$, $2 - acc$ and $with + 3$ (with valency Indexes as 1, 2, 3 respectively) in equation 2 would be replaced by *Arg0*, *Arg1* and *Arg2* respectively.
Finally, we replaced $Vsubj[NP]$ with *V* and removed all bracket symbols. Hence argument-pattern outlined as equation 2 would be translated as equation 3.

$$Q = ARG0 > V > ARG1 > ARG - LOC > ARG2 \quad (3)$$

3.2 Write Propbank Label order as FOL rule

Once having represented all argument-patterns (including alterations) for all lexical verb-forms of language *l* as allowed Propbank Label-orders, we rewrite each verb-form and Propbank Label-order pair as a FOL rule. For example the pair of verb-form ***tie*** and its corresponding allowed Propbank Label-order outlined as equation 4, is represented by the FOL rule indicated as equation 5.

$$f = baseForm(V, tie) \vee pattern(Y, Q) \quad (4)$$

Here Q is the Propbank label-order outlined in equation 3, and Y is the sequence of Propbank tag-sequence predicted by a neural-network model for any input token-seq. The logic-constraint in equation 5 would be true if the verb for which the arguments are being predicted is a variant of base verb-form *tie* and the predicted SRL tag sequence Y satisfies the label order Q.
While checking whether a predicted SRL tag sequence follows a specific order, we ignore the 'O' annotations ('O' indicates semantic role label 'NULL' in the Propbank Annotation scheme). For example the SRL tag sequences ***ARG0, ARG0, O, O, V, ARG1, ARG-LOC, O, ARG2*** follows the argument-pattern.
To check if the verb for which the arguments are being predicted is a morphological variant of the specific base verb-form, we perform stemming of both base verb-form and the token from the sentence which is tagged 'V' by the model. If the stem strings are equal we consider the verb token to be a variant of base verb-form.
If an argument-pattern (represented as Propbank label-order) is for a morpho-dependent alteration, then the morphological constraint is also added to the FOL rule representing the argument-pattern. For example, in table 1 the argument-pattern *Reflexive-Passive* is a morpho-dependent alteration. This argument-pattern is represented as FOL defined by equation 6.

$$f = baseForm(V, cuocere) \vee morphoForm(V, si) \vee pattern(Y, \hat{Q}) \quad (5)$$

Here $\hat{Q}$ represents the corresponding label-sequence for Argument-pattern. The rule $morphoForm(V, si)$ constraints the verb V to have morphene *si* for the rule to be true.
Hence we obtain a set of FOL rules F_l representing the entire Valpal database knowledge about language l (with each verb-form and argument-patterns pair provided in the Valpal database for the language l as a single FOL-rule $f \in F_l$). These FOL rules are used during the fine-tuning of a cross-lingual neural-network model for SRL in target-language l. During fine-tuning, the model is always rewarded if it predicts an SRL tag-seq Y which satisfies atleast one of the FOL rule $f \in F_l$, and penalised otherwise. Section 4.3 will explain the fine-tuning process in more detail.

4 Model

4.1 Base Approach

We utilized the state-of-the-art approach to Cross-lingual SRL in low-resource languages, proposed by (Cai and Lapata, 2020b) as our *Base Approach*. The approach comprises two key components namely *Semantic Role Labeler* and *Semantic Role Compressor*. The Semantic Role Labeler is a simple Bi-LSTM model with Biaffine Role Scorer (Dozat and Manning, 2016). Given input sentence $X = x_1...x_T$ of length T, the model accepts pre-trained multilingual contextualized word-embedding e_{x_i} and predicate indicator embedding p_{x_i} for all $x_i \in X$ as input. For each

word $x_i \in X$, the topmost biaffine layer computes the scores of all semantic roles to be assigned to x_i as $s_i \in R^{|n_r|}$ where n_r is the size of semantic role set. Hence the probability values of all SRL labels to be assigned to word x_i can be computed by applying the softmax function over s_i.
Subsequently, the Semantic Role Compressor is another Bi-LSTM model which compresses the useful information about arguments, predicates and their roles from the outputs of the Semantic Role Labeller (e.g., by automatically filtering unrelated or conflicting information) in a matrix $R \in R^{n_r * d_r}$ where d_r denotes the length of hidden representation for each semantic role.
The approach assumes the availability of a fully annotated source language corpus and parallel corpus of source-target sentences for training. Each model-training step involves two independent sequential sub-steps namely the *the supervised training* and *the cross-lingual training*.
In the source-language training sub-step, a batch is randomly selected from the annotated source-language corpus, to train both *Semantic Role Labeler* and *Semantic Role Compressor* simultaneously by minimizing the total loss computed by equation 3.

$$L_{total} = L_{CE} + L_{KL} \quad (6)$$

Here L_{CE} is the Cross-entropy loss between true labels and labels predicted by the Labeler whereas L_{KL} is the KL Divergence loss (Kullback and Leibler, 1951) between distributions predicted by the Compressor and the Labeler. After the *supervised training* sub-step, a batch from the parallel source-target data to perform the *cross-lingual training* sub-step. We refer to the original work (Cai and Lapata, 2020b) for the details of the *cross-lingual training* sub-step and the inference.

4.2 Training with Valpal knowledge

In this work we modified the training process described in section 4.1 to include the Valpal knowledge into the model parameters. Each training step in our proposed training step involves four independent sequential sub-steps.

Firstly, in the *Labeler pre-training* sub-step, we randomly sample a batch from the annotated source-language corpus and the Semantic Role Labeler is trained on it by minimizing the cross-entropy loss (L_{CE}) between true and predicted roles. Secondly, in the *Labeler fine-tuning*, the Valpal knowledge is injected in the parameters of the Semantic Role Labeler by the process described in section 4.3. Thirdly, in the *Compressor training* sub-step the *Semantic Role Compressor* is trained on the sampled source-language batch by minimizing the KL Divergence loss (L_{KL}) between distributions predicted by the Compressor and the fine-tuned Labeler (Labeler parameters are fixed in this sub-step). Finally we perform the *cross-lingual training* sub-step which is identical to as performed by the original authors (section 4.1)

4.3 Labeler fine-tuning with ValPal

This section describes the framework adopted by us to induce the target-language specific ValPal database knowledge expressed as a set of FOL rules F_l, into the pre-trained *Semantic Role Labeler*. Our framework is inspired by the *Deep Probabilistic Logic* (DPL) framework proposed by (Wang and Poon, 2018). The framework assumes the availability of only an unlabelled target-language corpus. Hence, for the *Labeler fine-tuning* sub-step, we randomly sample a batch from the already available parallel source-target data and utilised only the target language part of it.
Let $X = x_1 .....x_T$ be an input sentence and $Y = y_1.....y_T$ be any SRL-tag sequence. Further let Ψ be the pre-trained Bi-LSTM based *Semantic Role Labeler*, such that $\Psi(X, Y)$ denotes the conditional probability $P(Y|X)$ as outputted by the final softmax layer of Ψ.
The fine-tuning of this pre-trained Ψ to specific target-language l requires an unlabelled target-language training corpus. Given such unlabelled target-language-corpus X_{targ}, for each $X \in X_{targ}$ we input sentence X into the pre-trained Ψ to compute the most probable SRL-tag sequence Y as $Y = argmax_{\hat{Y}}(\Psi(x, \hat{Y}))$. Subsequently we input both the sentence X and it's predicted most-probable SRL tag-seq Y in all the FOL rules in F_l to compute their value (as 0.0 or 1.0). DPL framework defines the conditional probability distribution $P(F_l, Y|X)$ as equation 2.

$$P(F_l, Y|X) = \prod_{f \in F_l} \frac{exp(w.f(X,Y)).\Psi(X,Y)}{exp(w)} \quad (7)$$

The framework assumes the Knowledge-constraints to be log-linear thus defines each knowledge-constraint as $exp(w.f(X,Y))$ where $f \in F_l$ is the FOL rule representing the respective knowledge-constraint. Here w is the pre-decided reward-weight assigned to all constraints. Hence the predicted output-sequence Y would be rewarded (as its likelihood would increase by a factor of $exp(w)$) if it follows one of the defined argument-patterns in ValPal database for the respective verb for which the arguments are being predicted ($f(X, Y) = 1.0$). However no penalty is awarded for not following the correct Argument-pattern.

4.3.1 Learning

The ideal way to optimize the weights (fine-tune) of the model Ψ is by minimizing $P(F_l|X)$ and updating the parameters through back-propagation. We can compute $P(F_l|X)$ by summing over all possible SRL-tag sequences as $P(F_l|X) = \Sigma_Y P(F_l, Y|X)$. However computing $P(F_l, Y|X)$ by equation 4 with all possible output-sequences, and subsequently back-propagating through it, for each training example is computationally very inexpensive. Thus DPL framework also provides a more efficient EM-based approach (Moon, 1996) to the parameter fine-tuning which is adopted by us.

The full process of learning the parameters of Ψ (initialized with parameters pre-trained on source language) is outlined as Algorithm 1. For each

Algorithm 1 Fine-tuning of Semantic Role Labeller

Require: Target Language corpus X_{targ}; set of FOL rules F_l representing the entire Valpal database knowledge; Pre-trained LSTM based Semantic Role Labeller Ψ; Number of Epochs N;

repeat
  for each $X \in X_{targ}$ **do**
    ▷ **E-Step**
    $Y \leftarrow argmax_{\hat{Y}}(\Psi(X, \hat{Y}))$
    $q(Y) \leftarrow P(F_l, Y|X)$ ▷ by equation 7
    ▷ **M-Step**
    $\Psi \leftarrow argmin_{\hat{\Psi}}(D_{KL}(q(Y)||\hat{\Psi}(X, Y)))$
  end for
until convergence

training-example $X \in X_{targ}$, the Algorithm 1 implements three steps. In the first-step, it predicts the most probable SRL-tag sequence Y for the given training-example X as $Y = argmax_{\hat{Y}}(\Psi(x, \hat{Y}))$ with current parameter values for Ψ.

In the E-step, $q(Y) = P(F_l, Y|X)$ is computed by applying equation 4 with current parameters of Ψ. Finally in the M-step it keeps $q(Y)$ as fixed and updates parameters of Ψ by minimizing the KL-divergence (Kullback and Leibler, 1951) loss between $q(Y)$ and the probability of Y from $\Psi(X, Y)$ (i.e. $P(Y|X)$).

In other words, in each epoch step, the model first computes the joint likelihood of F_l and Y i.e $P(F_l, Y|X)$ with current model parameters, and subsequently it updates the parameters to predict likelihood of Y i.e., to be as close to $P(F_l, Y|X)$ as possible.

5 Experiments

This section described the experiments performed by us to evaluate the proposed model.

5.1 Dataset

We experimented with four languages namely *English* (en), *German* (de), *Chinese* (zh) and *Italian* (it) as these languages are covered in both the ValPal database as well as in the CoNLL 2009 Shared task (Hajic et al., 2009) dataset. The *Semantic Role Labeller* requires a fully-annotated training dataset in the high-resource source-language. We utilized the Universal Proposition Banks provided at `https://github.com/System-T/UniversalPropositions` provided for CoNLL 2009 Shared task, for training of the *Semantic Role Labeller* and the evaluation of various systems. On the other hand, the *Semantic Role Compressor* component requires sentence-paired parallel corpora in source and target languages. We used the Europarl parallel text-corpus (Koehn et al., 2005), and the large-scale EN-ZH parallel corpus (Xu, 2019) to train the *Semantic Role Compressor*, as used by (Cai and Lapata, 2020b). We used the target-language part of the same parallel-corpora independently for the Valpal knowledge induction, as the Valpal database knowledge induction simply requires unlabelled text-corpus in the target-language.

5.2 Model-configurations

We computed the language-independent BERT-Embeddings to be fed into the networks using pre-trained Multilingual BERT (mBERT) (Wu and Dredze, 2019) model. Given a sentence S, we tokenised the whole sentence using the WordPiece tokeniser (Wu et al., 2016). Subsequently we fed

Dropout prob.	0.01
Bach-size	32
Epochs	150
embeddings size	768
predicate indicator embed size	16
Bi-LSTM hidden states size	400
BiLSTM depth	3
hidden biaffine scorer size	300
Bi-LSTM hidden states size	256
BiLSTM depth	2
compressed role rep size	30
hidden biaffine scorer size	30

Table 2: Hyper-parameter settings for input and training (first block), semantic role labeler (second block) and semantic role compressor (third block). Semantic role labeler and Semantic role compressor are same as (Cai and Lapata, 2020b)

this token-sequence into pre-trained mBERT provided by (Turc et al., 2019). Embedding of any word $w \in S$ i.e. e_w is computed by taking average of mBERT outputs of all Wordpiece tokens corresponding to word w. Subsequently these word-embeddings are frozen during the training of the networks. Table 2 outlines the hyper-parameters used during training.

5.3 Baselines

We compared the performance of our proposed model against the base-model (4.1) as well as numerous other state-of-the-art baselines. These baselines include two annotation projection based models namely *Bootstrap* (Aminian et al., 2017) and *CModel* (Aminian et al., 2019b), as well as two strong mixture-of-experts models namely *MOE* (Guo et al., 2018) which focus on combining language specific features automatically as well as *MAN-MOE* (Chen et al., 2018) which learns language-invariant features with the multinomial adversarial network as a shared feature extractor. We also compared with PGN (Fei et al., 2020) which is the state-of-the-art translation-based model which translates the source annotated corpus into the target language, performs annotation projection, and subsequently trains the model on both source and the translated corpus. We utilised the source-code provided by the authors of each of these baselines to train and test them.

Algorithm 2 Full Training process. Here, the function *FineTune* represents the process outlined as algorithm 1 and function *CrossTrain* represents the cross-lingual training procedure adopted by (Cai and Lapata, 2020b). L_{CE} is cross-entropy loss and L_{KL} is KL divergence loss

Require: Annotated Source language corpus $\{X_{Tagged}, Y_{Tagged}\}$; Parallel Source-target Corpus $\{X^S_{Parallel}, X^T_{Parallel}\}$; set of FOL rules representing entire Valpal db knowledge of target language F_l; batch-size b; Number of Epochs E

Initialize:
  Semantic Role Labeler Ψ; Semantic Role Compressor Φ
  $steps \leftarrow |X_{Tg}|/b$
  for $epoch \leftarrow 1$ to E **do**
    for $step \leftarrow 1$ to $steps$ **do**
      $X, Y \leftarrow$ Sample($\{X_{Tg}, Y_{Tg}\}$,b)
      $X^S, X^T \leftarrow$ Sample($\{X^S_{Pr}, X^T_{Pr}\}$,b)
        ▷ **Labeler pre-training**
      $\Psi \leftarrow argmin_{\hat{\Psi}}(D_{CE}(Y||\hat{\Psi}(X)))$
        ▷ **Labeler Fine-tuning**
      $\Psi \leftarrow FineTune(X^T, F_L, \Psi, b)$
        ▷ **Compressor training**
      $\Phi \leftarrow argmin_{\hat{\Phi}}(D_{KL}(\Psi(X)||\hat{\Phi}(X)))$
        ▷ **Cross-lingual training**
      $\Phi, \Psi \leftarrow CrossTrain(X^S, X^T, \Psi, \Psi)$
    end for
  end for

6 Results

6.1 Monolingual training

In the first set of experiments we trained the models on a single source language English and tested these on the target languages *zh*, *it* and *de*. In these settings, we trained the models on English UPB train-dataset and tested them on the UPB test-sets of the target-languages. Table 3 shows the labeled F-scores achieved on each of these target-languages. In table 4, the *Base-wo-Compressor* refers to the base model without the SRL compressor, whereas *Base-full* refers to the full base model.

Results in Table 3, show that for both *Base-wo-Compressor* and *Base-full* model, adding Valpal database knowledge improved its performance on all three target languages. Furthermore, for all three target-languages, the improvement in performance of both *Base-wo-Compressor* and *Base-*

Model	it	de	zh	avg
Bootstrap	51.7	55.2	58.4	55.1
CModel	55.5	57.0	61.1	57.9
MAN-MOE	57.1	64.0	64.7	61.9
MoE	56.7	63.2	65.2	61.7
PGN	57.9	65.3	65.9	63.0
Base-wo-Compressor	37.1	49.7	45.3	44.0
Base-wo-Compressor+ Valpal	37.8	54.2	49.9	47.3
Increase	0.7	4.5	4.6	3.3
Base-full	57.2	65.1	68.8	63.7
Base-full+ Valpal	57.9	69.5	73.4	66.9
Increase	0.7	4.4	4.6	3.2

Table 3: Results for Monoloingual settings (with extended vocab for de and zh)

full models due to Valpal knowledge injection are same i.e 0.7 for *it*, 4.5 for *de* and 4.6 for *zh* (average 3.3). This provides the evidence that the improvement is indeed due to the Valpal Knowledge injection.

Model	it	de	zh	en	avg
MAN-MOE	57.7	66.2	65.9	66.0	63.9
MoE	57.1	63.5	66.1	64.1	62.7
PGN	58.0	65.7	66.9	67.8	64.6
Base-wo-Compressor	37.6	50.2	48.9	49.9	46.6
Base-wo-Compressor + Valpal	38.5	54.7	53.6	54.8	50.4
Increase	0.9	4.5	4.7	4.9	3.8

Table 4: Results in Polygot settings

6.2 Polyglot training

Table 4, outlines the results obtained under the polyglot training settings. For each experiment within these settings, the models are trained on a joint polyglot corpus of the three out of four languages namely *en*, *it*, *de* and *zh*, excluding the target language for which the results are outlined. For each experiment within these settings, the training corpus size is always fixed to 600,000 tokens to ensure controlled experiment-settings. We created such polyglot corpus by randomly sampling sentences from UPB train-set for each of the three source-languages until the token-size becomes approximately equal to 100,000, concatenated all these sampled datasets and randomly shuffled the order. *Alignment-projection* based approaches and the *Base-full* are not evaluated in the polyglot settings as these approaches require parallel-aligned source and target language sentence-pairs.

Results show that adding Valpal knowledge improves the performance of *Base-wo-Compressor* model, even within the polyglot settings, Furthermore, it is observed that although *Base-wo-Compressor* model performs better in polyglot training settings as compared to monolingual settings for most of the target languages, the improvement in performance of *Base-wo-Compressor* due to Valpal knowledge injection is same is both settings. This is because the fine-tuning of model with Valpal database knowledge is performed only with the unlabelled target-language corpus.

	it	de	zh
Vocab	125	128	122
Ext-vocab	–	975	415
Base-full	57.2	65.1	68.8
Base-full+ ValPal	57.9	65.9	68.7
Increase	0.7	0.8	0.9
Base-full+ ValPal-ext	–	69.5	73.4
Increase	0.7	4.4	4.6

Table 5: Results with and without ext-vocab

6.3 Performance with extended vocabularies

It can be observed in Tables 3 and 4 that the improvement on target-language is much lower than the improvements observed on zh, de and en. The reason being that we extended the Valpal vocabulary of en, zh and de using English Framenet (Barkley), Chinese Framenet (Yang et al., 2018) and German Framenet (of Texas) by the process described in section 2.4. However Italian Framenet is not publicly available.

We indeed performed experiments to analyze the impact of vocabulary extension on the performances. Table 5 outlines the results of these experiments. It can be observed in the table that extending the vocabulary of Valpal with the Framenet does lead to significant improvement in performance.

7 Conclusion

Valency Patterns Leipzig (ValPal) is a multilingual lexical database which provides the knowledge about the argument-patterns of various verb-forms in multiple languages including numerous low-resource languages. The database is originally created by the linguistic community to study the similarities and differences in the verb-patterns for various world's languages. In this work we utilised this database to improve the performance of the state-of-the-art cross-lingual model for SRL task.

We evaluated a framework to integrate the entire Valpal knowledge about any low-resource target-language into an LSTM based model. Our proposed framework only requires an unannotated target language corpus for the knowledge integration.

References

Alan Akbik, Laura Chiticariu, Marina Danilevsky, Yunyao Li, Shivakumar Vaithyanathan, and Huaiyu Zhu. 2015. Generating high quality proposition banks for multilingual semantic role labeling. In *Proceedings of the 53rd Annual Meeting of the Association for Computational Linguistics and the 7th International Joint Conference on Natural Language Processing (Volume 1: Long Papers)*, pages 397–407.

Maryam Aminian, Mohammad Sadegh Rasooli, and Mona Diab. 2017. Transferring semantic roles using translation and syntactic information. *arXiv preprint arXiv:1710.01411*.

Maryam Aminian, Mohammad Sadegh Rasooli, and Mona Diab. 2019a. Cross-lingual transfer of semantic roles: From raw text to semantic roles. *arXiv preprint arXiv:1904.03256*.

Maryam Aminian, Mohammad Sadegh Rasooli, and Mona Diab. 2019b. Cross-lingual transfer of semantic roles: From raw text to semantic roles. *arXiv preprint arXiv:1904.03256*.

ICSI Barkley. English framenet.

Emanuele Bastianelli, Giuseppe Castellucci, Danilo Croce, and Roberto Basili. 2013. Textual inference and meaning representation in human robot interaction. In *Proceedings of the Joint Symposium on Semantic Processing. Textual Inference and Structures in Corpora*, pages 65–69.

Rui Cai and Mirella Lapata. 2020a. Alignment-free cross-lingual semantic role labeling. In *Proceedings of the 2020 Conference on Empirical Methods in Natural Language Processing (EMNLP)*, pages 3883–3894.

Rui Cai and Mirella Lapata. 2020b. Alignment-free cross-lingual semantic role labeling. In *Proceedings of the 2020 Conference on Empirical Methods in Natural Language Processing (EMNLP)*, pages 3883–3894.

Xilun Chen, Ahmed Hassan Awadallah, Hany Hassan, Wei Wang, and Claire Cardie. 2018. Multi-source cross-lingual model transfer: Learning what to share. *ACL*.

Janara Christensen, Stephen Soderland, and Oren Etzioni. 2011. An analysis of open information extraction based on semantic role labeling. In *Proceedings of the sixth international conference on Knowledge capture*, pages 113–120.

Angel Daza and Anette Frank. 2019. Translate and label! an encoder-decoder approach for cross-lingual semantic role labeling. *arXiv preprint arXiv:1908.11326*.

Timothy Dozat and Christopher D Manning. 2016. Deep biaffine attention for neural dependency parsing. *arXiv preprint arXiv:1611.01734*.

Hao Fei, Meishan Zhang, and Donghong Ji. 2020. Cross-lingual semantic role labeling with high-quality translated training corpus. *arXiv preprint arXiv:2004.06295*.

Jiang Guo, Darsh J Shah, and Regina Barzilay. 2018. Multi-source domain adaptation with mixture of experts. *EMNLP*.

Jan Hajic, Massimiliano Ciaramita, Richard Johansson, Daisuke Kawahara, and Maria Antonia Martı. 2009. Lluıs marquez, adam meyers, joakim nivre, sebastian padó, jan štepánek, pavel stranák, mihai surdeanu, nianwen xue, and yi zhang. 2009. the conll-2009 shared task: Syntactic and semantic dependencies in multiple languages. In *Proceedings of the Thirteenth Conference on Computational Natural Language Learning (CoNLL 2009): Shared Task*, pages 1–18.

Iren Hartmann, Martin Haspelmath, and Bradley Taylor, editors. 2013. *The Valency Patterns Leipzig online database*. Max Planck Institute for Evolutionary Anthropology, Leipzig.

Luheng He, Kenton Lee, Mike Lewis, and Luke Zettlemoyer. 2017a. Deep semantic role labeling: What works and what's next. In *Proceedings of the 55th Annual Meeting of the Association for Computational Linguistics (Volume 1: Long Papers)*, pages 473–483.

Luheng He, Kenton Lee, Mike Lewis, and Luke Zettlemoyer. 2017b. Jointly predicting predicates and arguments in neural semantic role labeling. In *Proceedings of the 56th Annual Meeting of the Association for Computational Linguistics (Volume 2: Short Papers)*, pages 473–483.

Atif Khan, Naomie Salim, and Yogan Jaya Kumar. 2015. A framework for multi-document abstractive summarization based on semantic role labelling. *Applied Soft Computing*, 30:737–747.

Philipp Koehn et al. 2005. Europarl: A parallel corpus for statistical machine translation. In *MT summit*, volume 5, pages 79–86. Citeseer.

Mikhail Kozhevnikov and Ivan Titov. 2013. Cross-lingual transfer of semantic role labeling models. In *Proceedings of the 51st Annual Meeting of the Association for Computational Linguistics (Volume 1: Long Papers)*, pages 1190–1200.

Solomon Kullback and Richard A Leibler. 1951. On information and sufficiency. *The annals of mathematical statistics*, 22(1):79–86.

Ryan McDonald and Joakim Nivre. 2013. Yvonne irmbach-brundage, yoav goldberg, dipanjan das, kuzman ganchev, keith hall, slav petrov, hao zhang, oscar täckström, claudia bedini, núria bertomeu castelló, and jungmee lee. universal dependency annotation for multilingual parsing. In *Proceedings of the 51st Annual Meeting of the Association for Computational Linguistics*, pages 92–97.

Todd K Moon. 1996. The expectation-maximization algorithm. *IEEE Signal processing magazine*, 13(6):47–60.

University of Texas. German framenet.

Sebastian Padó and Mirella Lapata. 2009. Cross-lingual annotation projection for semantic roles. *Journal of Artificial Intelligence Research*, 36:307–340.

Jacob Persson, Richard Johansson, and Pierre Nugues. 2009. Text categorization using predicate-argument structures. In *Proceedings of the 17th Nordic Conference of Computational Linguistics (NODALIDA 2009)*, pages 142–149.

Dan Shen and Mirella Lapata. 2007. Using semantic roles to improve question answering. In *Proceedings of the 2007 joint conference on empirical methods in natural language processing and computational natural language learning (EMNLP-CoNLL)*, pages 12–21.

Swabha Swayamdipta, Miguel Ballesteros, Chris Dyer, and Noah A Smith. 2016. Greedy, joint syntactic-semantic parsing with stack lstms. *arXiv preprint arXiv:1606.08954*.

Iulia Turc, Ming-Wei Chang, Kenton Lee, and Kristina Toutanova. 2019. Well-read students learn better: On the importance of pre-training compact models. *arXiv preprint arXiv:1908.08962v2*.

Hai Wang and Hoifung Poon. 2018. Deep probabilistic logic: A unifying framework for indirect supervision. *arXiv preprint arXiv:1808.08485*.

Nan Wang, Jiwei Li, Yuxian Meng, Xiaofei Sun, and Jun He. 2021. An mrc framework for semantic role labeling. *arXiv preprint arXiv:2109.06660*.

Shijie Wu and Mark Dredze. 2019. Beto, bentz, becas: The surprising cross-lingual effectiveness of bert. *arXiv preprint arXiv:1904.09077*.

Yonghui Wu, Mike Schuster, Zhifeng Chen, Quoc V Le, Mohammad Norouzi, Wolfgang Macherey, Maxim Krikun, Yuan Cao, Qin Gao, Klaus Macherey, et al. 2016. Google's neural machine translation system: Bridging the gap between human and machine translation. *arXiv preprint arXiv:1609.08144*.

Bright Xu. 2019. Nlp chinese corpus: Large scale chinese corpus for nlp.

Tsung-Han Yang, Hen-Hsen Huang, An-Zi Yen, and Hsin-Hsi Chen. 2018. Transfer of frames from english framenet to construct chinese framenet: a bilingual corpus-based approach. In *Proceedings of the Eleventh International Conference on Language Resources and Evaluation (LREC 2018)*.

Jie Zhou and Wei Xu. 2015. End-to-end learning of semantic role labeling using recurrent neural networks. In *Proceedings of the 53rd Annual Meeting of the Association for Computational Linguistics and the 7th International Joint Conference on Natural Language Processing (Volume 1: Long Papers)*, pages 1127–1137.

How do Transformer-Architecture Models Address Polysemy of Korean Adverbial Postpositions?

Seongmin Mun
Chosun University, Republic of Korea
seongmin.mun@chosun.ac.kr

Guillaume Desagulier
Paris VIII University & UMR 7114, MoDyCo, France
guillaume.desagulier@univ-paris8.fr

Abstract

Postpositions, which are characterized as multiple form-function associations and thus polysemous, pose a challenge to automatic identification of their usage. Several studies have used contextualized word-embedding models to reveal the functions of Korean postpositions. Despite the superior classification performance of previous studies, the particular reason how these models resolve the polysemy of Korean postpositions is not enough clear. To add more interpretation, for this reason, we devised a classification model by employing two transformer-architecture models—BERT and GPT-2—and introduces a computational simulation that interactively demonstrates how these transformer-architecture models simulate human interpretation of word-level polysemy involving Korean adverbial postpositions *-ey*, *-eyse*, and *-(u)lo*. Results reveal that (i) the BERT model performs better than the GPT-2 model to classify the intended function of postpositions, (ii) there is an inverse relationship between the classification performance and the number of functions that each postposition manifests, (iii) model performance is affected by the corpus size of each function, (iv) the models' performance gradually improves as the epoch proceeds, and (vi) the models are affected by the scarcity of input and/or semantic closeness between the items.

1 Introduction

Polysemy, one type of ambiguity, occurs when one form delivers multiple, and yet related, meanings/functions(Glynn and Robinson, 2014). Traditional word-embedding models have shown an unsatisfactory level of performance in polysemy interpretation(e.g., Bae et al., 2014, 2015; Kim and Ock, 2016; Lee et al., 2015; Mun and Shin, 2020; Shin et al., 2005). This is mainly due to the technical nature of these models: they are *static* in that a single vector is assigned to each word (Desagulier, 2019; Ethayarajh, 2019; Liu et al., 2019a). To overcome this issue, recent studies have proposed a *contextualized* word-embedding model which considers neighborhood information about a polysemous word on the basis of sequences of words around the target word (Klafka and Ettinger, 2020; Loureiro and Jorge, 2019; Michalopoulos et al., 2021). These models have achieved a good level of performance in many natural language processing tasks (Devlin et al., 2018; Radford et al., 2018a; Liu et al., 2019b; Radford et al., 2018b; Lan et al., 2019). Among these models, transformer-architecture models such as Bidirectional Encoder Representations from Transformer (BERT; Devlin et al., 2018) and Generative Pre-Training 2 (GPT-2; Radford et al., 2018b) shows the best performance for this task of polysemy interpretation (Haber and Poesio, 2021; Soler and Apidianaki, 2021; Yenicelik et al., 2020).

Despite a good deal of research on transformer-architecture models in English, very few studies have investigated transformer-architecture-based polysemy interpretation in languages that are typologically different from English. We therefore attend to Korean, a Subject-Object-Verb language with overt case-marking through a postposition—a bound morpheme which adds grammatical functions to a content word where it is attached (Sohn, 1999). A Korean postposition normally involves many-to-many associations between form and function. As such a postposition is polysemous (Choo and Kwak, 2008). For example, an adverbial postposition *-(u)lo* (*-ulo* after a consonant) is interpreted as six major functions: criterion (CRT), direction (DIR), effector (EFF), final state (FNS), instrument (INS), and location (LOC) (Shin, 2008). For instance, the following sentence involving the postposition *-(u)lo* as a marker of INS (instrument) as in (1).

(1) 전선이 연줄로
censen-i yencwul-lo
wire-NOM connection.wire-INS

Proceedings of Deep Learning Inside Out (DeeLIO 2022):
The 3rd Workshop on Knowledge Extraction and Integration for Deep Learning Architectures, pages 11 - 21
May 27, 2022 ©2022 Association for Computational Linguistics

-ey		*-eyse*		*-(u)lo*	
Function	Frequency	Function	Frequency	Function	Frequency
LOC	1,780	LOC	4,206	FNS	1,681
CRT	1,516	SRC	647	DIR	1,449
THM	448			INS	739
GOL	441			CRT	593
FNS	216			LOC	158
EFF	198			EFF	88
INS	69				
AGT	47				
Total	4,715	Total	4,853	Total	4,708

Table 1: By-function frequency list of *-ey*, *-eyse*, and *-(u)lo* in cross-validated corpus

Note. Abbreviation: AGT = agent; CRT = criterion; DIR = direction; EFF = effector; FNS = final state; GOL = goal; INS = instrument; LOC = location; SRC = source; THM = theme

감겼다.
kam-ki-ess-ta.
wind-PSV-PST-DECL
'The wire wound around with the connection wire.'

Several studies have used transformer-architecture models to address the word-level polysemy of Korean adverbial postpositions (e.g., Bae et al., 2020a,b; Hong et al., 2020; Mun, 2021) with the model performance (measured through a *F*-score) ranging from 0.776 (Park et al., 2019) to 0.856 (Bae et al., 2020a). Notably, the particular reason for the transformer architecture's superior performance over the others is somewhat unclear (Puccetti et al., 2021; Yun et al., 2021). To add more interpretation of the model performance, we devised a classification model by employing BERT and GPT-2. In order to further understand how transformer-architecture models recognize word-level polysemy, we propose a transformer-architecture-based visualization system for polysemy interpretation of three adverbial postpositions, *-ey*, *-eyse*, and *-(u)lo*, which are frequently documented in the previous studies (e.g., Cho and Kim, 1996; Jeong, 2010; Nam, 1993; Park, 1999; Song, 2014).

2 Methods

2.1 Creating the Input Corpus

The Sejong primary corpus (Sejong corpus is available at: https://www.korean.go.kr), the representative corpus in Korean, does not code the information about the functions of postpositions directly in each sentence (which is necessary for model training). We thus annotated a portion of the original corpus data manually. For this purpose, we extracted sentences involving only one postposition and predicate. We did this treatment to control for additional confounding factors which might have interfered with the performance of our model. We then extracted 5,000 sentences randomly for each postposition from the initial dataset.

Three native speakers of Korean annotated each postposition for its function in this 15,000-sentence corpus. Fleiss' kappa scores were 0.948 (*-ey*), 0.928 (*-eyse*), and 0.947 (*-(u)lo*), which are considered

Index	Label	Sentence
1,862	1	[CLS] 한참 만에 오반장이 침묵을 깼다. [SEP]
1,863	1	[CLS] 정말 오랫만에 먹어보는 고기였다. [SEP]
1,864	1	[CLS] 옛날 구한말에 유명한 얘기가 있었죠? [SEP]
1,865	1	[CLS] 한밤중에 신나게 한바탕했지요. [SEP]
1,866	1	[CLS] 그런데 몇 시에 왔어? [SEP]
1,867	1	[CLS] 겨울에 꽃이라니요. [SEP]
1,868	1	[CLS] 아침에 엄마한테 돈을 달랬어요. [SEP]
1,869	1	[CLS] 결혼은 반드시 적령기에 해야 한다. [SEP]
1,870	1	[CLS] 한 달에 얼마씩은 정확하게 들어오니까. [SEP]
1,871	1	[CLS] 그럼 일 주일 후에 뵙겠습니다. [SEP]

Index	Label	Sentence
1,862	1	한참 만에 오반장이 침묵을 깼다.
1,863	1	정말 오랫만에 먹어보는 고기였다.
1,864	1	옛날 구한말에 유명한 얘기가 있었죠?
1,865	1	한밤중에 신나게 한바탕했지요.
1,866	1	그런데 몇 시에 왔어?
1,867	1	겨울에 꽃이라니요.
1,868	1	아침에 엄마한테 돈을 달랬어요.
1,869	1	결혼은 반드시 적령기에 해야 한다.
1,870	1	한 달에 얼마씩은 정확하게 들어오니까.
1,871	1	그럼 일 주일 후에 뵙겠습니다.

Figure 1: Example sentences used in the training for BERT (left) and GPT-2 (Right)

'almost perfect' according to the Kappa scale. We further excluded instances which showed disagreement among the human annotators. The final corpus consisted of 4,715 sentences for *-ey*, 4,853 sentences for *-eyse*, and 4,708 sentences for *-(u)lo*. Table 1 presents the detailed by-function frequency list of the three postpositions[1].

2.2 Creating Training and Test Sets

In order to make the training and test sets, we made three separate columns: index (the unique number of each sentence), label (the intended function of each postposition in each sentence), and sentence. For the sentence of BERT, we added [CLS] ('classification'; indicating the start of a sentence) before a sentence and [SEP] ('separation'; indicating the end of a sentence) after a sentence to indicate where the sentence starts and ends (Figure 1 left); no such addition occurred in GPT-2. We then split the corpus into two sub-sets, one with 90 per cent of the corpus for the training and with the remaining 10 per cent of the corpus for the testing.

2.3 Developing BERT and GPT-2 Models

For the BERT model training, we transformed the input data into three embedding types—*token* embedding, *position* embedding, and *segment* embedding (c.f., Devlin et al., 2018)—in the following ways. First, for the *token* embedding, we used *KoBertTokenizer* for the sentence tokenization; the maximum number of tokens for each sentence was set to 128. Second, for the *position* embedding, we converted each token into numeric values indicating unique indices of the tokens in the vocabulary of KoBERT. Third, for the *segment* embedding, we converted the number of tokens of each sentence into 128 numeric values using 0 (i.e., not existed) or 1 (i.e., existed). The labels of the data indicating the intended function of each postposition in the sentence were stored separately.

After the input creation, we set the parameters related to both of model training such as *batch size* (16), *epoch* (50), *seed* (42), *sequence length* (128), *epsilon* (0.00000008), and *learning rate* (0.00002), as advised by previous studies (e.g., McCormick, 2019; Vázquez et al., 2020; Wu et al., 2019). We then employed BERT and GPT-2 pre-trained language models in order to obtain high performance of outcomes: KoBERT (Jeon et al., 2019) for BERT and KoGPT-2-base-v2 (Jeon et al., 2021) for GPT-2. The BERT model training proceeded as follows. First, we loaded KoBERT through the function *BertForSequenceClassification* from *transformers* (Wolf et al., 2019). Second, we fine-tuned the pre-trained model by using the training set, with a view to reducing loss values and updating the *learning rate* for better classification performance of the model. Third, we loaded the testing set to evaluate whether the fine-tuned model successfully recognized the intended functions of each postposition in each sentence. In this part, the rates of F-score for each function and the total F-score rate (i.e., F-score) were calculated by comparing the intended function of each postposition in each test sentence against the parsed version returned by the model. Lastly, we employed t-distributed Stochastic Neighbor Embedding (t-SNE; Maaten and Hinton, 2008) for dimension reduction of classification embeddings from the postposition by each epoch. In addition, to statistically confirm the changes of sentence-level embedding outcomes by each epoch, we performed density-based clustering (Sander et al., 1998). These outcomes were fed into the visualization system [2].

The input treatment process and the training process of GPT-2 are almost the same as the BERT training process. For the input treatment, first, the BERT model used symbols to mark the start and the end of each input, but no such addition occurred in GPT-2 training. Second, BERT uses wordpiece algorithm for the *token* embedding (Sennrich et al., 2016), but GPT-2 uses byte pair encoding algorithm (Gage, 1994). For the training process, first, BERT operates on the basis of masked language modeling and next-sentence prediction for generating a pre-trained model, whereas GPT-2 uses general language modeling by using a huge size corpus. Second, the BERT model conducts learning in bi-direction, while GPT-2 conducts learning in uni-direction. In addition, GPT-2 loaded KoGPT2 through the function *GPT2ForSequenceClassification* and *PreTrainedTokenizerFast* from *transformers* (Wolf et al., 2019).

2.4 Developing the Visualization System

In order to better understand how BERT and GPT-2 recognize the word-level polysemy, we developed

[1] Our corpus is available at: https://github.com/seongminmun/Corpora/tree/main/APIK

[2] Code can be found at: https://github.com/seongminmun/Visualization/tree/master/2022/PostTransformers

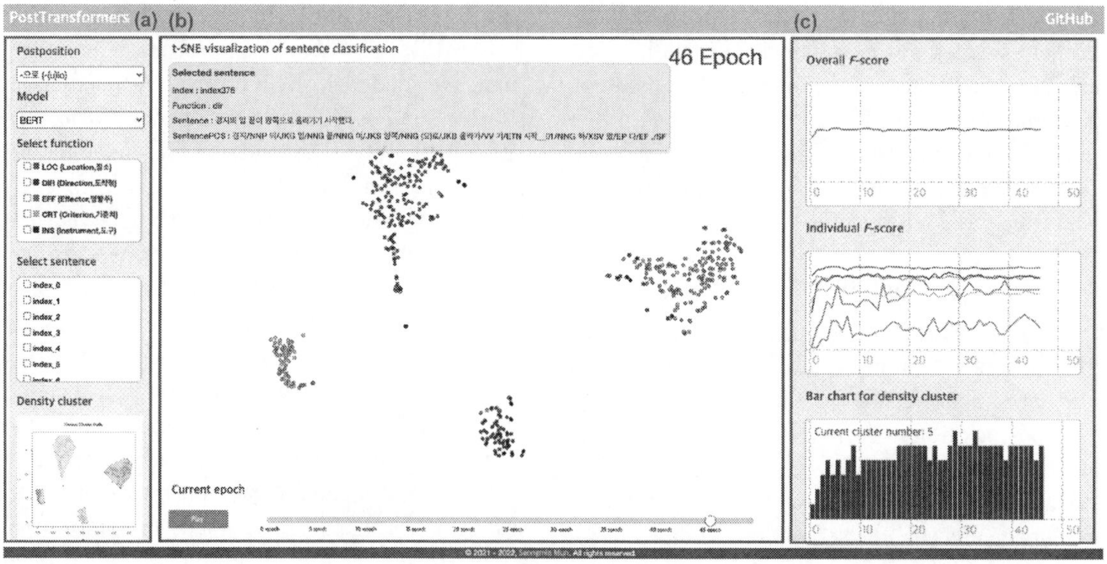

Figure 2: The overview interface of the visualization system

a visualization system by using the test set under the two-dimensional distribution. For the system interface, we created three areas for the demonstration of model performance: a distributional map for sentence-level embeddings, F-score charts relating to the model, and graphs for the density-based clustering[3].

2.4.1 Distributional Map for Sentence-Level Embeddings

The distributional map as in Figure 2b presents the relationship between the sentences with the selected postposition (represented as dots) involving different functions (represented as colors). A slider at the bottom of the map allows for changing the epochs; the patterns of clustering change as the slider moves. Each dot shows the details of the sentence (e.g., an index of the selected sentence, the intended function used in the sentence, the original sentence) once the mouse pointer is located on the dot. For the manipulating of visualization outcomes, Figure 2a provides options to select the checkboxes to highlight and tracking interesting sentences according to the function of these postpositions, the models, and the index number.

[3]The visualization system available at: https://seongmin-mun.github.io/Visualization/2022/PostTransformers/index.html

2.4.2 *F*-score Charts

The right side of the system as in Figure 2c provides users with various information about the model performance: overall F-score and by-function F-score in the classification task by epoch. This section also provides F-score rates of each function by hovering around the mouse pointer onto the specific-colored lines.

2.4.3 Graphs for the Density-Based Clustering

The bar chart at the bottom right side of the system presents the number of clusters produced by the

Epoch	Classification performance (*F*-score)								
	Overall	*AGT*	*CRT*	*EFF*	*FNS*	*GOL*	*INS*	*LOC*	*THM*
1	0.677	0	0.812	0.286	0	0.125	0	0.802	0.472
10	0.739	0.286	0.84	0.37	0.5	0.444	0.222	0.813	0.646
20	0.758	0.25	0.848	0.514	0.474	0.478	0.286	0.827	0.705
30	0.745	0.25	0.823	0.571	0.542	0.448	0.375	0.816	0.688
40	0.73	0.222	0.805	0.537	0.522	0.478	0.3	0.82	0.66
50	0.747	0.25	0.839	0.529	0.5	0.413	0.353	0.817	0.705
Average	0.744	0.217	0.837	0.531	0.499	0.435	0.29	0.823	0.651

Table 2: By-function F-score for the BERT model: *-ey*

Epoch	Classification performance (*F*-score)		
	Overall	*LOC*	*SRC*
1	0.893	0.94	0.509
10	0.88	0.933	0.431
20	0.874	0.93	0.358
30	0.87	0.927	0.376
40	0.878	0.931	0.468
50	0.87	0.928	0.364
Average	0.875	0.93	0.373

Table 3: By-function *F*-score for the BERT model: *-eyse*

Epoch	Classification performance (*F*-score)						
	Overall	*CRT*	*DIR*	*EFF*	*FNS*	*INS*	*LOC*
1	0.681	0.532	0.82	0	0.714	0.396	0
10	0.799	0.644	0.924	0.462	0.805	0.794	0.167
20	0.794	0.595	0.915	0.714	0.807	0.818	0.2
30	0.799	0.598	0.908	0.545	0.808	0.829	0.296
40	0.792	0.612	0.915	0.667	0.797	0.794	0.24
50	0.803	0.627	0.915	0.667	0.812	0.809	0.286
Average	0.795	0.626	0.911	0.604	0.805	0.803	0.233

Table 4: By-function *F*-score for the BERT model: *-(u)lo*

Epoch	Classification performance (*F*-score)								
	Overall	*AGT*	*CRT*	*EFF*	*FNS*	*GOL*	*INS*	*LOC*	*THM*
1	0.514	0	0.579	0	0	0	0	0.617	0
10	0.7	0	0.8	0.5	0.148	0.31	0	0.794	0.591
20	0.675	0	0.793	0.39	0.235	0.222	0	0.768	0.56
30	0.672	0	0.784	0.364	0.421	0.328	0.2	0.771	0.495
40	0.687	0	0.811	0.324	0.41	0.25	0	0.768	0.592
50	0.685	0	0.814	0.333	0.333	0.254	0	0.768	0.582
Average	0.68	0.003	0.796	0.386	0.335	0.24	0.061	0.769	0.546

Table 5: By-function *F*-score for the GPT-2 model: *-ey*

Epoch	Classification performance (*F*-score)		
	Overall	*LOC*	*SRC*
1	0.857	0.923	0
10	0.851	0.918	0.217
20	0.864	0.925	0.214
30	0.849	0.915	0.305
40	0.843	0.912	0.296
50	0.851	0.917	0.28
Average	0.844	0.912	0.272

Table 6: By-function *F*-score for the GPT-2 model: *-eyse*

model. This chart also provides a hovering function, providing the actual number of clusters per epoch. The particular hovering activity is interlocked with the density cluster view, located at the bottom left of the system, by presenting the clustering results according to the selected epoch.

Epoch	Classification performance (F-score)						
	Overall	*CRT*	*DIR*	*EFF*	*FNS*	*INS*	*LOC*
1	0.473	0.03	0.549	0	0.575	0.099	0
10	0.675	0.611	0.765	0.471	0.701	0.583	0.207
20	0.664	0.619	0.782	0.429	0.658	0.568	0.273
30	0.696	0.621	0.801	0.5	0.721	0.587	0.222
40	0.683	0.585	0.799	0.462	0.691	0.612	0.24
50	0.694	0.603	0.803	0.5	0.702	0.635	0.222
Average	0.676	0.588	0.782	0.425	0.69	0.591	0.226

Table 7: By-function F-score for the GPT-2 model: *-(u)lo*

3 Results: Four Case Studies

In order to report the transformer-architecture models' performance of classifying the functions of postpositions and assess how our visualization system works, we conducted four case studies.

3.1 Which Model is Better to Resolve the Polysemy of Korean Postposition?

Tables 2-7 show the classification performance (i.e., F-score) of the two models for each postposition. Results show that the overall F-score was the highest in BERT (0.875; for *-eyse*) and the lowest in GPT-2 (0.676; for *-(u)lo*)).

Comparison	$\|F\|$	p
Model	752.97	$< .001^{***}$
Postposition	1240.18	$< .001^{***}$
Model × Postposition	97.14	$< .001^{***}$

Table 8: Results of the two-way ANOVA for the overall comparison of two models

Note. $^{***} < .001$

To construct a global model, we performed a two-way ANOVA (2 models × 3 postpositions). As Table 8 shows, there are significant differences in the F-score across the models and postpositions. This indicates the classification performance differed between the BERT model and the GPT-2 model in all postpositions.

Comparison	$\|t\|$	p
BERT vs. GPT-2 (*-ey*)	14.506	$< .001^{***}$
BERT vs. GPT-2 (*-eyse*)	9.688	$< .001^{***}$
BERT vs. GPT-2 (*-(u)lo*)	21.337	$< .001^{***}$

Table 9: Statistical comparison between two models by each postposition: Two-sample t-test

Note. $^{***} < .001$

We further conducted post-hoc analyses through a two-sample t-test. As Table 9 shows, the model performance of BERT significantly differs from the GPT-2' performance. Considering the differences between two models for model training such as the different directions or pre-training tasks of two models (see Section 2.3), this can indicate that the different training processes of the two models influenced the classification performance by classifying the functions of the postpositions.

3.2 Does the Number of Functions Involving a Postposition Affect the Model Performance?

As shown in Tables 2-7, the BERT model performed better for *-eyse*, which has only two functions (SRC and LOC), than for the other two postpositions (*-ey* and *-(u)lo*). Similar to the BERT model, *-eyse* outperformed the other two postpositions in the GPT-2 model, as Tables 2-7 show. The overall classification F-score rates for *-ey*, *-eyse* and *-(u)lo* were around 0.744, 0.875 and 0.795 for BERT, 0.68, 0.844 and 0.676 for GPT-2.

Comparison	$\|F\|$	p
Postposition	22.941	$< .001^{***}$
Epoch	0.414	0.521
Postposition × Epoch	0.003	0.959

Table 10: Results of the two-way ANOVA for the BERT model

Note. $^{***} < .001$

Table 10 shows the two-way ANOVA for the comparison of the BERT classification performance. The result presents that the overall F-score levels of the postpositions were significantly different from each other. This indicates there is a difference in model performance between the three postposition types which have a different number of functions.

Comparison	$\|F\|$	p
Postposition	0.049	0.825
Epoch	1.690	0.196
Postposition × Epoch	0.355	0.552

Table 11: Results of the two-way ANOVA for the GPT-2 model

Unlike the results from the BERT model, the statistical analysis of two-way ANOVA for GPT-2 (Table 11) shows that there was no statistical significance in the performance across the postpositions/epochs. This indicates that GPT-2 is not affected by the number of functions of each postposition.

3.3 Do the Asymmetric Proportions of the Functions in Each Postposition Affect the Model Performance?

The answer is *they do*. For the BERT model, the overall classification F-score of each function for *-ey* was the highest for CRT (0.837) and the lowest for AGT (0.217); for *-eyse*, the performance was the highest in LOC (0.93) and the lowest in SRC (0.373); for *-(u)lo*, the classification performance was the highest in DIR (0.911) and the lowest in LOC (0.233) (Tables 2-4). Similar to the BERT model, the overall classification performance of GPT-2 for *-ey* was the highest in CRT (0.796) and the lowest for AGT (0.003); for *-eyse*, the F-score was the highest in LOC (0.912) and the lowest in SRC (0.272); for *-(u)lo*, the classification performance was the highest in DIR (0.782) and the lowest in LOC (0.226) (Tables 5-7).

As for the occurrences of individual functions per postposition, CRT for *-ey*, LOC for *-eyse*, and DIR for *-(u)lo* account for the larger portion of the entire corpus than other functions (see Table 1). This finding thus indicates that the model performance was affected by the asymmetric proportions of the functions comprising the use of each postposition.

3.4 How do the Transformer-Architecture Models Classify Sentences for Each Postposition Based on Function as the Epoch Proceeds?

Our visualization system showed that the model was able to recognize the functions of each postposition as the epoch progressed. Through the outcomes of the BERT model, for *-ey*, the number of clusters was one when the epoch was one, but as the epoch progressed, the sentences were divided into four in Epoch 8, five in Epoch 12, and six in Epoch 40. For *-eyse*, all of the sentences were grouped into one when the epoch was one, and there were two clusters since the epoch was two. For *-(u)lo*, the number of clusters increased, starting from one (Epoch 1) to four (Epoch 4), five (Epoch 9), and six (Epoch 29).

The GPT-2 model also showed a similar tendency with the BERT model. For *-ey*, all of the sentences were grouped into one when the epoch

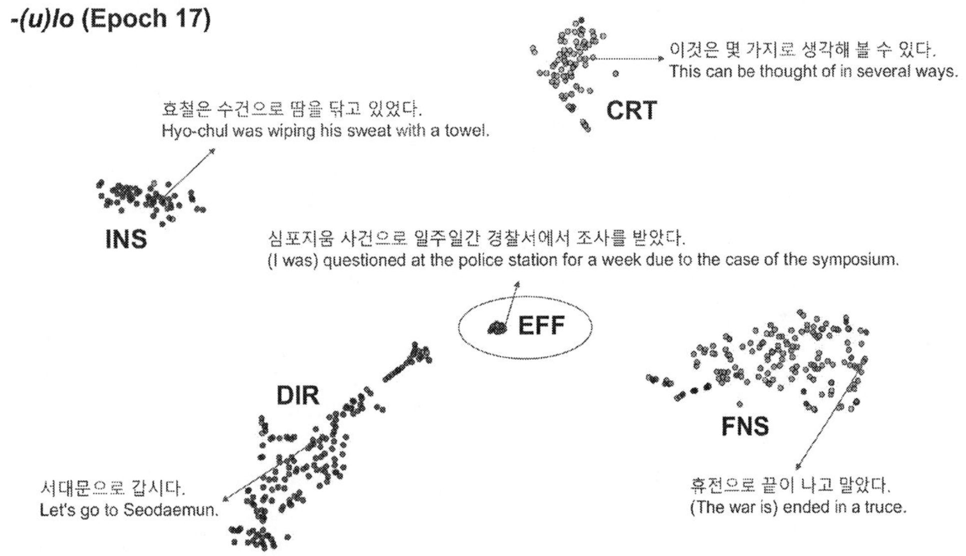

Figure 3: The t-SNE outcome of BERT model for *-(u)lo* in Epoch 17

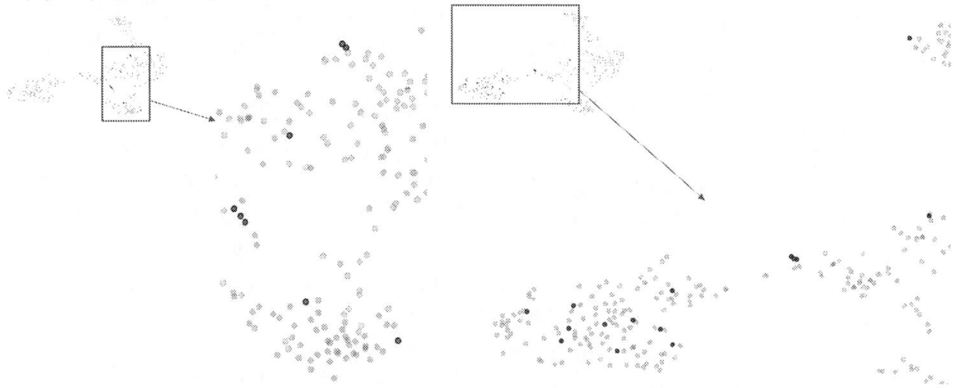

Figure 4: The t-SNE outcome of the GPT-2 model for *-(u)lo* in Epoch 50 (left: for highlighting the EFF instances; right: highlighting the LOC instances)

was one, but as the epoch progressed, the sentences were divided into two in Epoch 8, three in Epoch 23, four in Epoch 42, and five in Epoch 47. For *-eyse*, the number of clusters was one when the epoch was one, and there were two clusters since the epoch was 20. For *-(u)lo*, the number of clusters increased, starting from one (Epoch 1) to two (Epoch 3), three (Epoch 18), and four (Epoch 23).

In particular, by using visualization system, we found two interesting aspects. First, the BERT model in Epoch 17 (Figure 3) for *-(u)lo*, a cluster of EFF (the function with low-frequency occurrences in the data) emerged. This finding indicates that the BERT model can identify functions at a satisfactory level, even though they are relatively infrequent, as long as there are sufficient epochs provided. However, unlike the BERT model, the GPT-2 model did not recognize EFF as a designated function until Epoch 50 as shown in Figure 4 (left).

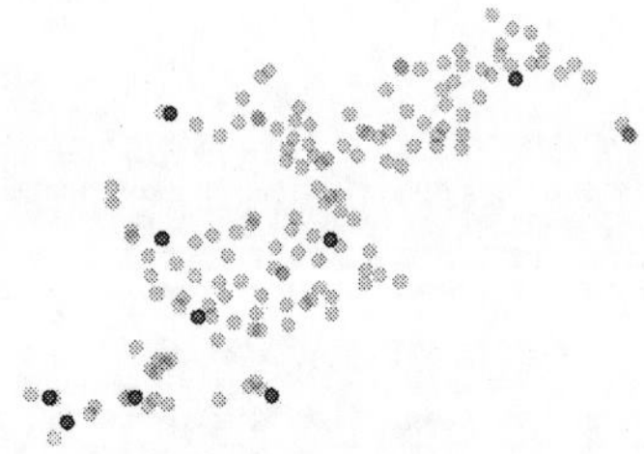

Figure 5: The DIR cluster in the t-SNE outcome of the BERT model for *-(u)lo* (Epoch 50) highlighting the LOC instances

Second, for both models, LOC could not form a designated cluster in the end. Zooming into the individual instances of LOC (Figure 4 (right) and Figure 5), we found that many of the LOC instances (11 out of 15) belonged to the DIR group. This may be due to (i) the low frequency of LOC in the data and (ii) the semantic closeness between DIR and LOC—they relate to a location and are often difficult to distinguish one from another. This finding indicates that there are still some limitations in regard to the identification of functions given the above complications.

4 Conclusion

In this study, we made five major findings. First, BERT performed better than GPT-2 in revealing the polysemy of Korean postpositions. Second, there was an inverse relation between the classification performance and the number of functions of each postposition. Third, the model was affected by the corpus size of each function. Fourth, the model was able to identify the intended functions of a postposition as the epoch progressed. Fifth, these models were affected by the rarely occurring input and/or semantic closeness between the items, limiting the performance of two models in the given task to some extent.

The findings of this study should be further verified by incorporating more postposition types that have similar degrees of polysemy that three adverbial postpositions demonstrate. Future study will also benefit from considering other contextualized word-embedding models such as GPT-3 (Brown et al., 2020) or ELECTRA (Clark et al., 2020) to better ascertain the advantage of transformer-architecture models in this kind of task.

We believe our visualization system will contribute to extending the current understanding of how transformer-architecture models work for language tasks (particularly in non-English settings).

Acknowledgments

We would like to thank Gyu-Ho Shin and the three anonymous reviewers for their comments and feedback. The research of Seongmin Mun was also supported by Basic Science Research Program through the National Research Foundation of Korea (NRF) funded by the Ministry of Education (2021R1I1A2051993) and Institute for Information communications Technology Planning Evaluation (IITP) grant funded by the Korea government (MSIT) (2019-0-01371, Development of brain-inspired AI with human-like intelligence).

References

Jangseong Bae, Changki Lee, Junho Lim, and Hyunki Kim. 2020a. Bert-based data augmentation techniques for korean semantic role labeling. pages 335–337.

Jangseong Bae, Changki Lee, and Soojong Lim. 2015. Korean semantic role labeling using deep learning. *Korean Information Science Society*, 6:690–692.

Jangseong Bae, Changki Lee, Soojong Lim, and Hyunki Kim. 2020b. Korean semantic role labeling with bert. *The Korean Institute of Information Scientists and Engineers*, 47(11):1021–1026.

Jangseong Bae, Junho Oh, Hyunsun Hwang, and Changki Lee. 2014. Extending korean propbank for korean semantic role labeling and applying domain adaptation technique. *Korean Information Processing Society*, pages 44–47.

Tom B. Brown, Benjamin Mann, Nick Ryder, Melanie Subbiah, Jared Kaplan, Prafulla Dhariwal, Arvind Neelakantan, Pranav Shyam, Girish Sastry, Amanda Askell, Sandhini Agarwal, Ariel Herbert-Voss, Gretchen Krueger, Tom Henighan, Rewon Child, Aditya Ramesh, Daniel M. Ziegler, Jeffrey Wu, Clemens Winter, Christopher Hesse, Mark Chen, Eric Sigler, Mateusz Litwin, Scott Gray, Benjamin Chess, Jack Clark, Christopher Berner, Sam McCandlish, Alec Radford, Ilya Sutskever, and Dario Amodei. 2020. Language models are few-shot learners. *CoRR*, abs/2005.14165.

Jeong-mi Cho and Gil-cheng Kim. 1996. A study on the resolving of the ambiguity while interpretation of meaning in korean. *The Korean Institute of Information Scientists and Engineers*, 14(7):71–83.

Miho Choo and Hye-young Kwak. 2008. *Using Korean*. Cambridge University Press, New York, NY.

Kevin Clark, Minh-Thang Luong, Quoc V. Le, and Christopher D. Manning. 2020. ELECTRA: pre-training text encoders as discriminators rather than generators. *CoRR*, abs/2003.10555.

Guillaume Desagulier. 2019. Can word vectors help corpus linguists? *Studia Neophilologica*, 91(2):219–240.

Jacob Devlin, Ming-Wei Chang, Kenton Lee, and Kristina Toutanova. 2018. BERT: pre-training of deep bidirectional transformers for language understanding. *CoRR*, abs/1810.04805.

Kawin Ethayarajh. 2019. How contextual are contextualized word representations? comparing the geometry of BERT, ELMo, and GPT-2 embeddings. In *Proceedings of the 2019 Conference on Empirical Methods in Natural Language Processing and the 9th International Joint Conference on Natural Language Processing (EMNLP-IJCNLP)*, pages 55–65, Hong Kong, China. Association for Computational Linguistics.

Philip Gage. 1994. A new algorithm for data compression. *C Users J.*, 12(2):23–38.

Dylan Glynn and Justyna Robinson. 2014. *Corpus Methods for Semantics*. Corpus Methods for Semantics. Quantitative studies in polysemy and synonymy. John Benjamins.

Janosch Haber and Massimo Poesio. 2021. Patterns of polysemy and homonymy in contextualised language models. In *Findings of the Association for Computational Linguistics: EMNLP 2021*, pages 2663–2676, Punta Cana, Dominican Republic. Association for Computational Linguistics.

Seung-Yean Hong, Seung-Hoon Na, Jong-Hoon Shin, and Young-kil Kim. 2020. Roberta and stack pointer network for korean semantic role labeling. *The Korean Institute of Information Scientists and Engineers*, pages 362–364.

Heewon Jeon, Hyung jun Kim, Seujung Jung, Muhyun Kim, Yunho Maeng, Kyeongpil Kang, and Sangwhan Moon. 2021. Kogpt2 ver 2.0.

Heewon Jeon, Donggeon Lee, and Jangwon Park. 2019. Korean bert pre-trained cased (kobert).

Byong-cheol Jeong. 2010. An integrated study on the particle '*-ey*' based on the simulation model. *The Linguistic Science Society*, 55:275–304.

Wan-su Kim and Cheol-young Ock. 2016. Korean semantic role labeling using case frame dictionary and subcategorization. *The Korean Institute of Information Scientists and Engineers*, 43(12):1376–1384.

Josef Klafka and Allyson Ettinger. 2020. Spying on your neighbors: Fine-grained probing of contextual embeddings for information about surrounding words. In *Proceedings of the 58th Annual Meeting of the Association for Computational Linguistics*, pages

4801–4811, Online. Association for Computational Linguistics.

Zhenzhong Lan, Mingda Chen, Sebastian Goodman, Kevin Gimpel, Piyush Sharma, and Radu Soricut. 2019. ALBERT: A lite BERT for self-supervised learning of language representations. *CoRR*, abs/1909.11942.

Changki Lee, Soojong Lim, and Hyunki Kim. 2015. Korean semantic role labeling using structured svm. *The Korean Institute of Information Scientists and Engineers*, 42(2):220–226.

Nelson F. Liu, Matt Gardner, Yonatan Belinkov, Matthew E. Peters, and Noah A. Smith. 2019a. Linguistic knowledge and transferability of contextual representations. In *Proceedings of the 2019 Conference of the North American Chapter of the Association for Computational Linguistics: Human Language Technologies, Volume 1 (Long and Short Papers)*, pages 1073–1094, Minneapolis, Minnesota. Association for Computational Linguistics.

Yinhan Liu, Myle Ott, Naman Goyal, Jingfei Du, Mandar Joshi, Danqi Chen, Omer Levy, Mike Lewis, Luke Zettlemoyer, and Veselin Stoyanov. 2019b. Roberta: A robustly optimized bert pretraining approach. Cite arxiv:1907.11692.

Daniel Loureiro and Alípio Jorge. 2019. Language modelling makes sense: Propagating representations through WordNet for full-coverage word sense disambiguation. In *Proceedings of the 57th Annual Meeting of the Association for Computational Linguistics*, pages 5682–5691, Florence, Italy. Association for Computational Linguistics.

Laurens van der Maaten and Geoffrey Hinton. 2008. Visualizing Data using t-SNE. *Journal of Machine Learning Research*, 9(Nov):2579–2605.

Chris McCormick. 2019. Bert fine-tuning tutorial with pytorch.

George Michalopoulos, Yuanxin Wang, Hussam Kaka, Helen Chen, and Alexander Wong. 2021. UmlsBERT: Clinical domain knowledge augmentation of contextual embeddings using the Unified Medical Language System Metathesaurus. In *Proceedings of the 2021 Conference of the North American Chapter of the Association for Computational Linguistics: Human Language Technologies*, pages 1744–1753, Online. Association for Computational Linguistics.

Seongmin Mun. 2021. *Polysemy resolution with word embedding models and data visualization : the case of adverbial postpositions -ey, -eyse, and -(u)lo in Korean.* Theses, Université de Nanterre - Paris X.

Seongmin Mun and Gyu-Ho Shin. 2020. Context window and polysemy interpretation: A case of korean adverbial postposition *-(u)lo*. In *IMPRS Conference 2020: Interdisciplinary Approaches to the Language Sciences, Max Planck Institute for Psycholinguistics.*

Ki-sim Nam. 1993. The use of the korean postposition: focus on '*-ey*' and '*-(u)lo*'. *sekwang hakswul calyosa.*

Chanmin Park, Yeongjoon Park, Youngjoong Ko, and Jungyun Seo. 2019. Semantic role labeling using the korean elmo embedding. *The Korean Institute of Information Scientists and Engineers*, pages 608–610.

Jeong-woon Park. 1999. A polysemy network of the korean instrumental case. *Korean Journal of Linguistics*, 24(3):405–425.

Giovanni Puccetti, Alessio Miaschi, and Felice Dell'Orletta. 2021. How do BERT embeddings organize linguistic knowledge? In *Proceedings of Deep Learning Inside Out (DeeLIO): The 2nd Workshop on Knowledge Extraction and Integration for Deep Learning Architectures*, pages 48–57, Online. Association for Computational Linguistics.

Alec Radford, Karthik Narasimhan, Tim Salimans, and Ilya Sutskever. 2018a. Improving language understanding by generative pre-training.

Alec Radford, Jeffrey Wu, Rewon Child, David Luan, Dario Amodei, and Ilya Sutskever. 2018b. Language models are unsupervised multitask learners.

Jörg Sander, Martin Ester, Hans-Peter Kriegel, and Xiaowei Xu. 1998. Density-based clustering in spatial databases: The algorithm gdbscan and its applications. *Data Mining and Knowledge Discovery*, 2(2):169–194.

Rico Sennrich, Barry Haddow, and Alexandra Birch. 2016. Neural machine translation of rare words with subword units. In *ACL (1)*. The Association for Computer Linguistics.

Hyo-pil Shin. 2008. The 21st sejong project : with a focus on selk (sejong electronic lexicon of korean) and the knc (korean national corpus). In *In The 3rd International Joint Conference on Natural Langauge Processing*.

Myung-chul Shin, Yong-hun Lee, Mi-young Kim, You-jin Chung, and Jong-hyeok Lee. 2005. Semantic role assignment for korean adverbial case using sejong electronic dictionary. *Korea Information Science Society*, pages 120–126.

Ho-Min Sohn. 1999. *The korean language*. Cambridge University Press, Cambridge, UK.

Aina Garí Soler and Marianna Apidianaki. 2021. Let's play mono-poly: BERT can reveal words' polysemy level and partitionability into senses. *CoRR*, abs/2104.14694.

Dae-heon Song. 2014. A study on the adverbial case particles of '*-ey*' and '*-eyse*' for korean language education. *The Association of Korean Education*, 101:457–484.

Raúl Vázquez, Alessandro Raganato, Mathias Creutz, and Jörg Tiedemann. 2020. A systematic study of inner-attention-based sentence representations in multilingual neural machine translation. *Computational Linguistics*, 46(2):387–424.

Thomas Wolf, Lysandre Debut, Victor Sanh, Julien Chaumond, Clement Delangue, Anthony Moi, Pierric Cistac, Tim Rault, Rémi Louf, Morgan Funtowicz, and Jamie Brew. 2019. Huggingface's transformers: State-of-the-art natural language processing. *CoRR*, abs/1910.03771.

Yu Wu, Wei Wu, Chen Xing, Can Xu, Zhoujun Li, and Ming Zhou. 2019. A sequential matching framework for multi-turn response selection in retrieval-based chatbots. *Computational Linguistics*, 45(1):163–197.

David Yenicelik, Florian Schmidt, and Yannic Kilcher. 2020. How does BERT capture semantics? a closer look at polysemous words. In *Proceedings of the Third BlackboxNLP Workshop on Analyzing and Interpreting Neural Networks for NLP*, pages 156–162, Online. Association for Computational Linguistics.

Zeyu Yun, Yubei Chen, Bruno Olshausen, and Yann LeCun. 2021. Transformer visualization via dictionary learning: contextualized embedding as a linear superposition of transformer factors. In *Proceedings of Deep Learning Inside Out (DeeLIO): The 2nd Workshop on Knowledge Extraction and Integration for Deep Learning Architectures*, pages 1–10, Online. Association for Computational Linguistics.

Query Generation with External Knowledge for Dense Retrieval

Sukmin Cho Soyeong Jeong Wonsuk Yang Jong C. Park*
School of Computing
Korea Advanced Institute of Science and Technology
{nelllpic,syjeong,derrick0511,park}@nlp.kaist.ac.kr

Abstract

Dense retrieval aims at searching for the most relevant documents to the given query by encoding texts in the embedding space, requiring a large amount of query-document pairs to train. Since manually constructing such training data is challenging, recent work has proposed to generate synthetic queries from documents and use them to train a dense retriever. However, compared to the human labeled queries, synthetic queries do not generally ask for hidden information, therefore leading to a degraded retrieval performance. In this work, we propose *Query Generation with External Knowledge* (QGEK), a novel method for generating queries with external knowledge related to the corresponding document. Specifically, we convert a query into a triplet-based template to accommodate external knowledge and transmit it to a pre-trained language model (PLM). We validate QGEK in both in-domain and out-domain dense retrieval settings. The dense retriever with the queries requiring external knowledge is found to make good performance improvement. Also, such queries are similar to the human labeled queries, confirmed by both human evaluation and unique & non-unique words distribution.

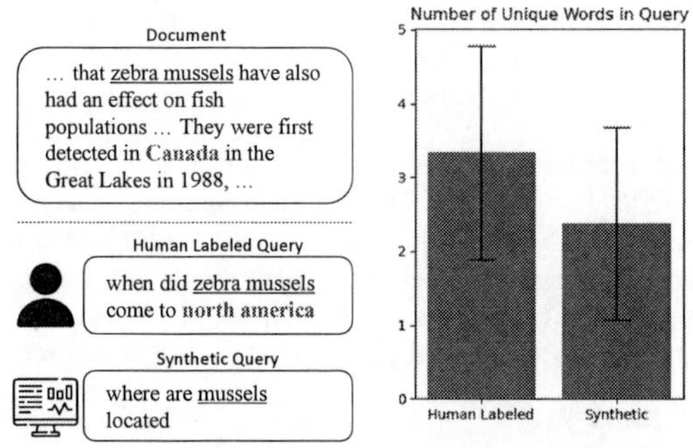

Figure 1: The analysis of human labeled query and synthetic query. (Left) Examples of the human labeled query and synthetic query. (Right) Average of unique words in human labeled query and synthetic query.

1 Introduction

Information retrieval (IR) is the task of collecting relevant documents from a large corpus when given a query. IR not only plays an important role in the search system by itself, but is also crucially applied to various NLP tasks such as Open-Domain QA (Kwiatkowski et al., 2019) and Citation-Prediction (Cohan et al., 2020) with its ability to find grounding documents. As the simplest retrieval method, traditional term-based sparse models such as TF-IDF and BM25 (Robertson and Zaragoza, 2009) are widely used. However, these sparse retrieval models are unable to capture the semantic similarities without explicit lexical overlaps between the query and its relevant documents. As a solution, dense retrieval models are recently proposed where query and document representations are embedded into the latent space (Gillick et al., 2018; Karpukhin et al., 2020), though they require a large amount of paired query-document training samples for notable performance, which is very challenging and expensive. In response, a zero-shot setting is often adopted, but dense retrievers are known to show poor performance on a new target domain (Ma et al., 2021; Wang et al., 2021; Xin et al., 2021).

One possible solution is to generate synthetic queries by fine-tuning a pre-trained language model (PLM) on a large IR benchmark dataset, and to use such queries for training dense retrievers (Ma et al., 2021; Thakur et al., 2021; Wang et al., 2021). However, this method does not yet provide synthetic queries whose quality is comparable to that of human labeled ones, thus hindering retrieval performance.

In particular, we argue that, for the effective training of dense retrievers, query samples should be allowed to contain external knowledge that is not explicitly shown in documents. As Figure 1

* Corresponding author

Proceedings of Deep Learning Inside Out (DeeLIO 2022): The 3rd Workshop on Knowledge Extraction and Integration for Deep Learning Architectures, pages 22 - 32
May 27, 2022 ©2022 Association for Computational Linguistics

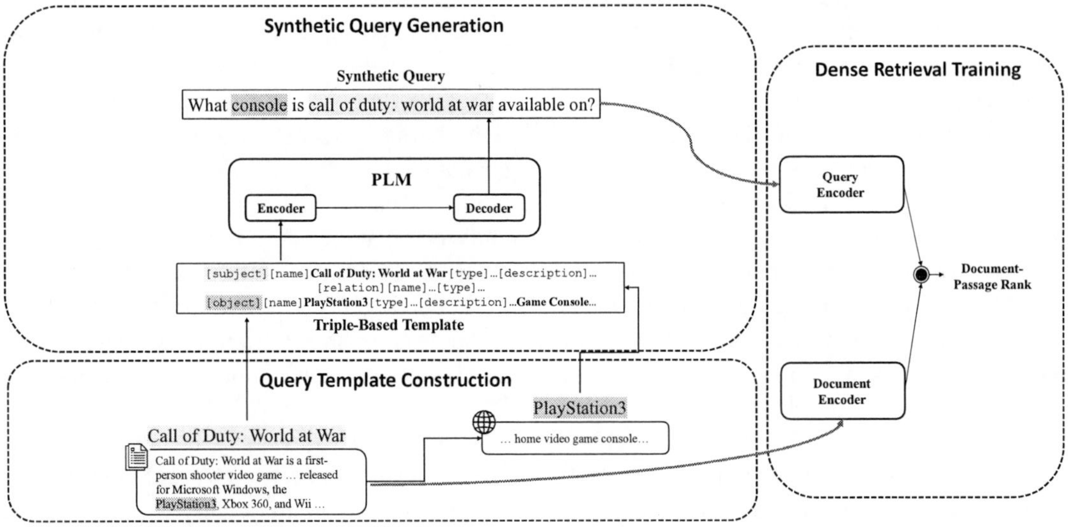

Figure 2: Overall methods of query generation with external knowledge and dense retrieval training with synthetic queries.

shows, the human labeled query contains the external knowledge that Canada and North America are related, which is easily grasped by humans but not by the machine. Also, unique words in the query, often considered as external knowledge, are more frequently included in the human labeled queries than in the synthetic queries. The dense retrievers would better capture semantic relations if they are trained with such queries that show more characteristics of human labeled ones.

In this paper, we focus on generating queries with external knowledge by employing a simple method of explicitly transmitting document-related information to a PLM. Even though PLMs can handle hidden information to some extent by learning from a large amount of data, we argue that transmitting additional pieces of external knowledge to a PLM contributes positively to generating queries requiring external knowledge. Specifically, we first interpret the given query into a triplet-based template to consider the given document and related external knowledge together. A PLM is then fine-tuned to generate queries from triplet-based templates, together with a processed KB-QA dataset. The dense retriever is trained with the synthetic queries from the template extracted from the given document and corresponding external knowledge. The proposed method, henceforth referred to as *Query Generation with External Knowledge* (QGEK), is schematically illustrated in Figure 2.

We validate QGEK in both in-domain and out-domain (zero-shot) dense retrieval settings with diverse evaluation metrics. The experimental results show that queries that require external knowledge to answer are helpful for improving retrieval performance. Furthermore, we provide detailed qualitative analyses of synthetic queries and discuss which aspects of queries should be considered when training dense retrieval models.

Our contributions in this work are threefold:

- We propose a generation method of queries that require hidden information, not present in the document, from external sources.
- We experimentally show that the generated queries are similar to the gold queries that are labeled by human annotators.
- We evaluate the quality of generated queries with respect to dense retrieval performance and distribution of unique words so as to find optimal queries in training a dense retriever.

2 Related Work

2.1 Dense Retriever

The sparse retriever, a traditional IR system, retrieves the target documents based on the lexical values such as frequency of terms and documents. BM25 (Robertson and Zaragoza, 2009) has been arguably the most frequently used method for such IR. However, as the retriever mainly handles the match of the lexical entries, 'semantically similar' but not the same lexical entries are not considered in the search for documents, affecting the user experience (Berger et al., 2000).

The dense retriever (Karpukhin et al., 2020) has received much attention as a solution to handle the problem, triggered by the Transformer (Vaswani et al., 2017) network and PLM. A dense retriever fetches the documents located closest to the query vector in the dense vector space with the results recorded in advance for retrieval performance. The model maps queries and documents to the dense vector space using a bi-encoder structure initialized from a PLM such as BERT (Devlin et al., 2019a).

The dense retriever requires a large-scale dataset for model training, and curating such datasets is a much arduous endeavor. Thakur et al. (2021) proposed a zero-shot setting where dense retrievers are trained on a single large IR corpus, rather than on every dataset. Nonetheless, retrieval in such setting is still quite challenging.

2.2 Query Generation

Query generation is a simple method that addresses the shortage of training data for a dense retriever (Ma et al., 2021; Thakur et al., 2021; Wang et al., 2021). The most commonly used method has been to fine-tune the T5-base model (Raffel et al., 2020) to the MS MARCO dataset (Nguyen et al., 2016) and create a synthetic query in the target domain. Exploiting the size and domain of MS MARCO, we can obtain an effective retrieval performance by fine-tuning the T5 model. Info-HCVAE (Lee et al., 2020) achieved good performance by designing the relationship between document, query, and answer as a probability distribution and learning the latent vectors based on an auto-encoder. Answers and documents are used as inputs when creating queries. In these two methods, however, the processing of hidden information in the document still depends only on PLMs.

The existing methods focus only on the given document when generating queries, without much consideration of hidden information. In contrast, QGEK includes not only the document but also the hidden information that can be inferred from the given document with external knowledge.

2.3 Exploiting External Knowledge

External knowledge has been widely used along with PLMs for several NLP tasks. (Wang et al., 2020) augmented PLMs using ConceptNet (Speer et al., 2017) for a commonsense question answering (QA) task and showed that KB, such as ConceptNet, contributes to the explicit grounding of the output, resulting in better reasoning abilities.

Furthermore, Zhou et al. (2018) proposed to generate knowledge-based dialogues for an Open-Domain Dialogue system. Dinan et al. (2019) confirmed that the additional external knowledge positively affects dialogue generation. In addition, Shuster et al. (2021) showed that the related external knowledge can be exploited to address critical issues, such as factual incorrectness and hallucination, in dialogue systems.

While external knowledge from KB has proved helpful in Commonsense QA and Open-Domain Dialogue domains, it is relatively underexplored for generating synthetic queries for dense retrieval. In this work, we adopt KB into a PLM for query generation and show the effectiveness of training dense retrievers with the synthetic queries on IR benchmark datasets.

3 Methods

QGEK is designed to generate a new synthetic query that requires an implicit inference process for the answer by exploiting both the given document and external knowledge hidden in the document. First, we interpret the query as the triplet $<S,R,O>$ that can easily utilize both of them, where the triplet is converted into a single-text template to simplify the transmission to a PLM. Then, we construct triplet-based template & query pairs as training datasets for fine-tuning a PLM. For generating a query from target documents, the triplet-based template is extracted from a general document.

3.1 Preliminaries

The dense retriever maps query q and document d into an n-dimensional vector space with query encoder $E_Q(\cdot, \theta_q)$ and document encoder $E_D(\cdot, \theta_d)$ where θ is the encoder's parameter. The similarity score $f(q, d)$ between query q and document d is computed as a dot product:

$$f(q, p) = E_Q(q, \theta_q)^T \cdot E_D(d, \theta_d)$$

Training the dense retriever targets the vector space of which the relevant query and document pairs have a high similarity score compared to irrelevant pairs. Given query q, let (D_q^+, D_q^-) be the pairs of the sets of relevant documents and irrelevant documents. The objective function of dense

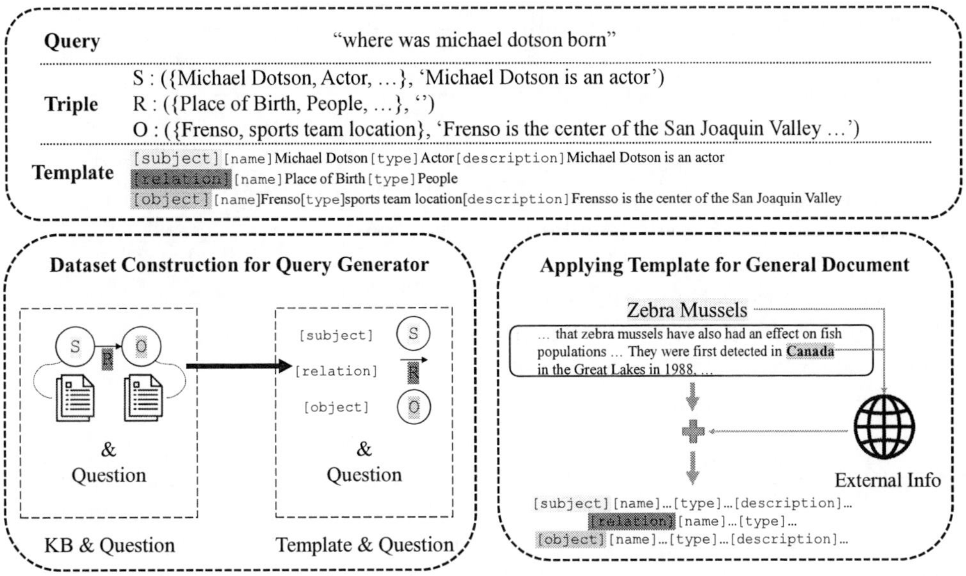

Figure 3: Overview of the Methods for Query Generation based on Triplet-based Template.

retriever is as follows:

$$\min_{\theta} \sum_{q} \sum_{d^+ \in D_q^+} \sum_{d^- \in D_q^-} L(f(q, d^+), f(q, d^-))$$

The loss L is the negative log likelihood of the positive passage.

3.2 Query Interpretation as Triplet Form

Queries can be simply mapped to the <S, R, O> triplet. The query <S, R, O> asks for the answer O, which has relationship R with subject S. For example, the query "big little lies season 2 how many episodes" and the answer "7 episodes" can be mapped to <"big little lies season 2", "number of episodes", "7 episodes">.

Information of each item in a triplet can be largely divided into sentences or words units. We use two types of information to express each item of a triplet in more detail. Let $W_x = \{w_x^1, \ldots, w_x^n\}$ and l_x be the set of word unit information and the single sentence unit information of the item x, respectively. Then, query Q can be interpreted as the triplet items with their own information:

$$Q = \{(W_S, l_S), (W_R, l_R), (W_O, l_O)\}$$

For generating a query that requires an implicit inference, a form of query that can utilize both the document and external knowledge is required. The proposed triplet simply handles both document and external knowledge by arranging information into the appropriate positions in the triplet. When transmitting such triplets to a PLM, we use the simple form of a single text template. The triplet-based template consists of triplet items delimited by special tokens as shown in Figure 3.

3.3 Dataset Construction for Query Generator

We construct a dataset consisting of triplet-query pairs for fine-tuning PLM. The KB based query can be converted into the proposed triplet. A canonical logical form of a KB based query is a representation that expresses the same meaning as the relationship between entities in KB. A simple interpretation of the proposed triplet can be seen as a canonical form consisting of two entities and a relationship between them.

For example, suppose that the entity, 'Michael Dotson', is first selected as subject S and has word unit information, 'Actor', and sentence unit information, 'Michael Dotson is an actor'. Suppose also that there is an entity, 'Frenso', linked by 'place-of-birth' relationship with 'Michael Dotson'. The other entity and relationship may have their own information from KB. The triplet-based template is created by combining all of them.

3.4 Applying Template for General Document

The fine-tuned PLM with the dataset constructed in Section 3.3 needs the triplet-based template to generate a query from a general document. We extract triplet items from the given document, and collect external knowledge to fill the template from the open web.

For example, suppose that there is a document about zebra mussels (cf. Figure 3). The subject S, relation R and object O are selected as 'zebra mussels', 'location' and 'Canada', respectively. The document alone is not enough to fill the information of object O, 'Canada'. The external knowledge, 'Canada is a country in North America', is extracted from the open web. Both given document and external knowledge are arranged into the appropriate positions in the template.

4 Experimental setups

We evaluate the performances of the dense retriever when trained with the synthetic queries compared to the human labeled queries. The dense retriever used in our experiments is the DPR (Karpukhin et al., 2020). The train dataset of the dense retriever is the pairs of the documents of Natural Question (NQ) (Kwiatkowski et al., 2019), also exploited as the source of the query generator, and the synthetic queries of the proposed method.

4.1 Datasets

We evaluate the effectiveness of the generated queries when using external knowledge on IR benchmark datasets. We conduct experiments in two settings: in-domain and out-domain (zero-shot). We measure the in-domain performance on the NQ and the out-domain performance on 13 representative IR datasets (Thakur et al., 2021).

In-Domain Dataset NQ (Kwiatkowski et al., 2019) is a benchmark dataset for the open-domain question answering task, fetched by Google search engine and from Wikipedia. We use the preprocessed version of the NQ following DPR (Karpukhin et al., 2020), which includes 58,880 training pairs and 7,405 test queries. The documents in NQ is used as input of query generator.

Out-Domain Dataset To validate the quality of generated queries for training the dense retriever, it is necessary to show the retrieval performance of diverse tasks. Each dataset used in out-domain experiments has diverse tasks and domains and requires retrieval models for finding grounding documents. They are shown in Table 1.

Task	Domain	Dataset
Argument Retrieval	Misc.	ArguAna (Wachsmuth et al., 2018)
	Misc.	Touche-2020 (Bondarenko et al., 2020)
Entity-Retrieval	Wikipedia	DBPedia (Hasibi et al., 2017)
Question Anwering	Wikipedia	HotpotQA (Yang et al., 2018)
	Finance	FiQA-2018 (Maia et al., 2018)
Duplicate-Question Retrieval	Quora	Quora (Thakur et al., 2021)
Fact Checking	Wikipedia	FEVER (Thorne et al., 2018)
	Wikipedia	Climate-Fever (Leippold and Diggelmann, 2020)
	Scientific	SciFact (Wadden et al., 2020)
Passage-Retrieval	Misc.	MS MARCO (Nguyen et al., 2016)
Citation-Prediction	Scientific	SCIDOCS (Cohan et al., 2020)
Bio-Medical IR	Bio-Medical	TREC-COVID (Voorhees et al., 2021)
	Bio-Medical	NFCorpus (Boteva et al., 2016)

Table 1: Datasets for Out-Domain Experiments

4.2 Metrics

We explain the metrics for evaluating the performance of a dense retriever. In the basic setting, the retriever searches for top k relevant documents on a given query. We employ 4 metrics for top k documents: ACC@k, MRR@k, MAP@k, and nDCG@k. The in-domain experiment is evaluated with these 4 metrics, and the out-domain performance is evaluated with only nDCG@10.

ACC@k is the percentage of whether the correct documents are included in the top-k hits. It ignores the rank of retrieved documents.

MRR@k (Mean Reciprocal Rank) computes the average of the ranks of the first correct document from top-k documents. The rest of the correct documents are not included in computing MRR.

MAP@k (Mean Average Precision) first computes the average precision score of the correct documents' ranks in top-k hits for a given query. The mean of the average precision scores is the value of the MAP@K.

nDCG@k (Normalised Cumulative Discount Gain) is similar to MAP@k, but reflects the fact that the more relevant document is the more highly ranked in top-k documents.

4.3 Implementation Details

Query Generator We used BART (Lewis et al., 2020), one of the widely used PLMs, to generate the synthetic query from the proposed template. BART based on the transformer seq2seq architecture is trained by reconstructing text from noised input. The de-noising ability of BART is suitable for generating queries from text with noise from the external source.

SimpleQuestions (Bordes et al., 2015) (SQ), a question answering dataset based on KB, is se-

In-Domain								
Train Query (↓)	**ACC@10**	**ACC@100**	**MRR@10**	**MRR@100**	**MAP@10**	**MAP@100**	**NDCG@10**	**NDCG@100**
Gold	.6374	.8974	.3372	.3493	.3146	.3296	.3892	.4543
QGEK	.4901	.7488	.2375	.2484	.2220	.2354	.2841	.3449
(-) Ext. Knowledge	.4860	.7285	.2348	.2457	.2162	.2295	.2745	.3357

Out-Domain														
Train Query (↓)	**Arguana**	**DBpedia**	**fiqa**	**HotpotQA**	**NFC**	**Quora**	**SciFact**	**Touche-2020**	**C-Fever**	**Fever**	**MS MARCO**	**SciDocs**	**TREC-COVID**	**Avg.**
Gold	.2203	.2585	.1763	.3205	.2226	.5778	.4476	.2334	.1609	.5160	.1858	.1022	.5152	.3029
QGEK	.0948	**.2733**	.1182	**.4226**	.1791	.4982	.3436	.2093	**.1754**	**.7731**	.1738	.0945	.4411	.2921
(-) Ext. Knowledge	.0568	.2555	.1138	**.4105**	.1876	.2366	.3001	.1890	**.1831**	**.7883**	.1757	.0800	.4427	.2630

Table 2: In-domain and Out-domain performance of DPR. The scores for out-domain denote nDCG@10. The scores over the gold query are marked in **bold**, and the better scores between queries from QGEK are underlined.

lected to convert the query's logical form into the proposed template. A query in SQ is generated from a one-to-one correspondence of KB entities, which is very similar to the form of our proposed triplet. The conversion process proceeds in the same way as mentioned in Section 3.3.

The BART-large ($d = 1024$) is fine-tuned for 5 epochs with 47,180 template-query pairs. For training the model, Adam optimizer (Kingma and Ba, 2015) is used with the batch size of 8, and the learning rate starts from 10^{-5}.

Query Generation We used the documents in the NQ train split (Kwiatkowski et al., 2019), exploited as a training dataset in DPR (Karpukhin et al., 2020), as the target dataset for query generation. The documents are converted into a template through the process described in Section 3.4. To obtain external knowledge of the subject and object, the first paragraph and category information of the Wikipedia documents are collected and inserted into the template. The generated queries and the corresponding NQ documents, input of the queries, are used in the training step of DPR.

Retriever model The dense retriever used in the training has the same structure proposed by DPR (Karpukhin et al., 2020), which has a bi-encoder structure that calculates the dot product between query and document embedding as the ranking score. The train dataset consists of the generated queries and the corresponding NQ documents for comparison with the human labeled queries of NQ. The encoder is initialized from BERT (base, uncased) (Devlin et al., 2019b). The retriever is trained with Adam optimizer (Kingma and Ba, 2015) for 25 epochs. The negative samples for contrastive learning are sampled from a single batch. The size of the train batch is 8 and the learning rate is initialized with $2 \cdot 10^{-5}$.

5 Result & Discussion

5.1 Overall Result

Our main results are shown in Table 2. We evaluate the retrieval performance of the dense retriever trained with the synthetic queries from QGEK against the gold query in the NQ train split. In the in-domain experiments, the dense retriever with the gold query of NQ showed superior performance over the retriever with QGEK. QGEK shows better performance in all metrics than the ablation case not including external knowledge in the proposed triplet. The average of NDCG@10 in out-domain experiments shows a small difference (-0.0108) between the gold queries and QGEK. In detail, the retriever trained with QGEK shows better performance on 4 datasets: DBpedia, HotpotQA, Fever, and Climate-Fever. The rest of the 9 datasets show that the retriever with the gold queries is more appropriate.

Using external knowledge gives rise to generating more appropriate queries for most datasets than not using one, though human labeled queries are more appropriate for training the dense retriever in the in-domain experiments. On the other hand, we see that QGEK gives comparable performance to the one with human labeled queries in the out-domain experiments and even outperforms on some datasets.

5.2 Analysis of Synthetic Queries

Experiments are conducted to compare against query generator baselines. We selected GenQ (Thakur et al., 2021) and Info-HCVAE (Lee et al., 2020) models as the baselines. The models receive the documents in NQ train split as input. The size

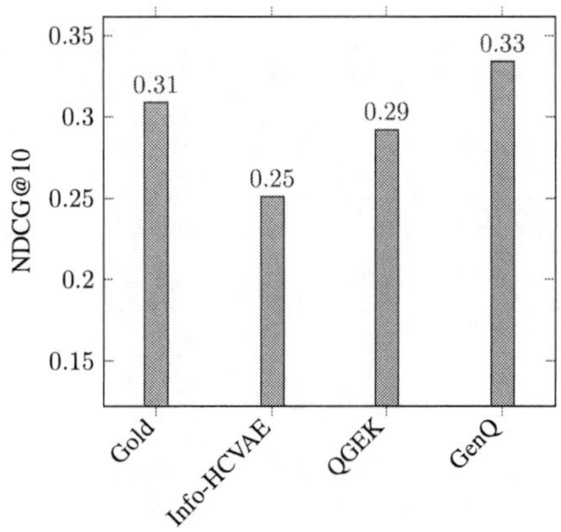

Figure 4: NDCG@10 average of the dense retrieval trained with various queries for NQ and 13 out-domain datasets.

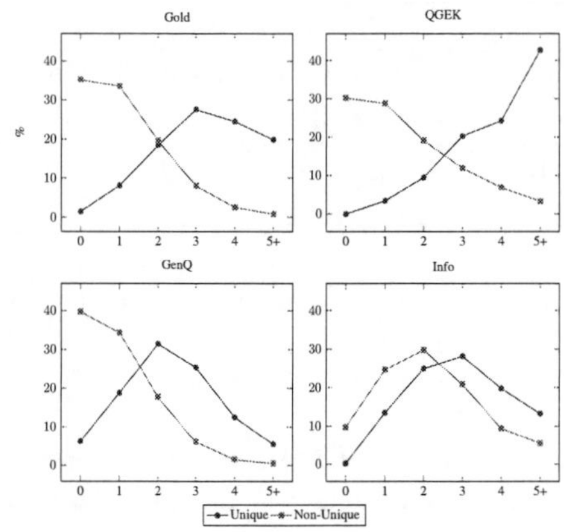

Figure 5: Distribution of unique & non-unique words in the queries.

and documents of the dataset are the same as those of the NQ train split except for synthetic queries.

Baseline Comparison A comparison with other query creation methods is made, as shown in Figure 4. The average of the NDCG@10 performance in in-domain and out-domain experiments is calculated by training the dense retriever through the generated queries. The models trained with synthetic queries are sorted as GenQ, QGEK, and Info-HCVAE in descending order. QGEK shows somewhat lower performance than the one with gold queries, but GenQ shows the best performance, indicating that many queries suitable for the IR tasks are generated by training on the MS MARCO dataset.

The MS MARCO dataset is most widely used for dense retriever training, and training a dense retriever with MS MARCO is known to give a higher performance than training it on other datasets such as NQ. Also, it has a huge amount of data, more than 500,000 pairs. This has the advantage of generating queries suitable for IR tasks based on abundant and task-appropriate data. However, the proposed method is trained on a relatively small amount of 47,180 data from SimpleQuestions, a KB-QA dataset. There is a possibility that the generated queries are largely incompatible with the IR task. However, the proposed method focuses on utilizing external knowledge, and it can be applied orthogonally to the MS MARCO dataset, which we leave for future work.

Unique & Non-Unique Words in Query We analyze whether the words in a query are from the corresponding documents. The implicitly inferring query has a higher probability of including unique words not present in the document. So, the distribution of unique & non-unique words can indirectly tell the existence of such queries. The stop words, such as the interrogative word and articles, in a query are excluded from the analysis.

The distribution of unique words in a query is shown in Figure 5. The 27% of gold labels of NQ contain 3 unique words, and 80% of the cases contain 4 or fewer unique words. QGEK shows a similar pattern of non-unique words compared with the gold, and over 40% of queries contain more than 5 unique words. The distribution of GenQ shows a similar pattern to that of the gold queries in both unique and non-unique words. Unlike other models, the Info most frequently includes 2 non-unique words.

Note that QGEK generates queries with more unique words than other queries, together with a similar distribution of non-unique words to that of gold queries. This implies that QGEK can generate queries requesting hidden information not present in the document. Given the performance of the dense retriever (Figure 4) and the distribution of unique & non-unique words (Figure 5), generating queries both close to the human labeled ones and appropriate to the IR tasks is an important factor for an optimal training of the dense retriever. Our future work includes generating queries not only close to human labeled ones but also optimized for IR tasks, such as exploiting the MS MARCO dataset.

Manual Evaluation We use human evaluation to check whether the synthetic queries are similar to human labeled ones. The randomly sampled 30

	Document 1	Document 2	Document 3
Document	(...) reporting having problems with their water treatment plants with the mussels attaching themselves to pipeworks. (...) They were first detected in Canada in the Great Lakes in 1988, in Lake St. Clair, located east/northeast of Detroit and Windsor. (...)	Call of Duty: World at War is a first-person shooter video game developed by Treyarch and published by Activision. It was released for Microsoft Windows, the PlayStation 3, Xbox 360, and Wii in November 2008. (...) "World at War" received ports featuring different storyline versions, while remaining in the World War II setting, for the and . (...)	(...) Call the Midwife is a BBC period drama series about a group of nurse midwives working in the East End of London in the late 1950s and early 1960s. It stars Jessica Raine, Miranda Hart, Helen George, Bryony Hannah, Laura Main, Jenny Agutter, Pam Ferris, (...) and Leonie Elliott. The series is produced by Neal Street Productions, a production company founded (...)
Gold Label	when did zebra mussels come to **north america**	who made call of duty world at war	where in london is call the midwife set
QGEK	What is the date zebra mussel was first detected in Canada?	What **console** is call of duty: world at war available on	who is the **actress** for call the midwife
(-) Ext. Knowledge	what country is zebra mussel found	what is the setting of call of duty: world at war	who produced call the midwife
Info-HCVAE	where did the lake st. clairs originate?	what setting was the setting for the game of the " world at war :"?	in what time period did the bbc's the midcene series take place?
GenQ	where are mussels located	what year did call of duty world at war come out	cast of call the midwife

Table 3: Examples of documents and the corresponding queries. The non-unique words are underlined, and the unique words are marked in **bold**.

documents and corresponding queries are given to three annotators fluent in English. After reading the given documents, annotators evaluated each query on a scale of 0-5 against three points: 1) how relevant a given query is to the document (Relevancy), 2) how grammatically natural it is (Grammaticality), and 3) how much reasoning is needed to answer (Difficulty).

Query	Relevancy	Grammaticality	Difficulty
Gold	3.95 (±1.38)	3.80 (±1.12)	2.10 (±1.43)
QGEK	3.66 (±1.50)	**4.07 (±1.04)**	**2.39 (±1.50)**
Info-HCVAE	3.66 (±1.45)	4.01 (±1.13)	2.31 (±1.52)
GenQ	4.12 (±1.20)	4.02 (±1.26)	1.90 (±1.21)

Table 4: The result of human evaluation. Statistically significant difference compared to gold via t-test ($p < 0.05$) is marked in **bold**.

As shown in Table 4, QGEK shows statistically higher degrees of grammaticality and difficulty than the gold labels. These results indicate that queries from QGEK need more hidden information not present in the documents compared to other queries.

Case Study Examples of the documents and corresponding queries are shown in Table 3.

Document 1 is about the water treatment problem caused by mussels. In answering the gold label, external knowledge that Canada is in North America is needed for the inference from the document. However, other generated queries do not require much external information. In the case of Document 2, the introduction of the game "Call of Duty", the gold label does not require hidden information in the document. However, in the case of GenQ, the additional information that PlayStation 3, Xbox 360, and Wii are gaming consoles is required for a suitable answer. This gives evidence that there are cases in which queries requiring inference from external knowledge are generated through the proposed method. In the case of Document 3, introduction of Call the Midwife, the query from QGEK needs external information about the gender of actors to answer.

Although QGEK generates the queries that need external knowledge to answer, they have a similar pattern that begins with an interrogative word. In the case of GenQ and Info-HCVAE, different patterns exist through the queries of Document 3. It can be inferred that the triplet-based template makes the logical structure simple, and that the syntactic diversity of the generated query tends to decrease. For future work, we plan to propose a template that can include more logical structures, developed from the current triplet-based template.

6 Conclusion

We presented a novel query generation method, QGEK, that generates synthetic queries in a form more similar to human labeled queries by using external knowledge. In order to use unprocessed external knowledge, we convert a query into a triplet-based template, which can include information of subjects and answers. Remarkably, when dense retrieval models are trained with the queries generated from QGEK, the performance has improved much compared to using the queries without external knowledge. Also, we have shown that including external knowledge give rises to the distribution of the unique words similar to that of the human labeled queries. We believe that QGEK can also be applied to the other generation methods by orthogonally adding some external knowledge processing modules. For future work, we plan to generate queries both close to human labeled ones and optimized for IR tasks and to allow the template to accept more general logical forms for diverse high-quality queries. The code and data will be made available for public access.

Acknowledgements

This work was supported by Institute for Information and communications Technology Promotion (IITP) grant funded by the Korea government (MSIT) (No. 2018-0-00582, Prediction and augmentation of the credibility distribution via linguistic analysis and automated evidence document collection).

References

Adam Berger, Rich Caruana, David Cohn, Dayne Freitag, and Vibhu Mittal. 2000. Bridging the lexical chasm: Statistical approaches to answer-finding. In *Proceedings of the 23rd Annual International ACM SIGIR Conference on Research and Development in Information Retrieval*, SIGIR '00, page 192–199, New York, NY, USA. Association for Computing Machinery.

Alexander Bondarenko, Maik Fröbe, Meriem Beloucif, Lukas Gienapp, Yamen Ajjour, Alexander Panchenko, Chris Biemann, Benno Stein, Henning Wachsmuth, Martin Potthast, and Matthias Hagen. 2020. Overview of touché 2020: Argument retrieval - extended abstract. In *CLEF*, pages 384–395.

Antoine Bordes, Nicolas Usunier, Sumit Chopra, and Jason Weston. 2015. Large-scale simple question answering with memory networks. *arXiv preprint arXiv:1506.02075*.

Vera Boteva, Demian Gholipour, Artem Sokolov, and Stefan Riezler. 2016. A full-text learning to rank dataset for medical information retrieval. In *Advances in Information Retrieval*, pages 716–722, Cham. Springer International Publishing.

Arman Cohan, Sergey Feldman, Iz Beltagy, Doug Downey, and Daniel Weld. 2020. SPECTER: Document-level representation learning using citation-informed transformers. In *Proceedings of the 58th Annual Meeting of the Association for Computational Linguistics*, pages 2270–2282, Online. Association for Computational Linguistics.

Jacob Devlin, Ming-Wei Chang, Kenton Lee, and Kristina Toutanova. 2019a. BERT: pre-training of deep bidirectional transformers for language understanding. In *Proceedings of the 2019 Conference of the North American Chapter of the Association for Computational Linguistics: Human Language Technologies, NAACL-HLT 2019, Minneapolis, MN, USA, June 2-7, 2019, Volume 1 (Long and Short Papers)*, pages 4171–4186. Association for Computational Linguistics.

Jacob Devlin, Ming-Wei Chang, Kenton Lee, and Kristina Toutanova. 2019b. BERT: Pre-training of deep bidirectional transformers for language understanding. In *Proceedings of the 2019 Conference of the North American Chapter of the Association for Computational Linguistics: Human Language Technologies, Volume 1 (Long and Short Papers)*, pages 4171–4186, Minneapolis, Minnesota. Association for Computational Linguistics.

Emily Dinan, Stephen Roller, Kurt Shuster, Angela Fan, Michael Auli, and Jason Weston. 2019. Wizard of wikipedia: Knowledge-powered conversational agents. In *International Conference on Learning Representations*.

Daniel Gillick, Alessandro Presta, and Gaurav Singh Tomar. 2018. End-to-end retrieval in continuous space.

Faegheh Hasibi, Fedor Nikolaev, Chenyan Xiong, Krisztian Balog, Svein Erik Bratsberg, Alexander Kotov, and Jamie Callan. 2017. Dbpedia-entity v2: A test collection for entity search. In *Proceedings of the 40th International ACM SIGIR Conference on Research and Development in Information Retrieval*, SIGIR '17, page 1265–1268, New York, NY, USA. Association for Computing Machinery.

Vladimir Karpukhin, Barlas Oguz, Sewon Min, Patrick Lewis, Ledell Wu, Sergey Edunov, Danqi Chen, and Wen-tau Yih. 2020. Dense passage retrieval for open-domain question answering. In *Proceedings of the 2020 Conference on Empirical Methods in Natural Language Processing (EMNLP)*, pages 6769–6781, Online. Association for Computational Linguistics.

Diederik P. Kingma and Jimmy Ba. 2015. Adam: A method for stochastic optimization. In *3rd International Conference on Learning Representations, ICLR 2015, San Diego, CA, USA, May 7-9, 2015, Conference Track Proceedings*.

Tom Kwiatkowski, Jennimaria Palomaki, Olivia Redfield, Michael Collins, Ankur Parikh, Chris Alberti, Danielle Epstein, Illia Polosukhin, Jacob Devlin, Kenton Lee, Kristina Toutanova, Llion Jones, Matthew Kelcey, Ming-Wei Chang, Andrew M. Dai, Jakob Uszkoreit, Quoc Le, and Slav Petrov. 2019. Natural Questions: A Benchmark for Question Answering

Research. *Transactions of the Association for Computational Linguistics*, 7:453–466.

Dong Bok Lee, Seanie Lee, Woo Tae Jeong, Donghwan Kim, and Sung Ju Hwang. 2020. Generating diverse and consistent QA pairs from contexts with information-maximizing hierarchical conditional VAEs. In *Proceedings of the 58th Annual Meeting of the Association for Computational Linguistics*, pages 208–224, Online. Association for Computational Linguistics.

Markus Leippold and Thomas Diggelmann. 2020. Climate-fever: A dataset for verification of real-world climate claims. In *NeurIPS 2020 Workshop on Tackling Climate Change with Machine Learning*.

Mike Lewis, Yinhan Liu, Naman Goyal, Marjan Ghazvininejad, Abdelrahman Mohamed, Omer Levy, Veselin Stoyanov, and Luke Zettlemoyer. 2020. BART: Denoising sequence-to-sequence pre-training for natural language generation, translation, and comprehension. In *Proceedings of the 58th Annual Meeting of the Association for Computational Linguistics*, pages 7871–7880, Online. Association for Computational Linguistics.

Ji Ma, Ivan Korotkov, Yinfei Yang, Keith Hall, and Ryan McDonald. 2021. Zero-shot neural passage retrieval via domain-targeted synthetic question generation. In *Proceedings of the 16th Conference of the European Chapter of the Association for Computational Linguistics: Main Volume*, pages 1075–1088, Online. Association for Computational Linguistics.

Macedo Maia, Siegfried Handschuh, André Freitas, Brian Davis, Ross McDermott, Manel Zarrouk, and Alexandra Balahur. 2018. Www'18 open challenge: Financial opinion mining and question answering. In *Companion Proceedings of the The Web Conference 2018*, WWW '18, page 1941–1942, Republic and Canton of Geneva, CHE. International World Wide Web Conferences Steering Committee.

Tri Nguyen, Mir Rosenberg, Xia Song, Jianfeng Gao, Saurabh Tiwary, Rangan Majumder, and Li Deng. 2016. Ms marco: A human generated machine reading comprehension dataset.

Colin Raffel, Noam Shazeer, Adam Roberts, Katherine Lee, Sharan Narang, Michael Matena, Yanqi Zhou, Wei Li, and Peter J. Liu. 2020. Exploring the limits of transfer learning with a unified text-to-text transformer. *Journal of Machine Learning Research*, 21(140):1–67.

Stephen Robertson and Hugo Zaragoza. 2009. The probabilistic relevance framework: Bm25 and beyond. *Foundations and Trends® in Information Retrieval*, 3(4):333–389.

Kurt Shuster, Spencer Poff, Moya Chen, Douwe Kiela, and Jason Weston. 2021. Retrieval augmentation reduces hallucination in conversation. In *Findings of the Association for Computational Linguistics: EMNLP 2021*, pages 3784–3803, Punta Cana, Dominican Republic. Association for Computational Linguistics.

Robyn Speer, Joshua Chin, and Catherine Havasi. 2017. Conceptnet 5.5: An open multilingual graph of general knowledge. In *Proceedings of the Thirty-First AAAI Conference on Artificial Intelligence*, AAAI'17, page 4444–4451. AAAI Press.

Nandan Thakur, Nils Reimers, Andreas Rücklé, Abhishek Srivastava, and Iryna Gurevych. 2021. BEIR: A heterogeneous benchmark for zero-shot evaluation of information retrieval models. In *Thirty-fifth Conference on Neural Information Processing Systems Datasets and Benchmarks Track (Round 2)*.

James Thorne, Andreas Vlachos, Christos Christodoulopoulos, and Arpit Mittal. 2018. FEVER: a large-scale dataset for fact extraction and VERification. In *Proceedings of the 2018 Conference of the North American Chapter of the Association for Computational Linguistics: Human Language Technologies, Volume 1 (Long Papers)*, pages 809–819, New Orleans, Louisiana. Association for Computational Linguistics.

Ashish Vaswani, Noam Shazeer, Niki Parmar, Jakob Uszkoreit, Llion Jones, Aidan N Gomez, Ł ukasz Kaiser, and Illia Polosukhin. 2017. Attention is all you need. In *Advances in Neural Information Processing Systems*, volume 30. Curran Associates, Inc.

Ellen Voorhees, Tasmeer Alam, Steven Bedrick, Dina Demner-Fushman, William R. Hersh, Kyle Lo, Kirk Roberts, Ian Soboroff, and Lucy Lu Wang. 2021. Trec-covid: Constructing a pandemic information retrieval test collection. *SIGIR Forum*, 54(1).

Henning Wachsmuth, Shahbaz Syed, and Benno Stein. 2018. Retrieval of the best counterargument without prior topic knowledge. In *Proceedings of the 56th Annual Meeting of the Association for Computational Linguistics (Volume 1: Long Papers)*, pages 241–251, Melbourne, Australia. Association for Computational Linguistics.

David Wadden, Shanchuan Lin, Kyle Lo, Lucy Lu Wang, Madeleine van Zuylen, Arman Cohan, and Hannaneh Hajishirzi. 2020. Fact or fiction: Verifying scientific claims. In *Proceedings of the 2020 Conference on Empirical Methods in Natural Language Processing (EMNLP)*, pages 7534–7550, Online. Association for Computational Linguistics.

Kexin Wang, Nandan Thakur, Nils Reimers, and Iryna Gurevych. 2021. Gpl: Generative pseudo labeling for unsupervised domain adaptation of dense retrieval. *arXiv preprint arXiv:2112.07577*.

Peifeng Wang, Nanyun Peng, Filip Ilievski, Pedro A. Szekely, and Xiang Ren. 2020. Connecting the dots: A knowledgeable path generator for commonsense question answering. In *EMNLP (Findings)*, pages 4129–4140.

Ji Xin, Chenyan Xiong, Ashwin Srinivasan, Ankita Sharma, Damien Jose, and Paul Bennett. 2021. Zero-shot dense retrieval with momentum adversarial domain invariant representations. *ArXiv*, abs/2110.07581.

Zhilin Yang, Peng Qi, Saizheng Zhang, Yoshua Bengio, William Cohen, Ruslan Salakhutdinov, and Christopher D. Manning. 2018. HotpotQA: A dataset for diverse, explainable multi-hop question answering. In *Proceedings of the 2018 Conference on Empirical Methods in Natural Language Processing*, pages 2369–2380, Brussels, Belgium. Association for Computational Linguistics.

Kangyan Zhou, Shrimai Prabhumoye, and Alan W Black. 2018. A dataset for document grounded conversations. In *Proceedings of the 2018 Conference on Empirical Methods in Natural Language Processing*, pages 708–713, Brussels, Belgium. Association for Computational Linguistics.

Uncovering Values: Detecting Latent Moral Content from Natural Language with Explainable and Non-Trained Methods

Luigi Asprino, Stefano De Giorgis and **Aldo Gangemi***
Università degli Studi di Bologna, Italy
name.surname@unibo.it

Luana Bulla, Ludovica Marinucci and **Misael Mongiovì**
ISTC - Consiglio Nazionale delle Ricerche, Rome and Catania, Italy
name.surname@istc.cnr.it

Abstract

Moral values as commonsense norms shape our everyday individual and community behavior. The possibility to extract moral attitude rapidly from natural language is an appealing perspective that would enable a deeper understanding of social interaction dynamics and the individual cognitive and behavioral dimension. In this work we focus on detecting moral content from natural language and we test our methods on a corpus of tweets previously labeled as containing moral values or violations, according to Moral Foundation Theory. We develop and compare two different approaches: (i) a frame-based symbolic value detector based on knowledge graphs and (ii) a zero-shot machine learning model fine-tuned on a task of Natural Language Inference (NLI) and a task of emotion detection. Our approaches achieve considerable performances without the need for prior training.

1 Introduction

Morality as a set of social and acceptable behavioral norms (Haidt, 2012) is part of the commonsense knowledge that determines dynamics of action among social agents in areas like societal interaction (Haidt, 2001), individual conception of rightness and wrongness (Young and Saxe, 2011), moral taste and emotions (Graham et al., 2009), political commitment (Clifford and Jerit, 2013), public figure credibility (Graham et al., 2012) and narratives for explainable causal dependence of events or processes (Forbes et al., 2020).

Understanding this pervasive moral layer in both in person and *onlife* (Floridi, 2015) interaction occurrences constitutes a pillar for a good integration of AI systems in human societal communication and cultural environment. However, the difficulties in identifying data with a latent moral content, as well as cultural dependence, political orientation and the inherent subjectivity of the annotation work, make this an especially tough undertaking. In our work we aim at addressing these critical issues in the most versatile and transparent way and, to the best of our knowledge, the two approaches we propose are unprecedented in moral values detection.

The first approach employs a zero-shot learning technique. This concerns a problem setup in which a model performs classification on labels it has never seen before. By correctly interpreting the meaning of the labels and text, the classifier decides the truth value of any incoming label. This opens to the fulfillment of tasks with controversial or scarce data. We enhance the model by adding to the original text some meaningful information concerning the emotional component.

The second approach is based on an unsupervised and domain-independent system which leverages semantic web technologies and existing linguistic resources. The implementation of this method meets the suggested explainability criteria by providing a semantic knowledge graph capable of clearly describing both lexical and conceptual triggers behind the prediction. Finally we test both methods on a relevant Twitter dataset previously labeled with Graham and Haidt's Moral Foundation Theory (MFT) (Graham et al., 2013).

Our key contributions are as follows:

- We evaluate a Zero-shot learning technique based on Natural Language Inference to detect latent moral values in unstructured linguistic data.

*The authors are listed in alphabetical order.

Proceedings of Deep Learning Inside Out (DeeLIO 2022): The 3rd Workshop on Knowledge Extraction and Integration for Deep Learning Architectures, pages 33 - 41

- We enhance the zero-shot technique by the addition of the emotional component detected in the input text. We further improve the results by combining the two methods (with and without emotions).
- As an alternative method, we propose a frame-based approach based on an unsupervised and domain-independent system that guarantee explainability in reading the results achieved.
- We evaluate the above approaches on a benchmark dataset for moral values based on Twitter data and discuss the results.

The paper is organized as follows. Section 2 summarizes the results achieved in this field at the current state-of-the-art. In Section 3 we describe some baseline models, tools and resources used in our methods. Section 4.1 briefly describes the Moral Foundation Theory theoretical background, while Section 4.2 and 4.3 focus on the Zero-shot and the frame based methods, respectively. In Section 6 results of the evaluation on a manually annotated Twitter dataset are provided and discussed, while in Section 7 we delineate some possible future improvements.

2 Related Works

Previous work on identifying moral values of MFT in texts was based on word count (Fulgoni et al., 2016) or used features based on embodiments of words and sequences (Garten et al., 2016; Kennedy et al., 2021). More generally, we have observed that the most common methodological approaches in this field are divided into unsupervised and supervised methods. Unsupervised methods rely on systems not supported by external framing annotations. This approach includes architectures based on the Frame Axis technique (Kwak et al., 2021), such as those of Mokhberian and colleagues (Mokhberian et al., 2020) and Priniski and colleagues (Priniski et al., 2021). This type of approach projects words onto microframe dimensions characterized by two opposing sets of words. A framing score Moral Foundations captures the ideological and moral inclination of the texts examined. Part of the studies take as a point of reference the extended version of the Moral Foundation Dictionary (MFD) (Hopp et al., 2021), which consists of words concerning the virtues and vices of the five dyads of MFT and a sixth dimension relating to the terms of general morality. The contribution of Kobbe and colleagues (Kobbe et al., 2020), which aims to link MFD entries to WordNet in order to extend and disambiguate the lexicon, is also placed in a dictionary-based approach framework. Another unsupervised approach is explained by the work of Hulpus and colleagues (Hulpuș et al., 2020), who provide a way to explore how moral values are captured by Knowledge Graphs. The study investigates and evaluates the relevance of the entities contained in WordNet 3.1, ConceptNet and DBpedia with respect to the MFT.

Supervised methods aim to create and optimize frameworks based on external knowledge databases. The main datasets in this field are: (i) the textual corpus (Johnson and Goldwasser, 2018), which contains 93,000 tweets from US politicians in the years 2016 and 2017, and (ii) the Moral Foundation Twitter Corpus (MFTC) (Hoover et al., 2020), which consists of 35,000 Tweets from 7 distinct domains. In this context, the work of Roy and colleagues (Roy and Goldwasser, 2021) extends the dataset created by Johnson and Goldwasser (Johnson and Goldwasser, 2018) and applies a methodology for identifying moral values based on DRaiL, a declarative framework for deep structured prediction proposed by Pacheco and Goldwasser (Pacheco and Goldwasser, 2021). The approach adopted is mainly based on the text and information available with the unlabeled corpus such as topics, political affiliations of the authors and time of the tweets.

Our research focuses on the use of unsupervised methods. In particular, our frame-based approach is close to the work of Hulpus and colleagues (Hulpuș et al., 2020) for the use of knowledge graphs to explore latent moral (and semantic) content. However, our work enables a greater degree of knowledge integration due to disambiguation of lexical units, frame evocation, factual knowledge integration and foundational alignments, part of the text exploration process through the creation of a knowledge graph. Finally, our work provides an alternative to Frame Axis's technique (Kwak et al., 2021). Nevertheless, unlike this methodology, which implements a method based on a predefined set of terms suited for the task, we use a technology that has no a priori affinity with the suggested work. This allows us to overcome the drawbacks of utilizing a well-defined dictionary as the foundation for the entire approach and investigate the more advanced possibilities offered by an unsupervised method.

3 Reference Models

We employ a Zero-shot model based on the method developed by (Yin et al., 2019), which involves the use of pre-trained NLI models as ready-made zero-shot sequence classifiers. The approach works by using the input text as an NLI premise to classify the sequence and by developing a hypothesis starting from every possible label. In particular, the authors discuss three different aspects of classification: topic, emotion and situation detection. For each task, the model is subjected to two distinct principles: (i) *Label-partially-unseen*, where labels concerned are partially exposed to the model during a further training step, and (ii) *Label-fully-unseen*, in which the model is completely unaware of the categories. Given the lack of a specific training phase, the second approach is particularly useful in the absence of large amounts of good quality data that can be used during model implementation.

Our frame-based value detector model is based on knowledge graph generation from natural language using the FRED tool (Gangemi et al., 2017) enriched with knowledge from Framester (Gangemi et al., 2016) as a strongly connected RDF/OWL (Motik et al., 2009) knowledge graph that can be queried via its online SPARQL endpoint[1]. FRED (Gangemi et al., 2017) is a system for hybrid knowledge extraction from natural language, based on both statistical and rule-based components, which generates RDF/OWL knowledge graphs, embedding entity linking, word-sense disambiguation, and frame/semantic role detection.

Framester is a linked data hub that provides a formal semantics for frames (Gangemi, 2020), based on Fillmore's frame semantics (Fillmore, 1982). It creates/reengineers linked data versions of linguistic resources, such as WordNet (Miller, 1995), OntoWordNet (Gangemi et al., 2003b), VerbNet (Schuler, 2005), BabelNet (Navigli and Ponzetto, 2010), etc, jointly with factual knowledge bases (e.g. DBpedia (Auer et al., 2007), YAGO (Suchanek et al., 2007)). Framester also includes ImageSchemaNet (De Giorgis et al., 2022), a cognitive layer connecting image schematic sensorimotor patterns to the above-mentioned linguistic resources.

[1] http://etna.istc.cnr.it/framester2/sparql

Recently, a novel layer, ValueNet[2], has been added on top of Framester. It includes moral and cultural values, and formalizes Haidt's (Graham et al., 2013) and Curry's theories (Curry et al., 2021), aligning values to Framester frames, along with a foundational ontology backbone, i.e. DOLCE-Zero (Gangemi et al., 2003a).

4 Methods

4.1 Theoretical Grounding

Through the reuse of ValueNet, our work solely focuses on Haidt's Moral Foundation Theory (MFT). MFT is grounded on the idea that, while morality could vary widely in its extension (for example, what is considered a harmful or caring behavior depends on geographical, temporal, cultural and many others dimensions), its intension presents some recurring patterns that allow to delineate a psychological system of "intuitive ethics" (Graham et al., 2013). MFT is "a nativist, cultural-developmentalist, intuitionist, and pluralist approach to the study of morality" (Graham et al., 2013): "nativist" in its neurophysiological grounding; "cultural-developmentalist" in including environmental variables in the morality-building process; "intuitionist" in declaring that there is no unique moral or non-moral trigger, but rather many patterns combining in a rationalized judgment; "pluralist" in considering that more than one narrative could fit the moral explanation process. At the core of MFT there are six dyads of values and violations:

- *Care / Harm*: a caring versus harming behavior, it grounds virtues of gentleness, kindness and nurturance.
- *Fairness / Cheating:* this foundation is based on social cooperation and typical nonzero-sum game theoretical situations based on reciprocal altruism. It underlies ideas of justice, rights and autonomy.
- *Loyalty / Betrayal:* this dyad is based on the positive outcome coming from cohesive coalition, and the ostracism towards traitors.
- *Authority / Subversion:* social interactions in terms of societal hierarchies, it underlies ideas

[2] Available via querying Framester SPARQL endpoint: http://etna.istc.cnr.it/framester2/sparql or here: https://github.com/StenDoipanni/ValueNet

of leadership and deference to authority, as well as respect for tradition.

- *Purity / Degradation:* derived from psychology of disgust, it implies the idea of a more elevated spiritual life, it is expressed via metaphors like "the body as a temple", including the more spiritual side of religious beliefs.

- *Liberty / Oppression:* it expresses the desire of freedom and the feeling of oppression when it is negated.

4.2 Zero-shot Models

Starting from the method developed by Yin et al. (2019), we adapt a checkpoint for BART-large[3] trained on the MultiNLI (MNLI) dataset (Kim et al., 2018). Since this model has been shown to perform well for topic labeling (Khan and Chua, December (2021) and for claim verification (Reddy et al., 2021), it is a reasonable candidate for our task.

In the first step, we examine the input text for any concept similarities between its content and the moral values denoted by the labels. To the premise represented by the original textual data, we place side by side the categories suggested by Haidt's taxonomy as plausible hypotheses. In other words, we verify how much every value in the MFT's set is semantically related to every tweet in the test set (e.g. we evaluate if the concept "care" is expressed in the text "Commitment to peace, healing and loving neighbors. Give us strength and patience."). The same tweet is flanked by all the remaining moral values in the same way. The structure is based on the technique of using pre-trained NLI models as ready-made zero-shot sequence classifiers to develop a hypothesis from every possible label. As the output of the classification, results are acquired according to the predicted degree of entailment. The result of the categorization is represented by labels with a compliance score of 90% or above.

In the second step, we improve the model's prediction performances by adding more information on the latent emotional component in the original text. The input premise was subjected to an emotional detection by a model trained for this purpose[4] and then augmented by the identification of the valence of the attitude represented. For example, given the tweet "Peace, Love And Unity <3" represented as a premise, we add to this text both (i) an emotion perception component such as "This sentence is about joy sentiment." and (ii) an information about its polarity "This is positive.".

In the third step, we combine the first and second methods by unifying the prediction results to increase the likelihood of success in the classification task. In this case the results achieved by the first step and the second step were compared, assuming as the final output of the classification the moral values envisaged by either approaches (i.e. the tweet "Prayers to our brave DPD officers! We support you!" was labeled "care" and "loyalty" during the first step and only "care" during the second. In this case, the third method takes as output both labels provided, hence "care, loyalty").

All these strategies assume that artificial intelligence models can capture the interactions and connections of social groups, as well as information about individuals. Consequently, it is argued that a model might be able to draw a line of similarity between morally connoted words and ideas depending on the lexical information provided in the training phase not directly attributable to a classification method.

4.3 Frame-based Value Reasoner

The frame-based value reasoner is a tool based on a frame semantics approach (Fillmore, 1982). Its pipeline consists of the following three main steps. The first one is knowledge graph generation from natural language: the input sentence is passed to FRED, which returns a knowledge graph that includes detected FrameNet frames and frame elements, VerbNet roles, and linking to DBpedia entities and WordNet synsets.

The second step consists in the actual moral value detection: relevant entities from FRED's knowledge graph are used to query Framester SPARQL endpoint in order to link the entities extracted by FRED to MFT moral values. The full graph and an extended description of the Moral Value ontological module in Framester are available on the ValueNet github repository.[5] The resulting knowledge graph is an enrichment of the original FRED graph with MFT moral values. If

[3] `https://huggingface.co/facebook/bart-large-mnli`

[4] `https://huggingface.co/bhadresh-savani/distilbert-base-uncased-emotion`

[5] ValueNet is available via Framester SPARQL endpoint: `http://etna.istc.cnr.it/framester2/sparql` and here: `https://github.com/StenDoipanni/ValueNet`

no value or violation is detected, the sentence is labeled as "non-moral".

This value detection process is heuristically transparent, since it keeps track of triggering elements (e.g. synset, linked entity, frame evocation, lexical unit, etc.), so providing a fully explainable moral value detector.

5 Experiments and Results

To examine the effectiveness of our approaches in the moral value detection task, we focus on the challenge of recognizing them in the Moral Foundation Twitter Corpus (MFTC) (Hoover et al., 2020).

The dataset, consisting of 35k tweets, is organized into seven distinct thematic topics covering a wide range of moral concerns. Each tweet is labeled from three to eight different annotators trained to detect and categorize texts following the guidelines outlined by Moral Foundation Theory. The MFTC includes ten different moral value categories, as well as a label for textual material that does not evoke a morally meaningful response. To account for their semantic independence, each tweet in the corpus was annotated with both values and violations. To set performance baselines, we treat the annotations of the tweets by calculating the majority vote for each moral value, where the majority is considered 50% (i.e. tweet "I have no respect for the *home run king*" is labeled by four different annotators. Two of them regard the text as "non-moral" while the others as "subversion". Hence, we consider the tweet labeled as "non-moral, subversion" because each of these labels corresponds to 50% of the annotation).

Table 1 shows the results obtained by our tools on a subset of 6,075 items representing the MFTC test set. We did not include the rest of the corpus in the evaluation since the process is time consuming, considering that the code is not optimized for efficiency. Each tool is evaluated in terms of precision, recall and F1 score in predicting each label. The overall results (All in the bottom) are calculated by averaging over all labels weighted by the support (i.e. the number of elements in the ground truth with each specific label). The choice to perform the tests on a small sample of the total dataset depends on the high data processing times of the FRED-based method and the ongoing goal of a comparison with a supervised approach. This methodology would require the use of a large part of the data contained in the MFTC during the model training phase.

The presented tests are carried out by evaluating different combinations suggested by the models mentioned in Sect. 4). In particular, the Emotion-Zero-shot model displays the results obtained by exposing the Zero-shot model to an input text that has had its emotional component explained. The Emotion-Zero-shot+ architecture refers to the combination of the two methods mentioned above and corresponds to the third approach discussed in Sect. 4.2. The frame-based system recalls the results obtained from the application of the tool described in Sect. 4.3.

Given the lack of a reasonable state-of-the-art baseline of non-trained systems, we report a Random lower-bound, obtained by predicting each label with a probability corresponding to the fraction of entries in the ground truth represented by the test set with that label. Finally, in Table 1 there is no reference to the *Liberty / Oppression* dyad. This happens coherently to the lack of this label in the MFTC, due to the late introduction of this value / violation opposition in an updated version of the MFT. Triggers of this dyad are still detected by the frame-based model, and could be explored in the extended file [6], since the Liberty and Oppression knowledge graphs are part of ValueNet, but they are not considered in the evaluation metrics.

Furthermore, since the original dataset is annotated considering a 50% percentage of agreement among annotators, some of the sentences shows a combination composed by "non-moral" + some other value or violation. While for the Zero-shot models the "non-moral" label is used as a feature itself, the combination of non-morality and any kind of morality was in conflict with the conceptual structure of the frame-based detector. We therefore modified the original dataset eliminating the "non-moral" label while co-occurring with some value or violation, and repeated the experiment. The results of all the applied methods can be explored in their extended files[7].

Although performances differ, the two methods perform similarly in terms of F1, with an overall score of 45%. Specifically, Emotion-Zero-shot+ and Frame-based outperform the other models for four out of eleven labels, with F1 scores ranging from 0.12 to 0.53 for the first and from 0.11 to 0.50

[6] https://github.com/StenDoipanni/MoralDilemmas

[7] https://github.com/StenDoipanni/MoralDilemmas

Moral Value	Metric	Random	Zero-shot	Emotion-Zero-shot	Emotion-Zero-shot+	Frame-based
	Precision	.09	.29	.51	.29	.29
Care	Recall	.18	.63	.36	.69	.57
	F1-score	.11	.40	**.42**	.41	.39
	Precision	.13	.30	.31	.29	.39
Harm	Recall	.24	.80	.59	.82	.70
	F1-score	.17	.44	.41	.43	**.50**
	Precision	.04	.07	.10	.07	.18
Purity	Recall	.08	.28	.30	.32	.20
	F1-score	.05	.11	.15	.12	**.19**
	Precision	.04	.12	.15	.12	.45
Degradation	Recall	.09	.63	.30	.66	.11
	F1-score	.06	**.20**	**.20**	**.20**	.18
	Precision	.07	.40	.73	.40	.40
Loyalty	Recall	.15	.45	.14	.46	.30
	F1-score	.10	.42	.24	**.43**	.34
	Precision	.05	.17	.37	.17	.57
Betrayal	Recall	.10	.44	.29	.44	.17
	F1-score	.07	.25	**.32**	.25	.27
	Precision	.07	.60	.85	.58	.16
Fairness	Recall	.15	.47	.26	.48	.11
	F1-score	.09	**.53**	.40	**.53**	.13
	Precision	.11	.54	.64	.54	.75
Cheating	Recall	.22	.29	.19	.29	.28
	F1-score	.15	.38	.30	.38	**.41**
	Precision	.04	.17	.40	.18	.15
Authority	Recall	.08	.28	.04	.29	.08
	F1-score	.05	.21	.07	**.22**	.11
	Precision	.08	.20	.15	.17	.28
Subversion	Recall	.16	.36	.39	.40	.17
	F1-score	.11	**.25**	.21	.24	.21
	Precision	.44	.40	.46	.47	.59
Non-moral	Recall	.66	.28	.86	.91	.72
	F1-score	.53	.33	.60	.62	**.65**
	Precision	.22	.35	.46	.38	.47
All	Recall	.36	.41	.52	.67	.48
	F1-score	.27	.35	.42	**.45**	.44

Table 1. Precision, Recall and F1 score for each model on the MFTC dataset.

for the second. These two architectures result in an improvement of 10 % compared to the Emotion-zero-shot model and 20 % compared to the Zero-shot model, and they performs vastly better than Random.

6 Discussion

As expected, the results for the single labels vary according to the difficulties encountered by classifiers in the interpretation of their meaning. For example, moral values such as "Harm" or "Care" convey more generic content and are therefore easier to identify. Conversely, concepts like "Degradation" or "Subversion" contain shades of meaning that are more difficult to grasp.

The results drawn from the Zero-shot models make this problem evident and difficult to solve as the intrinsic nature of machine learning models does not encompass a direct understanding of their decision-making phases. One possible solution would be to subject the models to few-shot learning, which is a fine-tuning with a little amount of data relevant for the moral values detection task. However, this would not be part of our main need, which is to develop flexible approaches that do not require training. Despite the task's complexity, the results imply that not only can moral values be detected in natural language texts, but also that models developed for NLI may be adapted to other tasks through the unintentional acquisition of abstract conceptions and concepts connected to the field of social value.

Results obtained from the frame-based value detector are provided as additional material[8]. Value triggers are listed in the "trigger" column, while value detection is shown in the "prediction" column. The full knowledge graph can be retrieved by passing the tweet content in column "tweet_text" as input to the FRED online demo[9], ticking the "align to Framester" option.

A necessary caveat is that, being the value labeling a subjective task, a certain amount of disagreement should always be taken into account. In this regard, the detection shows better results on those values whose extension seems more generic, e.g. a more broad concept like "harm", than a more opaque one like "purity", as described in Sect. 4.1. Additionally, the performance results could depend on two factors. The first factor is the success of the FRED tool in producing a knowledge graph from a fragmented syntax like the one used in tweets. In fact, even when a well formed graph is produced, if the value trigger is not in the main sentence e.g. it is an adjective of a pronoun in a subordinate sentence, it is possible that its disambiguation / frame evocation is not shown in the graph, due to internal FRED saliency heuristics. The second factor is that human value labeling is a task carried out with a certain subjective threshold. If we consider the example: "Horrible amount of anti-Islam bigotry are Paris attacks. ISIS murder more MUSLIMS than anyone else.", value labels for this sentence are "cheating" and "harm", while the detector predicts "cheating", "harm" and "purity". This happens because, along with triggers like the `fs:Offenses` and `fs:Killing` Framester frames, `wn:murder-noun-1` WordNet synset and the `dbr:Bigotry` DBpedia entity, the DBpedia entry `dbr:Muslim` is also retrieved, which according to "purity" definition (see Sect. 4.1) covers the semantics of a more spiritual aspect of life, and it is therefore a "purity" trigger.

7 Conclusions and Future Work

In our work we detect latent moral content from natural language in a versatile and transparent way, proposing two approaches (zero-shot and heuristic) that do not require training. The approaches assume Haidt's Moral Foundation Theory as a reference for moral values, and have been tested on the Moral Foundation Twitter Corpus.

Results are unprecedented in using domain independent methods. Future work will include improving the performance of the Zero-shot models through the creation of a technique capable of comprehending the intricacies of the most contentious moral values. Furthermore, we plan to build an implementation that gives greater weight to the most significant aspects of the sentence, in order to more simply detect the prevailing moral value.

For the frame-based value detector more precise results could be achieved via different refinements such as a set of heuristics based on the syntax, and consequently on the frame structure of the sentence, which would allow new and more complex inferences. The commitment to some value could, for example, be expressed by the negation of the value violation, or via a negative polarity of a verb which takes as argument some value trigger. Some

[8]https://github.com/StenDoipanni/MoralDilemmas

[9]http://wit.istc.cnr.it/stlab-tools/fred/demo/

other possibility to improve the results could be in a quantitative or qualitative way, namely introducing a scoring system based on the amount of trigger occurrences per value, or weighting differently the type of trigger (WordNet synset, FrameNet frame, etc.).

Finally, an interesting possibility is to conjugate the approaches and this could drive to various possibilities, for example the introduction of a layer in the aforementioned value trigger scoring system, able to guide the prediction of the final output, as well as using the knowledge base, in particular the extended lexical coverage from ValueNet graphs to improve Zero-shot models performance. A possible way could be to analyze the frame responsible for the value triggering by measuring its relevance inside the sentence via machine learning techniques. To conclude, further experiments can be done on different types of datasets as well as extending the employed dataset, and to compare with different methodological approaches, including supervised methods.

References

Sören Auer, Christian Bizer, Georgi Kobilarov, Jens Lehmann, Richard Cyganiak, and Zachary Ives. 2007. Dbpedia: A nucleus for a web of open data. In *The semantic web*, pages 722–735. Springer.

Scott Clifford and Jennifer Jerit. 2013. How words do the work of politics: Moral foundations theory and the debate over stem cell research. *The Journal of Politics*, 75(3):659–671.

Oliver Scott Curry, Mark Alfano, Mark J Brandt, and Christine Pelican. 2021. Moral molecules: Morality as a combinatorial system. *Review of Philosophy and Psychology*, pages 1–20.

Stefano De Giorgis, Aldo Gangemi, and Dagmar Gromann. 2022. Imageschemanet: Formalizing embodied commonsense knowledge providing an image-schematic layer to framester. *Semantic Web Journal*, forthcoming.

Charles J Fillmore. 1982. Frame semantics. In *Linguistics in the Morning Calm*, pages 111–138. Seoul: Hanshin.

Luciano Floridi. 2015. *The onlife manifesto: Being human in a hyperconnected era*. Springer Nature.

Maxwell Forbes, Jena D Hwang, Vered Shwartz, Maarten Sap, and Yejin Choi. 2020. Social chemistry 101: Learning to reason about social and moral norms. *arXiv preprint arXiv:2011.00620*.

Dean Fulgoni, Jordan Carpenter, Lyle Ungar, and Daniel Preoţiuc-Pietro. 2016. An empirical exploration of moral foundations theory in partisan news sources. In *Proceedings of the Tenth International Conference on Language Resources and Evaluation (LREC'16)*, pages 3730–3736.

Aldo Gangemi. 2020. Closing the loop between knowledge patterns in cognition and the semantic web. *Semantic Web*, 11(1):139–151.

Aldo Gangemi, Mehwish Alam, Luigi Asprino, Valentina Presutti, and Diego Reforgiato Recupero. 2016. Framester: a wide coverage linguistic linked data hub. In *European Knowledge Acquisition Workshop*, pages 239–254. Springer.

Aldo Gangemi, Nicola Guarino, Claudio Masolo, and Alessandro Oltramari. 2003a. Sweetening wordnet with dolce. *AI magazine*, 24(3):13–13.

Aldo Gangemi, Roberto Navigli, and Paola Velardi. 2003b. The ontowordnet project: extension and axiomatization of conceptual relations in wordnet. In *OTM Confederated International Conferences" On the Move to Meaningful Internet Systems"*, pages 820–838. Springer.

Aldo Gangemi, Valentina Presutti, Diego Reforgiato Recupero, Andrea Giovanni Nuzzolese, Francesco Draicchio, and Misael Mongiovì. 2017. Semantic web machine reading with fred. *Semantic Web*, 8(6):873–893.

Justin Garten, Reihane Boghrati, Joe Hoover, Kate M Johnson, and Morteza Dehghani. 2016. Morality between the lines: Detecting moral sentiment in text. In *Proceedings of IJCAI 2016 workshop on Computational Modeling of Attitudes*.

Jesse Graham, Jonathan Haidt, Sena Koleva, Matt Motyl, Ravi Iyer, Sean P Wojcik, and Peter H Ditto. 2013. Moral foundations theory: The pragmatic validity of moral pluralism. In *Advances in experimental social psychology*, volume 47, pages 55–130. Elsevier.

Jesse Graham, Jonathan Haidt, and Brian A Nosek. 2009. Liberals and conservatives rely on different sets of moral foundations. *Journal of personality and social psychology*, 96(5):1029.

Jesse Graham, Brian A Nosek, and Jonathan Haidt. 2012. The moral stereotypes of liberals and conservatives: Exaggeration of differences across the political spectrum. *PloS one*, 7(12):e50092.

Jonathan Haidt. 2001. The emotional dog and its rational tail: a social intuitionist approach to moral judgment. *Psychological review*, 108(4):814.

Jonathan Haidt. 2012. *The righteous mind: Why good people are divided by politics and religion*. Vintage.

Joe Hoover, Gwenyth Portillo-Wightman, Leigh Yeh, Shreya Havaldar, Aida Mostafazadeh Davani, Ying Lin, Brendan Kennedy, Mohammad Atari, Zahra Kamel, Madelyn Mendlen, Gabriela Moreno, Christina Park, Tingyee E. Chang, Jenna Chin, Christian Leong, Jun Yen Leung, Arineh Mirinjian, and Morteza Dehghani. 2020. Moral foundations twitter corpus: A collection of 35k tweets annotated for moral sentiment. *Social Psychological and Personality Science*, 11(8):1057–1071.

Frederic R Hopp, Jacob T Fisher, Devin Cornell, Richard Huskey, and René Weber. 2021. The extended moral foundations dictionary (emfd): Development and applications of a crowd-sourced approach to extracting moral intuitions from text. *Behavior research methods*, 53(1):232–246.

Ioana Hulpuș, Jonathan Kobbe, Heiner Stuckenschmidt, and Graeme Hirst. 2020. Knowledge graphs meet moral values. In *Proceedings of the Ninth Joint Conference on Lexical and Computational Semantics*, pages 71–80.

Kristen Johnson and Dan Goldwasser. 2018. Classification of moral foundations in microblog political discourse. In *Proceedings of the 56th Annual Meeting of the Association for Computational Linguistics (Volume 1: Long Papers)*, pages 720–730.

Brendan Kennedy, Mohammad Atari, Aida Mostafazadeh Davani, Joe Hoover, Ali Omrani, Jesse Graham, and Morteza Dehghani. 2021. Moral concerns are differentially observable in language. *Cognition*, 212:104696.

Qaisar Khan and Huina Chua. December (2021) 46 - 59. An automated topics labeling framework using zero-shot text classification. *Journal of Engineering Science and Technology Special Issue on ACSAT*.

Seonhoon Kim, Inho Kang, and Nojun Kwak. 2018. Semantic sentence matching with densely-connected recurrent and co-attentive information.

Jonathan Kobbe, Ines Rehbein, Ioana Hulpus, and Heiner Stuckenschmidt. 2020. Exploring morality in argumentation. Association for Computational Linguistics, ACL.

Haewoon Kwak, Jisun An, Elise Jing, and Yong-Yeol Ahn. 2021. Frameaxis: characterizing microframe bias and intensity with word embedding. *PeerJ Computer Science*, 7:e644.

George A. Miller. 1995. Wordnet: A lexical database for english. *Communications of the ACM*, 38(11):39–41.

Negar Mokhberian, Andrés Abeliuk, Patrick Cummings, and Kristina Lerman. 2020. Moral framing and ideological bias of news. In *International Conference on Social Informatics*, pages 206–219. Springer.

Boris Motik, Bernardo Cuenca Grau, Ian Horrocks, Zhe Wu, Achille Fokoue, Carsten Lutz, et al. 2009. Owl 2 web ontology language profiles. *W3C recommendation*, 27(61).

Roberto Navigli and Simone Paolo Ponzetto. 2010. Babelnet: Building a very large multilingual semantic network. In *Proceedings of the 48th annual meeting of the association for computational linguistics*, pages 216–225.

Maria Leonor Pacheco and Dan Goldwasser. 2021. Modeling content and context with deep relational learning. *Transactions of the Association for Computational Linguistics*, 9:100–119.

J Hunter Priniski, Negar Mokhberian, Bahareh Harandizadeh, Fred Morstatter, Kristina Lerman, Hongjing Lu, and P Jeffrey Brantingham. 2021. Mapping moral valence of tweets following the killing of george floyd. *arXiv preprint arXiv:2104.09578*.

Revanth Gangi Reddy, Sai Chinthakindi, Zhenhailong Wang, Yi R Fung, Kathryn S Conger, Ahmed S Elsayed, Martha Palmer, and Heng Ji. 2021. Newsclaims: A new benchmark for claim detection from news with background knowledge. *arXiv preprint arXiv:2112.08544*.

Shamik Roy and Dan Goldwasser. 2021. Analysis of nuanced stances and sentiment towards entities of us politicians through the lens of moral foundation theory. In *Proceedings of the Ninth International Workshop on Natural Language Processing for Social Media*, pages 1–13.

Karin Kipper Schuler. 2005. *VerbNet: A broad-coverage, comprehensive verb lexicon*. University of Pennsylvania.

Fabian M Suchanek, Gjergji Kasneci, and Gerhard Weikum. 2007. Yago: a core of semantic knowledge. In *Proceedings of the 16th international conference on World Wide Web*, pages 697–706.

Wenpeng Yin, Jamaal Hay, and Dan Roth. 2019. Benchmarking zero-shot text classification: Datasets, evaluation and entailment approach.

Liane Young and Rebecca Saxe. 2011. When ignorance is no excuse: Different roles for intent across moral domains. *Cognition*, 120(2):202–214.

Jointly Identifying and Fixing Inconsistent Readings from Information Extraction Systems

Ankur Padia*, Francis Ferraro and Tim Finin
University of Maryland, Baltimore County
Baltimore, MD 21250 USA
{pankur1, ferraro, finin}@umbc.edu

Abstract

Information extraction systems analyze text to produce entities and beliefs, but their output often has errors. In this paper we analyze the reading *consistency* of the extracted facts with respect to the text from which they were derived and show how to detect and correct errors. We consider both the scenario when the provenance text is automatically found by an IE system and when it is curated by humans. We contrast *consistency* with *credibility*; define and explore *consistency and repair tasks*; and demonstrate a simple, yet effective and generalizable, model. We analyze these tasks and evaluate this approach on three datasets. Against a strong baseline model, we consistently improve both consistency and repair across three datasets using a simple MLP model with attention and lexical features.

1 Introduction

Information Extraction (IE) systems read text to extract entities, and relations and create beliefs represented in a knowledge graph. Current systems though are far from perfect: e.g., in the 2017 Text Analysis Conference (TAC) Knowledge Base Population task, participants created knowledge graphs with relations like *cause of death* and *city of headquarters* from news corpora (Dang, 2017). When manually evaluated, no system had achieved an F1 score above 0.3 (Rajput, 2017).

One reason for such low scores is *inconsistency* between the text and the extracted beliefs. We consider a belief to be *consistent* if the text from which it was extracted linguistically supports it (regardless of any logical or real-world factual truth). We show the difference between consistent and inconsistent readings, along with a potential correction, in Fig. 1. In Fig. 1a, the system considered `Harry Reid` was charged with an `assault`, which is not consistent with the provenance sentence. In Fig. 1b the system is consistent in constructing its belief.

Belief learned by IE system:
`per:charges(Harry Reid, assault)`
Provenance identified by IE system:
Nevada's Harry Reid switches longtime stance to support assault weapon ban
Analysis output:
Is reading consistent: Inconsistent
Suggested relation: no repair

(a) An inconsistent reading with no correction.

Belief learned by IE system:
`per:cause_of_death(Edward Hardman, Typhoid fever)`
Provenance identified by IE system:
The Western Australian government agreed to offer the Government Geologist post to Hardman shortly before news of his death reached them . Early in April , he contracted typhoid fever , and died a few days later in a Dublin hospital on 6 April
Analysis output:
Is reading consistent: Consistent
Suggested relation: per:cause_of_death

(b) A consistent reading not requiring a correction. Notice the relation is unchanged.

Figure 1: Examples of beliefs extracted from real IE systems on the TAC 2015 English news corpus, demonstrating the *consistency* and *repair* tasks. Multiple sentences can contribute to a belief (1b).

We study two problems: (i) whether an extracted belief is consistent with its text (called consistency), and (ii) correcting it if not (called repair). We believe we are the first to study these problems jointly. We model these problems jointly, arguing that addressing both of these is important and can benefit one another. Our use of *consistency* here refers to a language-based sense that text supports the belief even if its contradicts world knowledge.

We are concerned with methods that can be *standalone*—that is, reliant on neither a precise schema (Ojha and Talukdar, 2017) nor an ensemble of IE systems, e.g., Yu et al. (2014); Viswanathan et al. (2015). Previous work on determining the

*This work was done while the first author was doing his Ph.D. at the University of Maryland, Baltimore County and before joining Philips Research North America.

Proceedings of Deep Learning Inside Out (DeeLIO 2022): The 3rd Workshop on Knowledge Extraction and Integration for Deep Learning Architectures, pages 42 - 52

consistency of an IE extraction was not standalone. We want a standalone approach because the results from non-standalone approaches cannot be applied when only the beliefs and associated provenance text is available without the IE ensemble systems and schema. (For this study we consider English beliefs and provenance sentences.) Parallel to the broad IE domain, schema-free and standalone systems have been developed to verify the credibility of news claims (Popat et al., 2018; Riedel et al., 2017a; Rashkin et al., 2017), but we are not aware of a study of their performance on IE system tasks. We incorporate these credibility systems into our study in order to determine their applicability for our tasks. We make the following contributions.

A study of real IE inconsistencies. We catalog and examine the understudied aspect of language-based consistency (§3).

A novel framework. To our knowledge we are the first to study and propose a framework for joint consistency and repair (§4).

Analysis of techniques. We show the effectiveness of straightforward techniques compared to more complicated approaches (§5).

Study of different provenance settings. We consider and contrast cases where provenance sentences are retrieved by an IE system (as in TAC) vs. where they are curated by humans (as in Zhang et al. (2017, TACRED)).

2 Task Setup

2.1 Consistency and Repair

We say the belief was consistently read if the text *lexically* supports the belief. While this can be viewed as a lexical entailment, it is not a logical, causal, or broader inferential/knowledge entailment. For example the belief `<Barack Obama,per:president_of,Kenya>` is consistent with a provenance sentence `"Barack Obama, president of Kenya, visited the U.S. for talks"` even though the sentence falsely claims that Obama is president of Kenya. .

The belief is considered repaired if the relation extracted by the IE system was not supported by the text, but when replaced by another relation that is supported by the text.

2.2 Datasets

We use three datasets: TAC 2015, TAC 2017, and a novel dataset we call TACRED-KG. All datasets use actual output from real IE systems. Each dataset is split into train/dev/test splits: in Table 2 (in the appendix) we show the size of each split, in terms of the number of provenance-backed beliefs.

TAC 2015 and 2017. These include the output of 70+ IE systems, from the TAC 2015 and TAC 2017 shared tasks, with belief triples supported by up to four provenance sentences. Each belief was evaluated by an LDC expert (Ellis, 2015a). We used these LDC judgments as the consistency labels for our experiments. For TAC 2015, 27% of the 34k beliefs are judged consistent; for TAC 2017, 36% of the 57k beliefs are judged consistent.

These TAC datasets do not, however, contain information on possible corrections when the belief is inconsistent. To overcome this limitation, we used negative sampling on the consistent beliefs with their provenance to create an inconsistent pair. We first selected an entity and then identified a set of relations that apply to the entity. We randomly chose one of the relations with uniform probability and shuffled it with another relation, keeping the provenance the same. For example, given two consistent beliefs `Barack_Obama,president_of,US`, and `Barack_Obama,school_attended,Harvard`, we swap `president_of` with `school_attended`, keeping the provenance unchanged. This yields inconsistent beliefs associated with corresponding provenance and the correct labels.

TACRED-KG. The TACRED-KG dataset is a novel adaptation from the existing TACRED (Zhang et al., 2017) relation extraction dataset. TACRED is focused on providing data for typical relation extraction systems. As such, it contains 4-tuples (subject, object, provenance sentence, correct relation), where relation extraction systems are expected to predict that relation for the given subject-object pair and the sentence. We turn this relation extraction dataset into a KG-focused dataset. We then used a relation extraction position-aware attention RNN model (Zhang et al., 2017) system on the TACRED data to produce 5-tuples (subject, object, provenance sentence, correct relation, predicted relation). From these we created a provenance-backed KG dataset, TACRED-KG, as (subject, predicted relation, object, provenance sentence). In TACRED-KG, we treat the gold standard relation as the repair label. We consider beliefs consistent when the predicted and gold standard relations are the same.

Category	Definition	Extracted Belief followed by IE extracted provenance text
Incorrect relation	subject & object present but relation not triggered/entailed	*Harry Reid per:charges assault* Nevada's Harry Reid switches longtime stance to support assault weapon ban
Subject missing	entity is not mentioned in provenance	*Eleanor Catton gpe:subsidiaries Bain* Buying into Canada Goose is the latest Canadian investment for Bain.
Misc	fact does not adhere to schema-specific guidelines and requirements	*Reginald Wayne Miller per:charges felony* Various news outlets have reported that federal agents have probable cause to charge Reginald Wayne Miller with forced labor, a felony that can carry up to a twenty-year prison sentence per charge.
Object missing	entity is not mentioned in provenance	*Kermit Gosnell per:cities_of_residence America* Historic crowdfunding for movie about abortionist Kermit Gosnell - YouTube

Table 1: Examples for each of the four identified error categories from the TAC 2015 dataset.

Observational Comparison. We note some qualitative observations about these datasets, though traceable back to how each dataset was constructed. First, TAC 2015 and TAC 2017 contain more provenance examples *per relation* than TACRED-KG. Second, because the provenance was provided by varied IE systems in TAC 2015/2017, the provenance may be the result of noisy extractions and matching: the provenance for TAC 2015/2017 is often noisier than TACRED-KG (e.g., portions of sentences vs. full sentences).

3 What Errors Do IE Systems Make?

We begin with an analysis of errors in the beliefs from actual IE systems. This analysis is enlightening, as each system used different approaches and types of resources to extract potential facts.

We sampled 600 beliefs and their provenance text each from the training portions of three different knowledge graph datasets: TAC 2015, TAC 2017, and TACRED-KG. As described in §2.2, they all contain provenance-backed beliefs that were extracted from actual IE systems (but ones which are generally not available for subsequent downstream examination). All of the beliefs are represented as a relation between two arguments. The authors manually assessed these according to available and published guidelines (Ellis, 2015a,b; Dang, 2017) to understand the kinds of errors made by the IE systems. We identified four types of errors: the subject (first argument) not present in the provenance text; the object (second argument) not present in the provenance; an insufficiently supported relation between two present arguments; and relations that run afoul of formatting requirements, e.g., misformed dates. We show examples of these in Table 1.

Our analysis, summarized in Fig. 2, found that the most frequent error type is an incorrect relation, followed by missing subject, missing object and (at a trace level) formatting errors. Though it varied

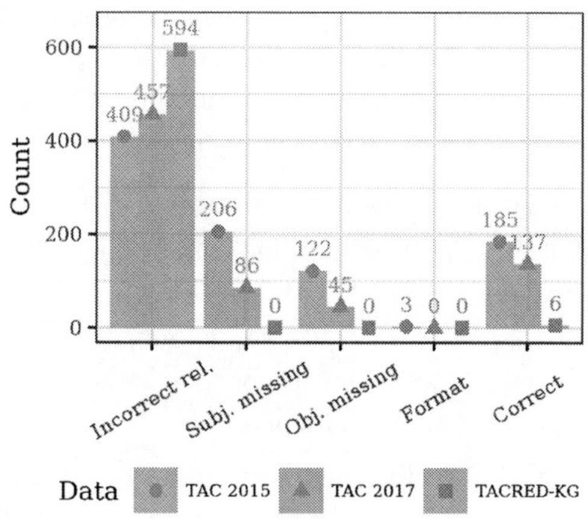

Figure 2: Error categorization of 600 beliefs extracted by IE systems on three datasets. Multiple categories can apply as beliefs can have incorrect relations and incomplete provenance.

based on dataset, approximately two-thirds of the sampled belief-provenance pairs had errors. The prevalence of incorrect relations **motivates the importance of the relation repair task**. It should be noted that while TAC 2015 and 2017 have a number of instances of missing subjects and objects, this is not the case for TACRED-KG. This illustrates a fundamental difference in selecting provenance information manually vs. automatically, and one that we observe to be experimentally important (§5.3), between TAC 2015/2017 and TACRED-KG.

4 Approach

Our approach computes both the consistency of a belief b_i and a "repaired" belief with respect to a given set of provenance sentences. We represent b_i as a triple $\langle \text{subject}_i, \text{predicate}_i, \text{object}_i \rangle$ and the set of provenance sentences as $S_{i,1}, S_{i,2}, ...S_{i,n}$. The system outputs two discrete predictions: (1) a binary one indicating whether the belief is consistent with the sentences, and (2) a categorical one sug-

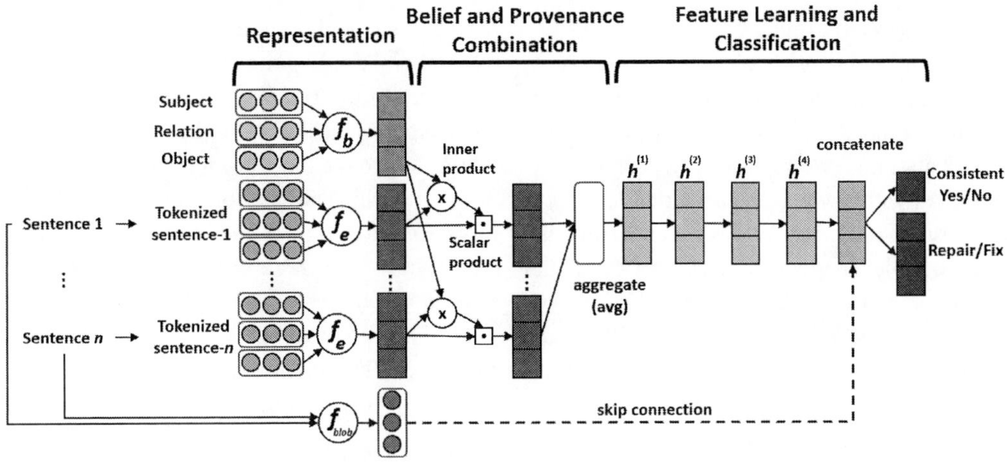

Figure 3: Given a belief and a set of n provenance sentences, our framework determines its consistency and suggests a repair when if is deemed inconsistent. Our approach has three main modules: representation (4.1), combination (4.2), and feature learning and classification (4.3).

gesting a repair. Fig. 3 illustrates our approach for representing and combining the beliefs and provenance sentences to jointly learn the two tasks.

Our approach has three main steps: embedding a belief and its provenance sentences in a vector space (§4.1), combining/aggregating these representations (§4.2), and using the result for additional feature learning and classification (§4.3). We describe our loss objective in §4.4. As we show, our framework can be thought of as generalizing high performing credibility models, such as DeClarE (Popat et al., 2018) or LSTM-text (Rashkin et al., 2017).

4.1 Belief & Provenance Representation

We process and tokenize a belief's arguments and relation. For example, the belief ⟨`Barack_Obama`, `per : president_of`, `United_States`⟩ yields a subject span ("Barack Obama"), a relation span ("president of"), and an object span ("United States"). We input processed text through an embedding function f_{belief} to get a single embedding $\boldsymbol{b}$ for the belief. Here, f_{belief} could be average of pretrained word embeddings, or final hidden state obtained from a sequence model (LSTM or Bi-LSTM) or the embedding from a transformer model (e.g., BERT (Devlin et al., 2019)). As we discuss in §5.2, we experiment with all of these.

We represent the provenance sentences at two granularities. The first is by representing each sentence separately. We get a representation $\boldsymbol{s}_i$ for each provenance sentence via an embedding function $f_{evidence}$ that embeds and combines them into a single vector. We define $f_{evidence}$ similarly to f_{belief}.

The second level considers all sentences at the same time. We refer to this as *blob*-level processing (rather than paragraph- or document-level) since the provenance sentences may come from different documents and we cannot assume any syntactic continuity between sentences. We obtain a representation of the blob from f_{blob}. In principle any method of distilling potentially disjoint text could be used here: we found TF-IDF to be effective, especially as multiple sentences of provenance selectively extracted from different sources could result in lengthy, but non-narratively coherent text (which can be problematic for transformer models).

4.2 Belief and Provenance Combination

Given the belief and provenance representations, we compute their similarity α_i as the cosine of the angle between their embedded representations: $\alpha_i = \frac{\boldsymbol{b}_i^T \boldsymbol{s}_i}{||\boldsymbol{b}_i|| \cdot ||\boldsymbol{s}_i||}$. The intuition is that sentences that are more consistent with the belief will score higher than those which are less. Scoring is important, as each IE system may give multiple provenance sentences (e.g., TAC allowed four). The sentences can be correct and support the belief, or be poorly selected and unsupportive. Higher scores suggest the provenance is related to the belief and helps differentiate supportive from unsupportive provenance. We use the computed similarity scores to combine the provenance representations and take a weighted average as our final input, capturing the semantics of the belief and provenance, as $\boldsymbol{x} = \frac{1}{n}\sum_i \alpha_i \cdot \boldsymbol{s}_i$. We pass the created representation $\boldsymbol{x}$ as the input to the feature learning module.

Though our computation of α_i and $\mathbf{x}$ operate at the sentence-level, our approach can also be applied to individual word representations. For this word-level attention, we replace each sentence representation s_i with a word representation w_{ij} in our computation of α_i and $\mathbf{x}$. While we experimented with this word-level attention we found the model had trouble learning, frequently classifying beliefs nearly all as consistent, or inconsistent with "no repair." We note that a similarly effective word-level attention was provided in DeClarE.

We selected a similarity-based, rather than position-based, attention. Applying position-based attention, as Zhang et al. (2017) did on the TACRED dataset, assumes that provenance sentences contain an explicit mention of the subject and object. In our setting that explicitly is not the case (recall the prevalence of missing arguments in our datasets, c.f. Fig. 2). There is also an assumption that there is exactly one provenance sentence as opposed to TAC, where an IE system can select up to four provenance sentences without explicitly mentioning either the subject or object.

4.3 Feature Learning and Classification

Prior to classification we may learn a more targeted representation $\mathbf{z}$ by, e.g., passing the combined representation $\boldsymbol{x}$ into a multi-layer perception. If we do not, then the consistency and repair classifiers operate directly on $\mathbf{z} = \mathbf{x}$.

We noticed through development set experiments that while adding additional layers initially helped, using more than three layers marginally decreased performance. For a k-layer MLP we obtained the projections $\boldsymbol{h}^{(j)}$, for $1 \leq j \leq k$, as: $\mathbf{h}^{(j)} = g\left(\boldsymbol{W}^{(j)}\boldsymbol{h}^{(j-1)} + \boldsymbol{b}^{(j)}\right)$. $\boldsymbol{h}^{(0)} = \boldsymbol{x}$ indicates the input, $\boldsymbol{W}^{(j)}$ and $\boldsymbol{b}^{(j)}$ are each layer's learned weights and biases (respectively), and g is the activation function. Through dev set experimentation we set g to be ReLU (Glorot et al., 2011). We found the MLP gave better performance (§5) and that it was parametrically and computationally efficient. We note that the effectiveness of an MLP was also noted by the two top systems from the Fake News Challenge (Hanselowski et al., 2018; Riedel et al., 2017b) for the verification task. On dev, we evaluated from one to five hidden layers and found the performance to be consistent after three layers, with the mean close the scores in Tables 3 and 4 and a maximum standard deviation across all the dataset and evaluation metrics to be less then one F1 point.

In addition to the learned features learned $\mathbf{h}^{(k)}$, we experiment with a lexically-based skip connection, where the input from the previous layer skips a few layers and is connected to a deeper one. We found this to be effective when making use of "blob" level features, computed via f_{blob}. We further found computing f_{blob} as the TF-IDF vector of all provenance text to be especially effective (§5.5). When using this connection, we compute $\mathbf{z} = \left[\boldsymbol{h}^{(k)}, f_{blob}(blob)\right]$. If this connection is not used, $\mathbf{z} = \boldsymbol{h}^{(k)}$.

Classification. We use the final representation $\mathbf{z}$ as input to the consistency ($\hat{y}_c = \texttt{sigmoid}\left(\boldsymbol{W}^c\boldsymbol{z} + \boldsymbol{b}^c\right)$) and repair classifiers ($\hat{\boldsymbol{y}}_r = \texttt{softmax}\left(\boldsymbol{W}^r\boldsymbol{z} + \boldsymbol{b}^r\right)$). The parameters W^c and W^r have sizes $1 \times (d_{\text{tf-idf}} + d_{\text{hidden}})$ and $d_{\text{relations}} \times (d_{\text{tf-idf}} + d_{\text{hidden}})$, respectively. Here $d_{\text{tf-idf}}$, d_{hidden}, and $d_{\text{relations}}$ are the dimension of the TF-IDF vector, hidden vector and number of relations considered by the IE systems.

4.4 Joint Optimization

We train the parameters using back propagation of both losses, $\mathcal{L}_{consistency}$ and $\mathcal{L}_{repair}$, jointly:

$$\mathcal{L} = \mathcal{L}_{\text{consistency}}\left(y_c, \hat{y}_c\right) + \mathcal{L}_{\text{repair}}\left(\boldsymbol{y}_r, \hat{\boldsymbol{y}}_r\right) \quad (1)$$

Each subloss is a cross-entropy loss between the true $(y_c, \boldsymbol{y}_r)$ and predicted $(\hat{y}_c, \hat{\boldsymbol{y}}_r)$ responses, weighted inversely proportional to the prevalence of the correct label. The tasks are not independent. In our formulation they share the same provenance and belief representations so learning both tasks jointly helps in learning these shared parameters.[1]

While in this paper we present a joint loss objective, we note that we separately experimented with alternative, non-joint approaches to Eq. (1). However, in development we found they performed worse than the joint approach. First we evaluated pipelined approaches, e.g., where the repair classifier also considered the output of the credibility model, but found its performance to be inferior to the joint approach. Second, we also tried using the repair output as input to the credibility classifier, and found that it resulted in high recall with poor precision, with inconsistent instances being classified as consistent. The shared abstract representation of belief and provenance used in our

[1]See §5 for discussion of alternative losses.

	TAC 2015	TAC 2017	TACRED-KG
Train	20575	45841	68124
Dev	6859	5734	22631
Test	6856	5729	15509

Table 2: Dataset statistics, in the number of provenance-backed beliefs, for the train/dev/test splits per dataset.

formulation presented above allows fine tuning for both subtasks. We also experimented on dev with other types of weighting, such as a uniform weighting. However, the inversely proportional weighting scheme we describe in the main paper is what performed best on dev experiments.

A Generalizing Framework. We note that we can represent DeClarE by defining the belief encoder f_{belief} as averaging word embeddings, a provenance encoder $f_{evidence}$ to be a Bi-LSTM, combining these representations with word level attention, and passing them to a two layer MLP without lexical skip connections. To achieve this specialization, we can optimize either $\mathcal{L}_{\text{consistency}}$ or $\mathcal{L}_{\text{repair}}$. Representing LSTM-text is similar. This shows that our framework encompasses prior work.

5 Experiments

We centered our study around four questions, answered throughout §5.3. **(1)** As our approach subsumes credibility models, can those credibility models also be used for the consistency and/or repair tasks (§5.3.1)? **(2)** What features and representations are important for the consistency and repair tasks (§5.3.2)? **(3)** How important is it to model the realized (sequential) order of words within the provenance sentences for our tasks (§5.3.3)? **(4)** What are the differences between relation repair and extraction (§5.3.4)?

5.1 Datasets and Hyperparameter Tuning

Table 2 provides statistics on the train/dev/test splits. On dev, we tuned hyper-parameters over all the models and datasets, using learning rates from $\{10^{-1},...,10^{-5}\}$ by powers of 10, dropout (Srivastava et al., 2014) from $\{0.0, 0.2\}$, and L2 regularizing penalty values from $\{0.0, 0.1..., 0.0001\}$ (powers of 10). We ran each model until convergence or for 20 epochs (whichever came first) with a batch size of 64.

5.2 Components

We evaluated the effect of each of the four major components mentioned below. We used Glove (Pennington et al., 2014) as pre-trained word embeddings, except for BERT models, where we used the uncased base model (Devlin et al., 2019).

Representations (Rep.): We evaluated three ways to represent beliefs and provenance text (compute f_{belief} and $f_{evidence}$): *Bag-of-Words (BoW) embedding* which is the average of Glove embeddings, the final output from the LSTM and Bi-LSTM models, and the BERT representation output. While an average of embeddings may seem simple, this approach has empirically performed well on other tasks compared to more complicated models (Iyyer et al., 2015).

Combining belief & provenance (Comb.): When beliefs and provenance are used, we considered similarity as sentence-level attention ("Yes (S)") as well as word-level attention ("Yes (W)").

Feature Learning (Feat.): In our primary experiments to do further feature learning we used a three layer multi-layer perceptron ("MLP") to do further feature learning. We indicate no further feature learning with a value of "None."

"Blob" Sparse Connection ("Sparse"): If used, we set f_{blob} to compute either a TF-IDF or binary-lexical vector based on the *blob* (concatenation of all sentences for a belief). This computed representation skips the feature learning component and is provided directly to the classifier.

5.3 Results

The overall test results across our three datasets are shown in Table 3 for the consistency task and Table 4 for the repair task. Each of the selected models was, prior to evaluation on the test set, chosen due to its performance on development data. The results are averaged across three runs.

5.3.1 Can Credibility Models be Used?

We first examine and compare our proposed framework against two different strong performing credibility models. These external methods are our baselines and we indicate them in Tables 3 and 4 by "♣" (Popat et al., 2018) and "♠" (Rashkin et al., 2017). We find they both perform poorly compared to other models, indicating that while both tasks learn similar functions the credibility models cannot be used "as-is" for consistency. This highlights the fact that the consistency task is sufficiently different from the existing credibility task.

Moreover, in examining whether credibility models transfer to the repair task, word level attention with a Bi-LSTM sentence encoder, as in DeClarE

f_{belief}	$f_{evidence}$	Comb.	Feat.	Sparse	TACRED-KG			TAC-17			TAC-15		
					P	R	F1	P	R	F1	P	R	F1
None	None	No	None	Binary	63.96	83.46	72.42	19.65	5.29	8.34	28.08	0.81	1.58
None	None	No	None	TF-IDF	63.95	**83.24**	**72.33**	**57.58**	30.66	14.05	22.68	15.08	18.12
None	♠ LSTM	No	MLP	No	42.59	66.66	51.98	52.05	30.76	27.78	17.01	9.21	11.95
BoW	♣ Bi-LSTM	Yes (W)	MLP	No	42.59	66.66	51.98	37.31	52.44	43.54	31.17	36.55	33.65
BERT	BERT	Yes (S)	MLP	TF-IDF	**66.42**	76.26	69.99	48.10	88.56	62.34	51.70	59.69	55.40
BoW	BoW	Yes (S)	MLP	TF-IDF	65.99	64.14	65.05	48.09	**98.03**	**63.17**	50.83	65.22	**57.13**

Table 3: Consistency performance (average of 3 runs) from our models (see §5.2 for a detailed explanation of the columns). We indicate existing credibility models with ♣ (Popat et al., 2018) and ♠ (Rashkin et al., 2017). BoW refers to bag of GLoVE embeddings.

f_{belief}	$f_{evidence}$	Comb.	Feat.	Sparse	TACRED-KG			TAC-2017			TAC-2015		
					Macro	Micro	MRR	Macro	Micro	MRR	Macro	Micro	MRR
None	None	No	None	Binary	2.16	41.65	0.83	44.86	53.10	0.83	22.78	16.50	0.19
None	None	No	None	TF-IDF	**14.50**	43.48	**0.83**	75.49	76.80	0.76	**76.35**	77.57	0.76
None	♠ LSTM	No	MLP	No	1.87	**78.56**	0.82	3.05	33.04	0.53	1.46	61.30	0.68
BoW	♣ Bi-LSTM	Yes (W)	MLP	No	1.24	52.39	0.8	1.04	32.02	0.43	1.46	61.30	0.66
BERT	BERT	Yes (S)	MLP	TF-IDF	4.10	7.72	0.28	72.17	81.85	0.89	54.91	58.61	0.69
BoW	BoW	Yes (S)	MLP	TF-IDF	7.22	64.43	0.74	**76.39**	**85.33**	**0.91**	65.76	**78.02**	**0.86**

Table 4: Repair Performance (averaged over 3 runs) of models with abbreviations as in Table 3.

f_{belief} and $f_{evidence}$	Comb.	Sparse	Consistency			Repair		
			P	R	F1	Macro	Micro	MRR
BoW	No	No	12.01	33.33	17.65	0.92	22.08	0.38
BoW	Yes (S)	No	12.01	33.33	17.65	0.89	21.16	0.34
BoW	No	TF-IDF	47.98	90.75	62.77	75.71	85.24	0.90
BoW	Yes (S)	TF-IDF	48.09	**92.03**	63.17	**76.39**	**85.33**	**0.91**
Bi-LSTM	Yes (S)	TF-IDF	**59**	87.71	**70.53**	75.76	83.86	0.89
BERT	Yes (S)	TF-IDF	48.11	91.47	63.06	76.30	85.25	0.91

Table 5: Consistency and repair performance ablation study, averaged over three runs. "Comb." is belief and provenance combination, and "Skip" is the use of skip connection. All use an MLP for feature learning. For space, we only consider TAC 2017 in these experiments.

(Popat et al., 2018, ♣), performs poorly in the repair task too (with one exception on TACRED-KG). These results highlight differences in the credibility vs. consistency tasks, and the applicability of existing credibility models to both consistency and repair, suggesting that a dedicated framework and study such as ours is needed.

5.3.2 What Representations are Effective?

Consistency: Both sentence attention and a TF-IDF sparse connection improve the overall F1 of our framework's embedding-based models. We noticed that precision and recall vary across the datasets due to their different characteristics. This can be seen with the two methods that rely only on the lexically-based sparse connections (the first two rows of Table 3): while performance was strong on TACRED-KG consistency, it was quite poor on TAC 2015 and 2017. These latter two datasets have more provenance sentences per belief, and make fewer assumptions about what must be contained in the provenance. Together, this results in greater lexical variety, which suggests that while non-neural lexical-based consistency approaches can be effective in settings with limited provenance, stronger approaches are needed for greater and more diverse provenance. Learning refined embeddings (rows 5 and 6) suggests that these pre-trained models are helpful in the task. BERT benefits from the less noisy provenance in TACRED-KG. However, similar or slightly better performance is achieved when simple word embeddings are used, especially for TAC 2015/2017, highlighting the difficulty of the consistency task with noisier provenance.

Repair: Perhaps surprisingly, an embedding model with a TF-IDF sparse connection yielded good performance. The sparse-based lexical features are most influential, as evident from when just TF-IDF or binary lexical features are used. Looking across the three datasets, we notice that a TF-IDF only model provides a surprisingly strong baseline, outperforming the existing credibility models in almost all cases. Using BoW embedding with sentence attention, MLP feature learning, and a TF-IDF sparse connection, we can surpass a sparse-only TF-IDF approach. The BERT-based representation, fine-tuned or not, performed nearly equally to a BoW embedding on the repair task, indicating both the effectiveness of its pre-trained model and highlighting the difficulty of this repair task.

Belief: *Marty Walsh; org:city_of_headquarters; Neighborhood House Charter School* **Summary**: (✓, *fixed*) **Human(C)**: No; **Predicted(C)**: No; **Human(R)**: org:founded_by; **Predicted(R)**: org:founded_by **Provenance**: Walsh was a founding board member of Dorchester's Neighborhood House Charter School, and makes clear that he would support lifting the cap on charters in the city, something that hardly wins him the favor of the Boston Teachers Union.
Belief: *Alan M. Dershowitz; per:title; professor* **Summary**: (✗, *incorrect_fixed*) **Human(C)**: Yes; **Predicted(C)**: No; **Human(R)**: per:title; **Predicted(R)**: per:religion **Provenance**: Harvard Law professor Alan Dershowitz said Sunday that the Obama administration was naive and had possibly made a "cataclysmic error of gigantic proportions" in its deal to ease sanctions on Iran in exchange for an opening up of the Islamic Republic s nuclear program.

Figure 4: Examples of our model's predictions on the TAC 2015 datasets. Human: gold standard label, Predicted: our model's label, C: Consistency, R: Repair, Human(C): Human Consistency label, and Predicted(C): Predicted consistency label. Similarly for repair. Summary indicates overall prediction analysis of example. (✓, fixed) means consistency correctly predicted and incorrect belief was fixed.

5.3.3 How Helpful Is Sequential Modeling?

As indicated by Zhang et al. (2017), the sentences in TACRED and TAC are long. Consistency and repair models must be able to handle that. Note that BoW representation methods do not consider word order, while LSTM, Bi-LSTM and BERT embeddings do. From Tables 3 and 4, we see that TF-IDF sparse features and a sentence level combination of the belief and provenance give the best performance on both tasks when using a BoW representation, as compared to an LSTM, Bi-LSTM with word attention, and BERT. This indicates that for consistency and repair, **unordered lexical features can be sufficient to get better performance**.

We further examine this in Table 5, where due to space we focus on TAC 2017. Notice that while sequence-based encodings can improve some aspects (e.g., precision and F1 for consistency), there are not across-the-board improvements. We experimented with replacing the BoW embedding with a sentence-level Bi-LSTM representation. A Bi-LSTM representation with just attention and TF-IDF sparse features gives better consistency precision and F1 compared to BoW embedding approaches. However, the Bi-LSTM results in overall lower performance for repair. While the differences are not very large, they indicate that **simple methods can outperform, or perform competitively with, sequential and autoencoding methods**.

5.3.4 Relation Repair vs. Re-Extraction

While the repair task *can* be viewed as relation re-extraction, we examine the implications of this. Tables. 3 and 4 show a large performance drop for TACRED-KG vs. TAC 2015/2017. First, TACRED was created from a TAC dataset and modified and augmented by crowd-sourced workers. When the belief was found with abstract or generalized provenance, workers were shown a set of sentences containing the subject-object pairs and asked to pick the representative sentence which was most specific. Second, each sentence is guaranteed to include the subject and object mentions, which is not always true for TAC 2015 and 2017, where a significant number of TAC provenance sentences were missing one or both the subject and object mentions. This highlights some of the differences in the core assumptions made in the construction of a relation extraction dataset.

5.4 Prediction Error Analysis

Fig. 4 demonstrates our framework's performance on some examples from TAC 2015. The first example describes the case where the belief was consistent with the provenance information and there was no recommendation of an alternate relation. Depending on the provenance the fix may not be appropriate, as in the second example of per:title vs. per:religion where we believe an indicative word like "Islamic" influenced the repair prediction.

5.5 Ablation Study

Our results show the strength of attention with lexical features. We further examine the impact of lexical features, using the first four rows of Table 5.

Lexical Impact on Consistency. From the first row of Table 5, we see BoW embedding for both the belief and provenance results in low precision and recall. While adding attention does not help, using TF-IDF sparse features drastically improves performance. Meanwhile, removing sentence-based attention only has a small impact on performance. All together this indicates the provenance found by the IE system is *more lexically systematic*.

Lexical Impact on Repair. A similar trend is seen for the repair task: our combined representation with TF-IDF is better than relying only on embeddings. Combining belief and provenance sentences gets slightly better micro overall compared to macro. This affects the MRR score too. However, the best performance is achieved when all components are combined.

6 Related Studies

There has been research on determining the consistency of beliefs using either schemas or ensembles, but none that are language-based, do not require access to IE system details, or attempt to repair inconsistent facts. Our work addresses all these.

Schema and Ensemble Based approaches: Previous work by Ojha and Talukdar (2017) and Pujara et al. (2013) determined the consistency of the extracted belief using a schema as the side information and coupling constraints to satisfy the schema's axioms. Rather than applying schemas, Yu et al. (2014) proposed an unsupervised method applying linguistic features to filter credible vs. non-credible belief. However, it required access to multiple IE systems with different configuration settings that extracted information from the same text corpus. Viswanathan et al. (2015) used a supervised approach to build a classifier from the confidence scores produced by multiple IE systems for the same belief. These are not *standalone* systems, as they assume the availability of multiple IE systems.

Language based approaches: The FEVER (Thorne et al., 2018) fact-checking study proposes a framework for credibility task and performs provenance-based classification without attempting to repair errors. This task has inspired a number of efforts (Yin and Roth, 2018, i.a.,), including Ma et al. (2019) who tackle a problem similar to our consistency. Guo et al. (2022) outlines additional language-based approaches for consistency prediction (they term it "verdict prediction"). However, a crucial difference is that we aim to operate on KG tuple outputs as the belief (not sentences).

Overall, our study differs from previous ones in two important ways. (1) We address the problem of determining consistency and potential corrections without access to an underlying semantic schema. (2) Our standalone approach treats the underlying IE systems as *blackboxes* and requires no access to the original IE systems or detailed system output containing confidence scores.

7 Conclusions

We propose a task of refining the beliefs produced by a blackbox IE system that provides no access to or knowledge of its internal workings. First we analyze the types of errors made. Then we propose two subtasks: determining the consistency of an extracted belief and its provenance text, and suggesting a repair to fix the belief. We present a modular framework that can use a variety of representation, and learning techniques, and subsumes prior work. This framework provides effective techniques for the consistency and repair tasks.

Acknowledgements

We would also like to thank the anonymous reviewers for their comments, questions, and suggestions. This material is based in part upon work supported by the National Science Foundation under Grant Nos. IIS-1940931, IIS-2024878, and DGE-2114892. Some experiments were conducted on the UMBC HPCF, supported by the National Science Foundation under Grant No. CNS-1920079.This material is also based on research that is in part supported by the Army Research Laboratory, Grant No. W911NF2120076, and by the Air Force Research Laboratory (AFRL), DARPA, for the KAIROS program under agreement number FA8750-19-2-1003. The U.S.Government is authorized to reproduce and distribute reprints for Governmental purposes notwithstanding any copyright notation thereon. The views and conclusions contained herein are those of the authors and should not be interpreted as necessarily representing the official policies or endorsements, either express or implied, of the Air Force Research Laboratory (AFRL), DARPA, or the U.S. Government.

References

Hoa Trang Dang, editor. 2017. *Proceedings of the 10th Text Analysis Conference*. NIST.

Jacob Devlin, Ming-Wei Chang, Kenton Lee, and Kristina Toutanova. 2019. Bert: Pre-training of deep bidirectional transformers for language understanding. In *NAACL*.

Joe Ellis. 2015a. TAC KBP 2015 assessment guidelines. Technical report, Linguistic Data Consortium.

Joe Ellis. 2015b. TAC KBP 2015 slot descriptions. Technical report, Linguistic Data Consortium.

Patrick Ernst, Cynthia Meng, Amy Siu, and Gerhard Weikum. 2014. Knowlife: a knowledge graph for health and life sciences. In *30th International Conference on Data Engineering*, pages 1254–1257. IEEE.

Tim Finin, Dawn Lawrie, James Mayfield, Paul McNamee, and Cash Costello. 2017. HLTCOE participation in TAC KBP 2017: Cold start TEDL and low-resource EDL. In *Proceedings of the Text Analysis Conference (TAC2017)*. NIST.

Xavier Glorot, Antoine Bordes, and Yoshua Bengio. 2011. Deep sparse rectifier neural networks. In *Proceedings of the 14th International Conference on Artificial Intelligence and Statistics*, pages 315–323.

Zhijiang Guo, Michael Schlichtkrull, and Andreas Vlachos. 2022. A Survey on Automated Fact-Checking. *Transactions of the Association for Computational Linguistics*, 10:178–206.

Andreas Hanselowski, Avinesh PVS, Benjamin Schiller, Felix Caspelherr, Debanjan Chaudhuri, Christian M. Meyer, and Iryna Gurevych. 2018. A retrospective analysis of the fake news challenge stance-detection task. In *Proceedings of the 27th International Conference on Computational Linguistics*, pages 1859–1874. Association for Computational Linguistics.

Mohit Iyyer, Varun Manjunatha, Jordan Boyd-Graber, and Hal Daumé III. 2015. Deep unordered composition rivals syntactic methods for text classification. In *Proceedings of the 53rd Annual Meeting of the Association for Computational Linguistics and the 7th International Joint Conference on Natural Language Processing (Volume 1: Long Papers)*, volume 1, pages 1681–1691.

Jing Ma, Wei Gao, Shafiq Joty, and Kam-Fai Wong. 2019. Sentence-level evidence embedding for claim verification with hierarchical attention networks. In *Proceedings of the 57th Annual Meeting of the Association for Computational Linguistics*.

T. Mitchell, W. Cohen, E. Hruschka, P. Talukdar, J. Betteridge, A. Carlson, B. Dalvi, M. Gardner, B. Kisiel, J. Krishnamurthy, N. Lao, K. Mazaitis, T. Mohamed, N. Nakashole, E. Platanios, A. Ritter, M. Samadi, B. Settles, R. Wang, D. Wijaya, A. Gupta, X. Chen, A. Saparov, M. Greaves, and J. Welling. 2015. Never-ending learning. In *Proceedings of the 29th AAAI Conference on Artificial Intelligence*.

Prakhar Ojha and Partha Talukdar. 2017. KGEval: Accuracy estimation of automatically constructed knowledge graphs. In *Conf. on Empirical Methods in Natural Language Processing*. ACL.

Ankur Padia. 2019. *Joint Models to Refine Knowledge Graphs*. Ph.D. thesis, University of Maryland, Baltimore County.

Jeffrey Pennington, Richard Socher, and Christopher Manning. 2014. Glove: Global vectors for word representation. In *Conf. on Empirical Methods in Natural Language Processing*, pages 1532–1543. ACL.

Kashyap Popat, Subhabrata Mukherjee, Andrew Yates, and Gerhard Weikum. 2018. DeClarE: Debunking fake news and false claims using evidence-aware deep learning. In *Proceedings of the Conference on Empirical Methods in Natural Language Processing*, pages 22–32. Association for Computational Linguistics.

Jay Pujara, Hui Miao, Lise Getoor, and William Cohen. 2013. Knowledge graph identification. In *Int. Semantic Web Conf.*, pages 542–557. Springer.

Shahzad Rajput. 2017. Overview of the cold start knowledge base construction and slot filling tracks. Slides from the U.S. National Institute of Standards and Technology.

Hannah Rashkin, Eunsol Choi, Jin Yea Jang, Svitlana Volkova, and Yejin Choi. 2017. Truth of varying shades: Analyzing language in fake news and political fact-checking. In *Proceedings of the 2017 Conference on Empirical Methods in Natural Language Processing*, pages 2931–2937. Association for Computational Linguistics.

Benjamin Riedel, Isabelle Augenstein, Georgios P Spithourakis, and Sebastian Riedel. 2017a. A simple but tough-to-beat baseline for the fake news challenge stance detection task. *arXiv preprint arXiv:1707.03264*.

Benjamin Riedel, Isabelle Augenstein, Georgios P. Spithourakis, and Sebastian Riedel. 2017b. A simple but tough-to-beat baseline for the Fake News Challenge stance detection task. *CoRR*, abs/1707.03264.

Nitish Srivastava, Geoffrey Hinton, Alex Krizhevsky, Ilya Sutskever, and Ruslan Salakhutdinov. 2014. Dropout: A simple way to prevent neural networks from overfitting. *The Journal of Machine Learning Research*, 15(1):1929–1958.

Fabian M Suchanek, Gjergji Kasneci, and Gerhard Weikum. 2007. Yago: a core of semantic knowledge. In *Proceedings of the 16th international conference on World Wide Web*, pages 697–706. ACM.

Mihai Surdeanu, David McClosky, Julie Tibshirani, John Bauer, Angel X Chang, Valentin I Spitkovsky, and Christopher D Manning. 2010. A simple distant supervision approach for the TAC-KBP slot filling task. https://nlp.stanford.edu/pubs/kbp2010-slotfilling.pdf.

James Thorne, Andreas Vlachos, Christos Christodoulopoulos, and Arpit Mittal. 2018. FEVER: a large-scale dataset for fact extraction and verification. *arXiv preprint arXiv:1803.05355*.

Vidhoon Viswanathan, Nazneen Fatema Rajani, Yinon Bentor, and Raymond Mooney. 2015. Stacked ensembles of information extractors for knowledge-base population. In *ACL*.

Wenpeng Yin and Dan Roth. 2018. TwoWingOS: A two-wing optimization strategy for evidential claim verification. In *Proceedings of the Conference on Empirical Methods in Natural Language Processing*.

Dian Yu, Hongzhao Huang, Taylor Cassidy, Heng Ji, Chi Wang, Shi Zhi, Jiawei Han, Clare Voss, and Malik Magdon-Ismail. 2014. The wisdom of minority: Unsupervised slot filling validation based on multi-dimensional truth-finding. In *25th Int. Conf. on Computational Linguistics*, pages 1567–1578.

Yuhao Zhang, Victor Zhong, Danqi Chen, Gabor Angeli, and Christopher D Manning. 2017. Position-aware attention and supervised data improve slot filling. In *Proceedings of the Conference on Empirical Methods in Natural Language Processing*, pages 35–45.

KIQA: Knowledge-Infused Question Answering Model for Financial Table-Text Data

Rungsiman Nararatwong[1], Natthawut Kertkeidkachorn[2], Ryutaro Ichise[4,1,3]
[1]National Institute of Advanced Science and Technology, Japan
[2]Japan Advanced Institute of Science and Technology
[3]National Institute of Informatics, Japan
[4]Tokyo Institute of Technology
r.nararatwong@aist.go.jp, natt@jaist.ac.jp
ichise@iee.e.titech.ac.jp

Abstract

While entity retrieval models continue to advance their capabilities, our understanding of their wide-ranging applications is limited, especially in domain-specific settings. We highlighted this issue by using recent general-domain entity-linking models, LUKE and GENRE, to inject external knowledge into a question-answering (QA) model for a financial QA task with a hybrid tabular-textual dataset. We found that both models improved the baseline model by 1.57% overall and 8.86% on textual data. Nonetheless, the challenge remains as they still struggle to handle tabular inputs. We subsequently conducted a comprehensive attention-weight analysis, revealing how LUKE utilizes external knowledge supplied by GENRE. The analysis also elaborates how the injection of symbolic knowledge can be helpful and what needs further improvement, paving the way for future research on this challenging QA task and advancing our understanding of how a language model incorporates external knowledge.

1 Introduction

Decades of development in question-answering research have seen numerous methods focusing on unstructured text, structured knowledge bases, or semi-structured tables. Recent work (Zhu et al., 2021) has discovered a new challenge in applying these techniques to the financial domain. The study proposed a QA task on financial reports compiled as a Tabular And Textual dataset for Question Answering (TAT-QA). Each question has an associated table and multiple paragraphs, making a hybrid data structure. TAT-QA requires a certain level of financial knowledge to extract evidence from tables and texts, making it an appropriate choice for our study. Our motivation is to examine whether injecting symbolic knowledge help the model better understand financial concepts.

As shown in Figure 1, we can inject the entity information of companies (dbpedia:BCE_Inc), financial terms (dbpedia:Share_repurchase), and common knowledge (dbpedia:Europe), among others. The coverage and accuracy of the information depend on the entity linking method. Nevertheless, we expect certain common entities to appear in a text-question or table-question pair. We hypothesized that this commonality helps the QA model to focus on the target answer spans, and our analysis provided evidence to confirm the hypothesis.

In summary, we introduced the knowledge-infused question answering (KIQA) model for tabular-textual data. We designed our experiment to evaluate the end-to-end results and investigate the strengths and weaknesses of the injection method to provide insights for future research. Our main contributions are as follows:

- We proposed, evaluated, and compared KIQA in different settings, improving the performance of the baseline method.
- We conducted an exhaustive attention-weight analysis of the entity-linking model we applied to our study.

Our analysis aims at understanding how language models utilize symbolic knowledge. We intend for this work to stimulate more studies into the mechanism of these models as we advance their capabilities and applications.

2 Related Works

2.1 Question Answering

Numerous QA datasets focus on textual data, such as SQuAD (Rajpurkar et al., 2016), tabular data, such as SQA (Iyyer et al., 2017) and a mixture of tables and texts (Chen et al., 2020). TAT-QA combines both tabular and textual input and requires numerical reasoning. We are interested in TAT-QA due to its practical applications since it consists of

Proceedings of Deep Learning Inside Out (DeeLIO 2022):
The 3rd Workshop on Knowledge Extraction and Integration for Deep Learning Architectures, pages 53 - 61
May 27, 2022

Text

In 2018, BCE repurchased 3,085,697 common shares for a total cost of $175 million through a NCIB.

Table

Year Ended December 31,	2019	2018
...		
Europe		
Travel	32,081	30,856
Local	4,817	5,293
Total Europe revenues	36,898	36,149
...		

Question

Q1: How many common shares did BCE repurchase in 2018?

Q2: In 2019, how many geographic regions have total revenues of more than $20,000?

Entities

dbpedia:BCE_Inc dbpedia:Share_repurchase

dbpedia:Common_stock dbpedia:Total_cost

dbpedia:Europe > dbpedia:region

dbpedia:Total_revenue

Figure 1: KIQA injects entity information commonly found in TAT-QA's tables, texts, and questions into the QA model. Some questions may require external knowledge to reason. For example, to answer Q2, the model needs to understand which cells in the table refer to a region.

real-world financial reports annotated and verified by experts. It also requires the model to understand financial concepts, making it suitable for our purposes.

TAT-QA proposed a baseline model called TagOp, which performs sequence tagging and symbolic reasoning using operators. Their experiment includes baseline textual QA models, a tabular model, and a hybrid model. TagOp significantly outperformed all baseline models; thus, we decided to base our model on it.

2.2 Entity Linking

There are several entity-retrieval models currently available, e.g., BLINK (Li et al., 2020), EntQA (Zhang et al., 2022). However, we decided to use LUKE (Yamada et al., 2020), a pre-trained language model with entity-aware self-attention, since it outputs contextualized representations of words and entities, which we can adapt to TagOp's architecture. LUKE, adapting RoBERTa's architecture (Liu et al., 2019), consists of a modified multi-layer bidirectional transformer that takes words and entities as input tokens. The modified transformer adds query matrices that allow the *entity-aware* attention mechanism to attend to both words and entities as it computes the attention scores. This additional calculation allows LUKE to directly model the relationships among words and entities.

While masked entities are part of LUKE's pre-training data, its experiment showed that explicitly adding entity information to the model's input yielded the best result. Thus, we used the GENRE (Generative ENtity REtrieval) (Cao et al., 2021) model to retrieve entities in TAT-QA and input the additional information to LUKE. Based on a pre-trained language model BART (Lewis et al., 2020), GENRE retrieves entities by generating their unique names autoregressively using constrained beam search. Given an input text sequence, the model outputs the same sequence with special tokens indicating mentions, followed by the entity's unique Wikipedia page title after each mention. For example, an output for "*In 2018, BCE repurchased 3,085,697 ...,*" is "*In 2018, **[BCE]**(BCE_Inc) **[repurchased]**(Share_repurchase) 3,085,697 ...*"

3 KIQA Model

KIQA is a QA model built from TagOp, a baseline model for the TAT-QA dataset, to evaluate symbolic knowledge injection into a QA model for a domain-specific dataset with tabular and textual structure. With the stated objective, we strictly applied the architecture of TagOp but replaced the underlying LM, RoBERTa, with LUKE to obtain knowledge-infused representations. Following TagOp, KIQA consists of three main components: 1) Evidence Extraction, 2) Reasoning and 3)Knowledge Injection.

3.1 Evidence Extraction

The evidence extraction module predicts answer spans using sequential Inside-Outside (IO) tagging Ramshaw and Marcus, 1999. TagOp takes in an input sequence of the question, flattened table, and relevant paragraphs. The preprocessing step concatenates all table cell tokens into a continuous string without separating tokens. We split KIQA into two modules, shown in Figure 2; the first module ($\text{KIQA}^{\text{TagOP}}$) is identical to TagOp, while the second module ($\text{KIQA}^{\text{Text}}$) only processes the ques-

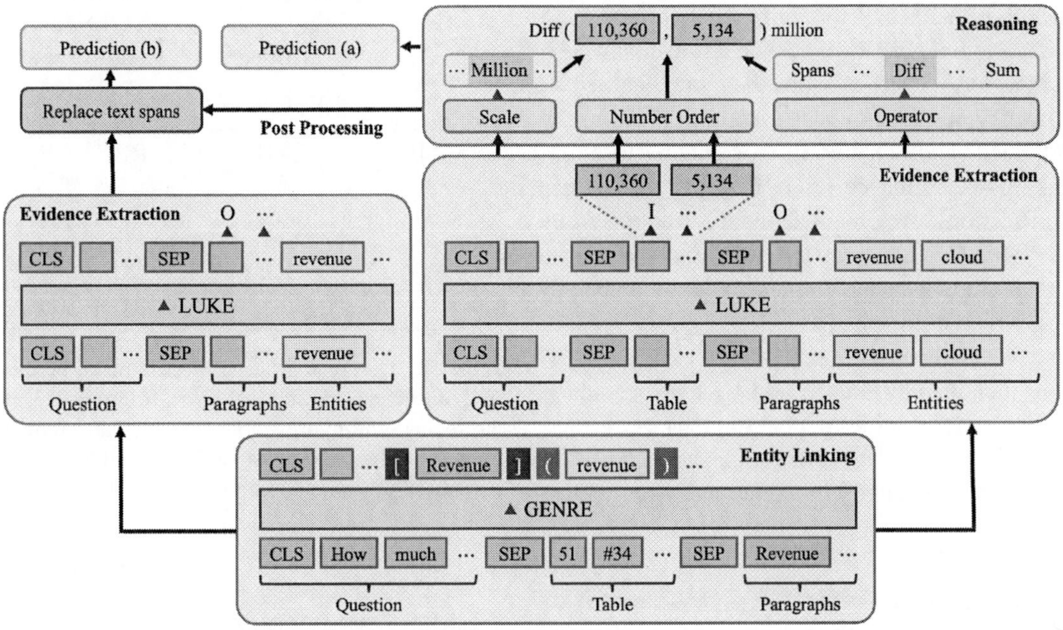

Figure 2: KIQA adopts TagOp's architecture with additional modules to handle knowledge injection. We used GENRE to retrieve entities (bottom block) and then extracted answer spans using LUKE (middle blocks). The model performs reasoning (upper-right block) on the hybrid answer spans (middle-right block). These two blocks on the right side without entity injection are comparable to TagOp. We replaced the reasoner's text span predictions with outputs from the text-only extractor (middle-left block) in certain experimental conditions.

tion and paragraphs. Our decision to introduce ($\text{KIQA}^{\text{Text}}$) stemmed from our preliminary investigation, which indicated that LUKE and GENRE did not perform as well on the tabular data as on the textual data. The idea was to replace KIQA ^{TagOp}'s prediction on textual input with $\text{KIQA}^{\text{Text}}$'s output and measure the difference. Although the inputs are different, we applied the same two-layer feed-forward network (FFN) with GELU Hendrycks and Gimpel, 2016 activation for tag prediction:

$$\mathbf{p}_{\mathrm{t}}^{\mathrm{tag}} = \mathrm{softmax}(\mathrm{FFN}(h_t)) \quad (1)$$

where h_t is the representation of sub-token t.

3.2 Reasoning

Reasoning in TAT-QA's context involves identifying and applying an operation, such as arithmetic calculation, to the tagged sequence. Three TAGOP's components perform symbolic reasoning: operator, number order, and scale classifiers. All three classifiers are two-layer feed-forward networks with GELU activation. TagOp defines ten operators: *span-in-text*, *cell-in-table*, *spans*, *sum*, *count*, *average*, *multiplication*, *division*, *difference*, and *change ratio*. Following our early investigation, we decided to merge span-based prediction, i.e., KIQA outputs all predicted answer spans when it predicts the operator as *span-in-text*, *cell-in-table*, or *spans*. The number order classifier determines the positions of two tokens with the highest probability for *division*, *difference*, and *change-ratio* operations (e.g., the numerator and denominator in the case of division). Lastly, the scale classifier can output *none*, *thousand*, *million*, *billion*, or *percent*. Since $\text{KIQA}^{\text{Text}}$ only performs sequence tagging, it does not require the reasoning classifiers. To clarify, following TagOp's definitions,

$$\mathbf{p}^{\mathrm{op}} = \mathrm{softmax}(\mathrm{FFN}([\mathrm{CLS}])) \quad (2)$$

$$\mathbf{p}^{\mathrm{order}} = \mathrm{softmax}(\mathrm{FFN}(\mathrm{avg}(h_{t1}, h_{t2}))) \quad (3)$$

$$\mathbf{p}^{\mathrm{scale}} = \mathrm{softmax}(\mathrm{FFN}([[\mathrm{CLS}]; h_{tab}; h_p])) \quad (4)$$

where [CLS] is a sentence-level classification token, "avg" is averaging, h_{t1}, h_{t2}, h_{tab}, and h_p are the output representations of the top two tokens and the averaged representations of the table and paragraphs respectively.

3.3 Knowledge Injection

We injected symbolic knowledge to TagOp by introducing entity information obtained from GENRE to

LUKE. LUKE's transformer-based architecture allows us to fine-tune the model on downstream tasks such as QA. However, while the model learned to utilize symbolic knowledge from pre-training, it still needs additional entity information to maximize its performance (more detail in the discussion section). We obtained this information from GENRE (Cao et al., 2021). The entity retrieval model outputs unique entities' Wikipedia page titles, which we mapped to LUKE's entity vocabulary. We could map 76.92% of entities in the questions identified by GENRE to LUKE's vocabulary, averaging 1.78 entities per question. The coverage is 78.42% (0.62 entities per cell) and 64.03% (2.91 entities per paragraph) for tables and paragraphs.

3.4 Training

We trained $\text{KIQA}^{\text{TagOp}}$ and $\text{KIQA}^{\text{Text}}$ separately to measure the effect of the flattened tables, where the input contains minimal syntactic structure, and observe how LUKE and GENRE learn and generalize. Following TagOp, KIQA uses the sum of sequence tagging, operator, scale, and order classification losses (negative log-likelihood) in its optimization. We used the development set of TAT-QA for evaluating our fine-tuning to ensure consistency.

4 Experiments and Results

Our experimental settings aim to measure the effect of injecting symbolic knowledge into a domain-specific tabular/textual QA model. We chose the financial domain for evaluation since research involving knowledge-infused language models in this domain is still limited. As for the dataset, TAT-QA provides extensive and high-quality samples with complex and realistic tabular and textual data.

4.1 Dataset

TAT-QA (Tabular And Textual dataset for Question Answering) presents the challenges of performing QA on tabular/textual financial reports. The dataset consists of 16,552 questions with 2,757 hybrid contexts from 182 financial documents. Each sample contains a question, a table with $3 \sim 30$ rows and $3 \sim 6$ columns, and a minimum of two relevant paragraphs. Also included in the sample are the answer and derivation, which explain the calculation steps required to derive the answer. TAT-QA splits into three parts, i.e., training (80%), development (10%), and testing (10%). The labels in the test set are not publicly available.

Group	TagOp-based Models	Text Span Replacement
I	RB, L, L&G	-
II	RB L L&G	RB → RB L → L L&G → L&G
III	RB	RB → L RB → L&G

Table 1: The TagOp-based models make prediction on both tabular and textual data. In group II and III, we replace the hybrid models' text span predictions with text-only models' outputs (indicated by →). RB = RoBERTa, L = LUKE, L&G = LUKE & GENRE.

4.2 Pipelines

We defined three groups of pipelines, each containing an ensemble of the three models we investigated. The first group includes three pipelines evaluating RoBERTa, LUKE, and LUKE with the extra entity information from GENRE (L&G). The second group replaces $\text{KIQA}^{\text{TagOp}}$'s answer span predictions from the first group with their corresponding $\text{KIQA}^{\text{Text}}$'s predictions for the *span-in-text* operator. Specifically, we replaced $\text{KIQA}^{\text{TagOp}}_{\text{RoBERTa}}$ with $\text{KIQA}^{\text{Text}}_{\text{RoBERTa}}$ and the same for LUKE and L&G. The third group is a follow-up experiment based on our analysis of the results from the first and second groups. In this last group, we paired $\text{KIQA}^{\text{TagOp}}_{\text{RoBERTa}}$ with $\text{KIQA}^{\text{Text}}_{\text{LUKE}}$ and $\text{KIQA}^{\text{Text}}_{\text{L\&G}}$ individually. We summarized our pipelines in Table 1.

4.3 Data Preprocessing

TagOp uses an automated approach to create labels for sequence tagging. We found that their algorithm does not always produce correct labeling. Therefore, we performed a simple check by extracting answer spans indicated in the labels, then executed the operations and compared the predicted answers with gold answers. Once we had identified the discrepancies, we manually examined and corrected them. However, due to the design of TagOp, we could not fix all the errors. For example, TagOp considers a table cell as a word, but some answers do not cover the entire cell. Nevertheless, since most labels are already valid, we have decided not to pursue further correction for this study. The strategy we employed was to train our models with correct samples, then validate and test the models with the entire development and test sets.

4.4 Evaluation

Table 2 shows the test set's results. The first row, TagOp, is the scores reported in the TAT-QA paper. The first pipeline of group I, RB or RoBERTa, is our reimplementation of TagOp. We attribute the boost from the original implementation to our data preprocessing algorithm, including labeling correction and elimination of invalid samples. The change we made to the prediction, i.e., outputting all answer spans for *span-in-text*, *cell-in-table*, and *spans*, also contributed to the improvement.

Although the changes we made helped increase the model's performance, it appeared that injecting external knowledge did not lead to further overall improvement. More importantly, RoBERTa seemed to outperform LUKE and GENRE on tabular data (table and hybrid). However, we noticed that LUKE & GENRE consistently exceeds RoBERTa in arithmetic operations and single-span prediction. While the arithmetic score results from multi-step prediction involving reasoning, single-span answers are more straightforward to isolate and measure the effect of knowledge infusion.

Based on group I and II results, we created the third group of pipelines consisting of KIQA$^{\text{TagOp}}_{\text{RoBERTa}}$ paring with the text-based models KIQA$^{\text{Text}}_{\text{RoBERTa}}$, KIQA$^{\text{TagOp}}_{\text{Luke}}$, and KIQA$^{\text{Text}}_{\text{L\&G}}$. The results indicate that injecting external knowledge into the textual part of the data improves the QA model. Nonetheless, due to the hybrid nature of the dataset, the overall improvement is less dramatic. According to our analysis of the training data, it is likely that the high variance in the counting columns is due to the small number of samples in this category.

5 Analysis

We have learned from our experimental results that injecting entity information helped improve the model's performance on textual data. This conclusion seems reasonable given that we did not provide the model with the same information for the tabular input. However, in some cases, the infused text-only entity information negatively affects the model's ability to handle tabular input. Our analysis attempts to answer the following questions:

- **Q1:** How does the injected external knowledge contribute to the improvement?
- **Q2:** Why do the knowledge-infused models underperform the baseline model on tabular data?

5.1 Attention Weights

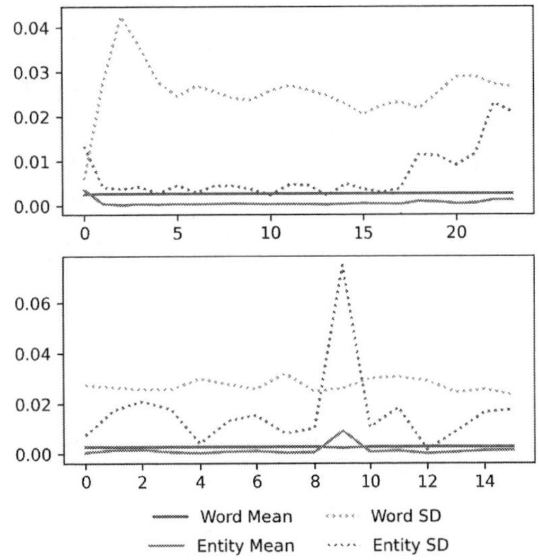

Figure 3: Top: Average and standard deviation of attention scores by layer (0 ~23). Bottom: Average and standard deviation of layer 22's attention scores by attention head (0 ~15).

We investigated Transformers' (Vaswani et al., 2017) attention weights α in different levels of aggregation to determine how LUKE utilizes entity information. Each Transformers layer consists of multiple attention heads. LUKE employs entity-aware self-attention, meaning that the model computes the weights from both word and entity tokens:

$$\text{Attention}(\mathbf{Q}, \mathbf{K}, \mathbf{V}) = \alpha \mathbf{V} \quad (5)$$

$$\alpha = \text{softmax}(\frac{\mathbf{Q}\mathbf{K}^{\text{T}}}{\sqrt{L}}) \quad (6)$$

where the query matrix $\mathbf{Q} \in \mathbb{R}^{L \times D}$ can be one of $\mathbf{Q}_{w2w}$, $\mathbf{Q}_{w2e}$, $\mathbf{Q}_{e2w}$, or $\mathbf{Q}_{e2e}$, depending on the types of tokens (word or entity). $\mathbf{K} \in \mathbb{R}^{L \times D}$ and $\mathbf{V} \in \mathbb{R}^{L \times D}$ denote key and value matrices. L is the dimension of input embedding, and D is the dimension of output embedding.

LUKE and RoBERTa (large model) consist of 24 layers of Transformers with 16 attention heads on each level. RoBERTa has an input length of 512 tokens, while LUKE extends it to 549 to handle the entity input, resulting in up to 549 $\times$ 549 attention matrix. Taken together with the 1,668 samples in TAT-QA's development set, the analysis would involve 12-billion data points.

The most straightforward approach is to average the weights by layer, head, and sample. However,

Model	EM	F1	Table A	Table C	Table M	Table S	Hybrid A	Hybrid C	Hybrid M	Hybrid S	Text A	Text M	Text S
TagOp	50.1	58.0	41.1	63.6	66.3	56.5	46.5	62.1	**63.2**	68.2	27.3	19.0	45.2
Group I: TagOp-based Models													
RB	57.2	67.2	51.6	36.4	**72.3**	**60.7**	**63.3**	**79.3**	60.4	68.8	18.2	19.1	51.1
LUKE	54.3	64.8	47.4	**72.7**	65.1	57.8	48.9	62.1	**62.3**	**75.5**	27.3	14.3	51.1
L&G	56.4	66.4	**53.7**	27.3	65.1	59.0	55.4	51.7	58.5	72.9	27.3	19.1	52.3
Group II: TagOp-based & Text Models													
RB	57.3	67.2	51.6	63.7	68.7	58.3	62.3	65.5	**62.3**	73.4	27.3	19.1	50.8
LUKE	56.4	66.1	52.8	45.5	68.7	55.4	58.6	34.5	61.3	75.0	27.3	19.1	51.1
L&G	57.2	66.6	**53.7**	27.3	65.1	59.5	55.4	51.7	58.5	75.0	27.3	19.1	54.8
Group III: TagOp-based (RB) & Text Models (LUKE & L&G)													
RB	57.3	67.2	51.6	63.7	68.7	58.3	62.3	65.5	**62.3**	73.4	27.3	19.1	50.8
LUKE*	57.6	67.1	•	•	•	59.0	•	•	•	74.5	•	•	51.7
L&G*	**58.2**	**67.4**	•	•	•	59.0	•	•	•	73.0	•	•	**55.3**

Table 2: Evaluation of the first and second groups on the test set. The abbreviations are: RB = RoBERTa, A = Arithmetic, C = Counting, M = Multi-span extraction, S = Single-span extraction. The detailed scores are exact match (EM) scores. The underlined scores are the top scores in the group, and the top scores across all groups are in bold. The test set does not include samples with the counting operation, so we removed them from the table. * For group III, since we only replaced RoBERTa's text span outputs with the text-only LUKE and L&G's outputs, the scores for A, C, and M are the same as those of RoBERTa (indicated by •).

since most tokens are unrelated to the entities, averaging the entire input sequence would dampen any indication of high attention paid to the entities. We instead narrowed our focus to tokens within the correct answer spans. In other words, where does the model pay attention when it computes output representations of the answer tokens?

Given an input sequence $\mathbf{x} = (x_1, ..., x_n)$ and a target output $\mathbf{y} = (y_1, ..., y_n) \in \{0, 1\}$, where $y_i = 1$ if y_i belongs to an answer span $s \in S$, let $\mathbf{A} \in \mathbb{R}^{n \times n}$ be an attention-weight matrix. We selected $\mathbf{a}_i \in \mathbf{A}$ where $y_i = 1$ to form a reduced matrix $\tilde{\mathbf{A}} \in \mathbb{R}^{k \times n}$, then averaged $\tilde{\mathbf{A}}$ along the first dimension to produce vector b, representing averaged attention weights of the answer tokens. Since we are interested in all m samples individually, we based our analysis on matrix $\mathbf{B} = [\mathbf{b}_1, ..., \mathbf{b}_m]$, where:

$$\mathbf{b} = \frac{\sum_{j=1}^{k} \tilde{\mathbf{a}}_j}{k}, \tilde{\mathbf{A}} = [\tilde{\mathbf{a}}_1, ..., \tilde{\mathbf{a}}_n] \quad (7)$$

First, we looked for the layers where the model pays heightened attention to the entities. We obtained this information by averaging $\mathbf{B}$ over each layer's attention heads, as shown in Figure 3 (a). Interestingly, the standard deviations indicate that the model pays special attention to the entities on its top layers. In Figure 3 (b), we took a closer look at layer 22 and found that attention head 9 seemed to specialize in the infused knowledge. We observed a similar trend on layer 23 but chose to analyze layer 22 as its standard deviation was the highest among all layers.

5.2 Visualizing Attention

Figure 4 shows averaged attention weights by sample. We sorted the samples by their maximum attention score among the entities since the model tends to pay attention to specific entities rather than all of them when computing the representations of the target tokens. We refer to these maximum scores as *relevance* scores. Since RoBERTa does not have entity inputs, we sorted the samples based on LUKE's scores. While the sequence lengths are varied, they all start with the sentence-level classification token, followed by the question, flattened table, and paragraphs. LUKE has additional attention weights starting from b_{513} to b_{549}. We included Figure 6 as a reference for tabular and textual input boundaries.

Since we only injected entity information to the textual part of the data, it is reasonable that the model would pay more attention to the entities for samples where the answer spans are in paragraphs.

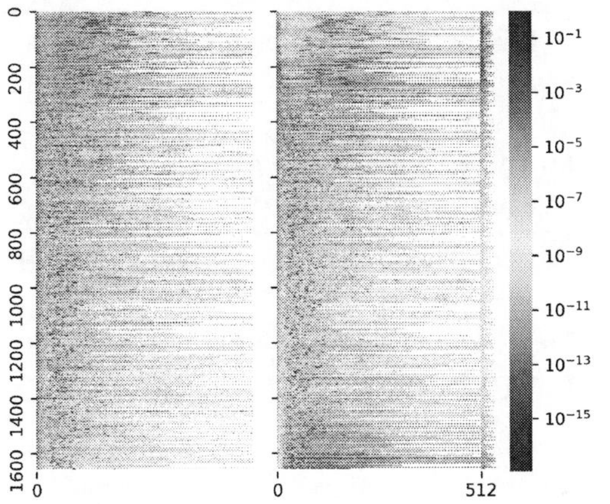

Figure 4: Attention weights of samples sorted by the relevance scores, the maximum attention scores among entities. The left side (a) is a heat map in log scale for $\text{KIQA}^{\text{TagOp}}_{\text{RoBERTa}}$ and the right side (b) is for $\text{KIQA}^{\text{TagOp}}_{\text{L\&G}}$.

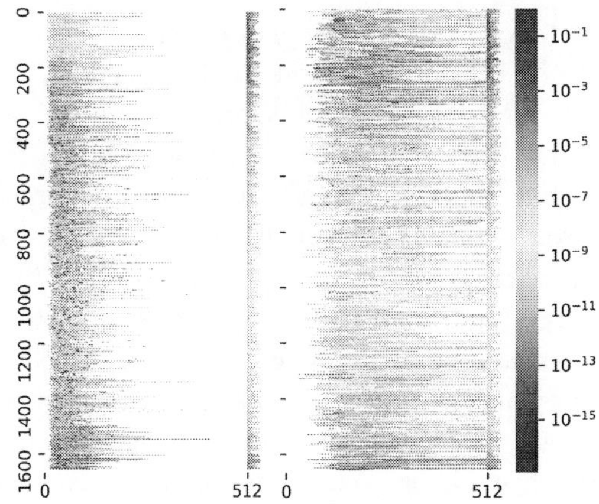

Figure 6: Table and paragraph boundaries in terms of attention weights. The left side (a) includes the scores of the sentence-level classification tokens, questions, and flattened tables. The right side (b) is the paragraph tokens' scores.

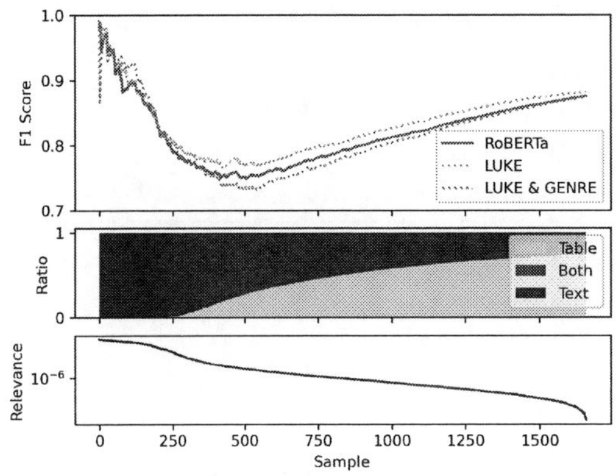

Figure 5: From top to bottom: (a) The average of accumulated F1 scores sorted by the relevance score, (b) the accumulated ratio of answer span locations in the input sequences, (c) the relevance score (in log scale) computed from the maximum attention weight among entities.

This pattern is most visible in Figure 6 (a), where the entity's attention weights decrease as the model attends more to the tabular part.

In Figure 4, we observed a pattern of difference in attention weights among samples where LUKE pays more attention to the entities. While the answer spans in these samples are in the paragraphs, RoBERTa seems to pay considerable attention to the tabular inputs. On the other hand, LUKE seems more focused on the textual part. This pattern clearly shows that the infused knowledge helps guide the model to narrow its focus to the more relevant section. While we did not observe the opposite effect since we did not inject entity information into the tabular part, with an entity retrieval model capable of linking tabular data, there is a possibility that the model may behave as expected. Nevertheless, this observation warrants further study on integrating entity retrieval models specializing in tabular data.

5.3 Interpretation

We learned from the previous section that the entity information helps guide the model to pay attention to the more relevant part of the input. The next and crucial question is whether or not this change of focus translates into improved accuracy. We used the F1 score that exclusively measures sequence-tagging prediction and omitted the reasoning operations to isolate the effect of knowledge infusion. Our objective is to find patterns in the model's performance (Figure 5) in relation to how the model utilizes the entity information (Figure 4) that could explain the two questions we posed at the beginning of the analysis.

We created the accumulated F1-score chart in Figure 5 (a) based on the sorted attention weight vectors as in the heat map in Figure 2. To clarify, the score at the ith position on the x-axis is the average of F1 scores from the first sample to the ith sample. The corresponding ratio chart (b) is also an accumulated ratio of the same sequence of samples, i.e., the ratio of text and tabular-based questions in the top-i^{th} samples. However, the relevance score is of the individual sample at the ith position.

The F1-score chart exhibits different patterns at different sample ranges; therefore, we divided our interpretation into four parts. The first part starts from the first sample to roughly the 50th sample. While the F1 scores within this range are high, their margin is minuscule, indicating that the questions are relatively easy enough that the baseline language model can predict the correct answers without help from the infused knowledge.

The second part (approximately $50^{th}{\sim}200^{th}$) is where LUKE & GENRE has the most advantage. The rapid drop in the F1 scores across all models means that the text-based questions are much more difficult. The exact section in Figure 4 shows that the infused knowledge is still highly relevant in directing the model's attention until this point. We sampled question-answer pairs with the entity and attention information from this part and will discuss them in the following section.

The majority of the samples in the third part ($200^{th}{\sim}1000^{th}$) are table-based questions, as indicated by the steady increase in their ratio. According to Figure 2, the model pays less attention to the entities than the first two parts, although still noticeably higher than the fourth part. Since the answers are in the tables but the entities link to mentions in the paragraphs, they are not particularly useful. On the contrary, the potentially unrelated information weakens LUKE's performance considerably.

The last part ($1000^{th}{\sim}1668^{th}$), also primarily table-based, is easier to answer than the previous one. As the model mostly ignores entity information, LUKE & GENRE's performance recovers steadily due to less interference.

Q-113: Why did the cloud license segments total margin increase ...?
Mention: ... due to expenses growth.
Entity: Expense
F1 scores: L&G = 1.00, RB = 0.54

Q-139: When is the impairment of goodwill and tangible assets tested?
Mention: intangible assets is tested annually
Entity: Intangible asset
F1 scores: L&G = 0.38, RB = 0.00

Q-156: What was the reason for the increase in the Adjusted EBITDA?
Mention: Adjusted EBITA was on the ...
Entity: Earnings before interest, taxes, depreciation, and amortization
F1 scores: L&G = 1.00, RB = 0.68

Q-178: When does the company record an accrued receivable?
Mention: ... prior to invoicing ...
Entity: Contractual term
F1 scores: L&G = 1.00, RB = 0.39

Table 3: Example KIQA$^{TagOp}_{L\&G}$s, including the entity with maximum α and its corresponding mention.

5.4 Examples

Our examples, shown in Table 3, are from the third part of our interpretation, where the injection of external knowledge contributes most to the model's performance. We only include the entity with the highest attention score and its corresponding mention in the text for each example. These examples represent some aspects of the differences the infusion made. In the first example, according to the correct answer, the margin increased because the total margin decreased slightly due to expenses growth. RoBERTa was able to correctly predict the first half of the answer span ("Excluding the effects of currency rate fluctuations, our cloud and license segment's total"), which does not include the primary point. The entity "Expense" seems to highlight the relevance of the latter half, resulting in LUKE's complete prediction.

The second example is a precise instance of the more concentrated attention weights pattern we observed in Figure 4. Although this seems to be a complex case since no model could achieve a high score, LUKE could partially predict the correct answer. On the other hand, we examined RoBERTa's attention scores and found that the model was paying attention to the tabular part of the input.

In our opinion, while GENRE provided the precise information for EBITA, it does not seem to contribute significantly to the improvement. RoBERTa already partially captured the main reason for the increase, while the mention "EBITA" only completes the beginning of the sentence (LUKE's answer: "Adjusted EBITA was on the prior-year level as ... [main reason]"). Nonetheless, LUKE also included the entire reason while RoBERTa missed part of it, thus achieving a much better score on this sample.

In the last example, while RoBERTa correctly located the correct answer span, it also included irrelevant adjacent text, negatively affecting the F1 score considerably.

6 Discussion

The QA model used the infused knowledge to focus on the more relevant information (**Q1**). However, only 25.20 % of the answers are in the paragraphs, explaining the limited improvement. We did not anticipate the margin to be substantial since LUKE's EM score on the development set of the SQuAD 1.1 dataset (Rajpurkar et al., 2016) was only 1.01 % (88.9 $\rightarrow$ 89.8). Injecting entity information to LUKE resulted in 0.21 % improvement (94.8 $\rightarrow$ 95.0). However, since our baseline score is much lower, it was reasonable to expect a higher increase (RoBERTa $\rightarrow$ LUKE & GENRE: 8.86 % for single text spans). Our analysis revealed that the irrelevant entity information interfered with the model's decision, which is why the knowledge-infused models underperformed the baseline model (**Q2**).

There is still a gap in TAT-QA's tabular data where GENRE did not perform well, requiring further study involving entity-linking models specialized in tabular data. Solving the problem of unrelated entity information interfering with the model's prediction is also another challenge.

7 Conclusion

We investigated the effect of external knowledge infusion on a hybrid tabular/textual QA model in the financial domain. The results indicated an improvement, especially to the textual part of the data. Our attention-weight analysis shows the model's ability to utilize the injected knowledge and reveals the challenges involving the hybrid structure of the data. As a result, this study has paved the way for future research to incorporate entity-linking models specialized in tabular data and find a solution that enables the model to integrate tabular and textual symbolic knowledge more efficiently.

References

Nicola De Cao, Gautier Izacard, Sebastian Riedel, and Fabio Petroni. 2021. Autoregressive entity retrieval. In *International Conference on Learning Representations*.

Wenhu Chen, Hanwen Zha, Zhiyu Chen, Wenhan Xiong, Hong Wang, and William Wang. 2020. HybridQA: A dataset of multi-hop question answering over tabular and textual data. In *Findings of the Association for Computational Linguistics: EMNLP*.

Dan Hendrycks and Kevin Gimpel. 2016. Bridging nonlinearities and stochastic regularizers with gaussian error linear units. *arXiv:1606.08415*.

Mohit Iyyer, Wen-tau Yih, and Ming-Wei Chang. 2017. Search-based neural structured learning for sequential question answering. In *Proceedings of the 55th Annual Meeting of the Association for Computational Linguistics (Volume 1: Long Papers)*, pages 1821–1831.

Mike Lewis, Yinhan Liu, Naman Goyal, Marjan Ghazvininejad, Abdelrahman Mohamed, Omer Levy, Ves Stoyanov, and Luke Zettlemoyer. 2020. BART: Denoising sequence-to-sequence pre-training for natural language generation, translation, and comprehension. In *Proceedings of the 58th Annual Meeting of the Association for Computation Linguistics*.

Belinda Z. Li, Sewon Min, Srinivasan Iyer, Yashar Mehdad, and Wen-tau Yih. 2020. Efficient one-pass end-to-end entity linking for questions. In *Proceedings of the 2020 Conference on Empirical Methods in Natural Language Processing*.

Yinhan Liu, Myle Ott, Naman Goyal, Jingfei Du, Mandar Joshi, Danqi Chen, Omer Levy, Mike Lewis, Luke Zettlemoyer, and Veselin Stoyanov. 2019. Roberta: A robustly optimized bert pretraining approach. *arXiv preprint arXiv:1907.11692*.

Pranav Rajpurkar, Jian Zhang, Konstantin Lopyrev, and Percy Liang. 2016. SQuAD: 100,000+ questions for machine comprehension of text. In *Proceedings of the 2016 Conference on Empirical Methods in Natural Language Processing*.

Lance A Ramshaw and Mitchell P Marcus. 1999. Text chunking using transformation-based learning. In *Natural language processing using very large corpora*, pages 157–176. Springer.

Ashish Vaswani, Noam Shazeer, Niki Parmar, Jakob Uszkoreit, Llion Jones, Aidan N Gomez, Łukasz Kaiser, and Illia Polosukhin. 2017. Attention is all you need. *Advances in neural information processing systems*, 30.

Ikuya Yamada, Akari Asai, Hiroyuki Shindo, Hideaki Takeda, and Yuji Matsumoto. 2020. LUKE: Deep contextualized entity representations with entity-aware self-attention. In *Proceedings of the 2020 Conference on Empirical Methods in Natural Language Processing*.

Wenzheng Zhang, Wenyue Hua, and Karl Stratos. 2022. EntQA: Entity linking as question answering. In *International Conference on Learning Representations*.

Fengbin Zhu, Wenqiang Lei, Youcheng Huang, Chao Wang, Shuo Zhang, Jiancheng Lv, Fuli Feng, and Tat-Seng Chua. 2021. TAT-QA: A question answering benchmark on a hybrid of tabular and textual content in finance. In *Proceedings of the 59th Annual Meeting of the Association for Computational Linguistics and the 11th International Joint Conference on Natural Language Processing (Volume 1: Long Papers)*.

TRANS-KBLSTM: An External Knowledge Enhanced Transformer BiLSTM model for Tabular Reasoning

Yerram Varun [1*], Aayush Sharma[1*], Vivek Gupta[2*†]
[1]Indian Institute of Technology, Guwahati ; [2]School of Computing, University of Utah
vgupta@cs.utah.edu; {y.varun, aayushsharma}@iitg.ac.in

Abstract

Natural language inference on tabular data is a challenging task. Existing approaches lack the world and common sense knowledge required to perform at a human level. While massive amounts of KG data exist, approaches to integrate them with deep learning models to enhance tabular reasoning are uncommon. In this paper, we investigate a new approach using BiLSTMs to incorporate knowledge effectively into language models. Through extensive analysis, we show that our proposed architecture, Trans-KBLSTM improves the benchmark performance on INFOTABS , a tabular NLI dataset.

1 Introduction

Understanding tabular or semi-structured knowledge presents a reasoning challenge for modern natural language processing algorithms. Recently, Chen et al. (2020) through TabFact and Gupta et al. (2020) via INFOTABS presented this problem as a natural language inference problem (NLI, Dagan et al., 2013; Bowman et al., 2015, many others), where a model is asked to determine whether a hypothesis is entailed or refuted by a premise, or is unrelated to it (c.f. Table 1). One technique for modeling such tabular reasoning problems is to rely on the success of contextualized representations for the sentential variant of the problem (e.g., Devlin et al., 2019; Liu et al., 2019, etc.). To convert tabular data into a format suitable for these models, they are flattened using heuristics into phrases.

Recently, Neeraja et al. (2021) highlight the significance of adding world knowledge for the tabular inference task (c.f. Table 1). Their approach develops a knowledge addition strategy, namely *KG Explicit*, which expands the keys of a tabular premise with its definitions obtained from Wordnet and Wikipedia articles. These definitions are appended as a suffix to the original input as additional context. With this added additional knowledge, the model outperforms the original baseline. Despite improved effectiveness, knowledge addition has the following drawbacks: (a) **Knowledge Extraction.** *KG Explicit* disambiguates multiple key definitions using the table context, ignoring the hypothesis content entirely. Additionally, the extended definition contains hypothesis-unrelated and unnecessary additional functional terms. All of these factors contribute to erroneous key-sense disambiguation and additional noise. (b) **Knowledge Addition.** *KG Explicit* adds knowledge by appending a suffix definition to existing inputs instead of using more effective semantic representations such as Knowledge Embedding (Graph Embedding or Learned representations). (c) **Knowledge Integration.** Finally, utilizing tokenized input BERT (Devlin et al., 2019) to fuse word-pair relations yields considerably weaker semantic linkages between premise, hypothesis, and the external knowledge.

In this work, we propose a solution to these issues. We drew inspiration from Chen et al. (2018) and utilize relational connections between premise and hypothesis to extract important knowledge relations from ConceptNet (Speer et al., 2017) and

	James Hetfield
Birth Name	James Alan Hetfield
Born	Aug. 3, 1963(age 58), California, U.S.
Genres	Heavy metal, thrash metal, hard rock
Occupation(s)	Musician, Singer
Instruments	Vocals, Guitar
Years active	1978-present
Labels	Warner Bros, Elektra, MegaForce
Hypothesis	James Hetfield was born on the west coast of the USA.
Focused Relation	coast $\xleftarrow{AtLocation}$ california
Human	Entailment
RoBERTa	Neutral
Trans-KBLSTM	Entailment

Table 1: An INFOTABS example demonstrating the need of knowledge augmentation. Predicting the Gold label requires broad understanding of *California* is located on the *Coast.* In the table, for each row the first column represents the keys (unique identifiers) and the second column represents their corresponding values (attributes).

*Equal Contribution †Corresponding Author

Proceedings of Deep Learning Inside Out (DeeLIO 2022): The 3rd Workshop on Knowledge Extraction and Integration for Deep Learning Architectures, pages 62 - 78
May 27, 2022 ©2022 Association for Computational Linguistics

Wordnet (Miller (1992)). This enhancement reduces noise in knowledge addition, resulting in improved **Knowledge Extraction**. We embed relational terms in sentences using sentence transformers (Reimers and Gurevych, 2019) to encode semantic representations of the relation, comparable to Gajbhiye et al. (2021), culminating in successful **Knowledge Addition**. Finally, for effective **Knowledge Integration**, we combine these relational embeddings into a word-level language model, using BiLSTM (Hochreiter and Schmidhuber, 1997), and backpropagate using our proposed BiLSTM and transformer architecture together to enhance model inferencing capabilities.

Our proposed model, Trans-KBLSTM, outperforms the earlier baseline, i.e., *KG Explicit* in full as well as limited supervision setting, substantially for some specific categories. Furthermore, knowledge addition via Trans-KBLSTM improve model *lexical*, *multi-row* and *Numerical* reasoning. We also performed a detailed ablation study to understand the importance of each component. Our contributions are as follows:

1. We address the challenges inherent in existing techniques, e.g., KG Explicit, for explicit knowledge addition in tabular reasoning.
2. We investigate a more efficient knowledge extraction method that involves using knowledge embeddings rather than directly appending them to the input.
3. We propose a novel architecture, namely Trans-KBLSTM, for integrating word-level knowledge effectively with BiLSTM's encoders with state-of-the-art transformers such as BERT.
4. Through extensive experiments, analysis and ablation studies, we demonstrate that Trans-KBLSTM improves reasoning for INFOTABS dataset.

The dataset, and associated scripts, are available at `https://trans-kblstm.github.io/`.

2 Proposed Trans-KBLSTM Model

We highlight the main model components and their implementation details in this section. We begin with a description of the knowledge relations retrieval technique, followed by a discussion of the model architecture's core components.

2.1 External Knowledge Relations Retrieval

It is challenging to retrieve contextually relevant knowledge relations from the knowledge graphs.

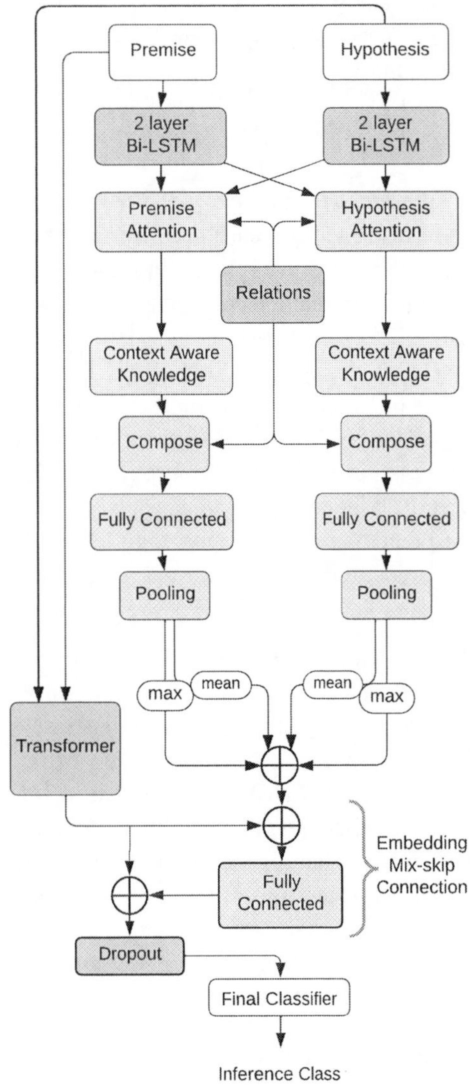

Figure 1: High level flowchart of Trans-KBLSTM.

The challenge is to retrieve task-relevant knowledge relations from massive volumes of noisy Knowledge Graph data. Our method is inspired by Chen et al. (2018), which considers a connection to be significant if the knowledge graph contains the term pair relations.

Relational Connections We define relational connections between two sentences through external relational knowledge between each pair of words in the sentences. The token level relation connections are based on word triples derived from the knowledge graphs.

Relational Connections Retrieval Stop words and punctuation are first removed from the premise and hypothesis. Then, we analyze the knowledge relational connections between the premise and hypothesis token pairs and compute the relationship attention matrix, A^r_{ij}, as follows:

$$A^r_{ij} = \begin{cases} 1 & i^{th} \text{ and } j^{th} \text{ words are } \textbf{related} \\ 0 & i^{th} \text{ and } j^{th} \text{ words are } \textbf{not related} \end{cases}$$

Each knowledge relational triple, consisting of two token terms (one from each premise and hypothesis) and their respective relationship is transformed into a complete grammatical sentence. For instance, the triple {Day, *Antonym*, Night} is transformed into "*Day* is the *opposite* of *Night*". For a complete list of knowledge templates refer to table 5 in Appendix §B. We utilize sentence transformers, as presented in Reimers and Gurevych (2019), to convert the relationship phrase e.g. *"is opposite of"* in the preceding example into high-level semantic representations. The contextual representations denote the relational pair's across relational pairs.

Relational Connection Embedding The contextual knowledge connections between premise and hypothesis token pairs are used to generate a relational vector, R_{ijk}. Each marginal vector R_{ij} is the k dimension BERT representation for the *"Relation Connection Sentence"* in the previously described sentential form constructed using the relationship between the ith premise word and the jth hypothesis word. For words whose relations are absent from knowlege source, we initialize the R_{ij} vector with 'zero' values.[1]

2.2 Model Architecture Details

Next, we described several components of our proposed model. Figure 1 describe the high level architecture of the **Trans-KBLSTM** model.

Transformer We encode the premise and hypothesis using RoBERTa(Liu et al., 2019) to generate contextual word embeddings. Consider $P = \{p_i\}_{i=1}^{m}$ as table premise of length m and $H = \{h_j\}_{j=1}^{n}$ as hypothesis of length n. We input these premise-hypothesis pairs to RoBERTa as :

$S =$ [<s> P </s> H </s>] ; $T_r =$ RoBERTa(S)

Here, T_r denotes the context-aware representations of the premise and hypothesis sentence.

Encoding Premise and Hypothesis The encoder approach is inspired from Chen et al. (2018). We encode the Premise, $P = \{p_i\}_{i=1}^{m}$ and Hypothesis, $H = \{h_j\}_{j=1}^{n}$ using bidirectional LSTMs (BiLSTMs). We embed p_i and h_i into d_e dimensional vectors $[\mathbf{E}(p_1), ...\mathbf{E}(p_m)]$ and $[\mathbf{E}(h_1), ...\mathbf{E}(h_n)]$ using embedding matrix $\mathbf{E} \in \mathbb{R}^{d_e \times |V|}$, where $|V|$ is the Vocabulary size and $\mathbf{E}$ can be initialized with pretrained embeddings. We feed the premise-hypothesis pairs into BiLSTM encoders (Hochreiter and Schmidhuber (1997)) to generate context-aware hidden states p^s and h^s.

$$p^s = \text{BiLSTM}(\mathbf{E(p)}, i) \;\; ; \;\; h^s = \text{BiLSTM}(\mathbf{E(h)}, i)$$

$$p^s \in \mathbb{R}^{m \times l_k} \text{ and } h^s \in \mathbb{R}^{n \times l_k}$$

Here, l_k is the LSTM hidden state size. Following that we apply embedding dropout (Gal and Ghahramani (2016)) to enhance variation and prevent overfitting (Zaremba et al. (2014)).

Premise and Hypothesis Attention Module To assess the contribution of external knowledge to the premise (and hypothesis), we utilize the Multi-Head dot-product attention (Vaswani et al., 2017) across knowledge representations and premise-hypothesis encoding. We calculate premise hypothesis relation values by normalizing relational connection embedding (R_{ijk}) with respect to column-axis (1), to obtain $R^{prem}_{jk} \in \mathbb{R}^{n \times k}$ which is the average premise relation for every hypothesis word.

$$R^{prem}_{jk} = \sum_{i=1}^{m} \frac{R_{ijk}}{m}$$

To apply dot product attention, we then reduce the dimension of the relation matrix to BiLSTM hidden state dimension, i.e., l_k.

$$R^r_{jk} = F^r_P(R^{prem}_{jk}) \quad \in \mathbb{R}^{n \times l_k}$$

where, F^r_P is a single layer neural network.

To highlight the importance of premise and its relations to hypothesis we utilise the premise attention head. The context-aware hypothesis hidden state h^s is used as queries, premise hidden state is used as keys and reduced premise hypothesis relation values are used as values. The attention function can be defined as follows:

$$\text{Attention}(h^s, p^s, R^r_{jk}) = \text{softmax}(\frac{h^s p^{sT}}{\sqrt{l}}) R^r_{jk}$$

where, the multi-head attention is defined:

$$\begin{aligned} h^{att}_p &= \text{MH}(h^s, p^s, R^r_{jk}) \\ &= \text{Concat}(\text{head}_1, \ldots, \text{head}_h) W^o \end{aligned}$$

[1] Experiment with non-zero random initialization ref §3.3.

Here, $\text{head}_i = \text{Attention}(h^s W_i^q, p^s W_i^k, R_{jk}^r W_i^v)$ and W_i^q, W_i^k, and W_i^v are projection matrices and i is the number of attention heads. The output $h_p^{att} \in \mathbb{R}^{n \times l_k}$ is a context matrix that is attention-weighted according to the strength of the premise and its relationships to each of the hypothesis words. We also extract P^{att}, the premise multi-head attention attention weights. In hypothesis attention module, we use hypothesis attention head to highlight the importance of hypothesis and its relations to premise. Similar to the premise attention module, we calculate[2] $p_h^{att} \in \mathbb{R}^{m \times l_k}$, attention-weighted context matrix measuring the importance of premise and relations to each of the hypothesis. We also extract H^{att}, the hypothesis multi-head attention attention weights.

Context Aware External Knowledge ExBERT (Gajbhiye et al., 2021) uses a mixture model to weigh the balance of external relations and premise-hypothesis during inference. We construct attention-weighted external knowledge relations using Multi-head attention weights obtained in the attention modules.

$$P^{CE} = \sum_{k=1}^{h} P_{ij}^{att} R_{ijk} \ ; \ H^{CE} = \sum_{k=1}^{h} H_{ij}^{att} R_{ijk}$$

Composition Layer p^s encodes the individual word representations of the premise while p_h^{att} is the context representation of the premise aligned to the hypothesis. We can obtain word-level inference information for each word in the premise by composing them together with attention weights and context-aware external knowledge. We can do the same calculation for hypothesis, h^s and h_p^{att}:

$$p^m = G_P([p^s; p_h^{att}; p^s - p_h^{att}; p^s * p_h^{att}; \sum_{j=1}^{n} P_{ij}^{CE}])$$

$$h^m = G_H([h^s; h_p^{att}; h^s - h_p^{att}; h^s * h_p^{att}; \sum_{j=1}^{n} H_{ij}^{CE}])$$

Here, G_P and G_H are 2-layer neural networks with Dropout and ReLU activation (Agarap (2018)) that compose the knowledge relations and premise-hypothesis contextual vectors into a unified knowledge aware context vector.

Pooling Layer The pooling layer creates fixed-length representations from the knowledge-aware premise and hypothesis context vectors.

$$p_{mean} = \text{MeanPool}(p^m) \ ; \ p_{max} = \text{MaxPool}(p^m)$$

$$h_{mean} = \text{MeanPool}(h^m) \ ; \ h_{max} = \text{MaxPool}(h^m)$$

[2] More details can be found in section A in §Appendix

Embedding mix-skip connection To effectively integrate transformer embeddings with representations from premise and hypothesis, we introduce an Embedding mix-skip connection, where the embeddings are concatenated and passed through a fully connected layer with a skip connection to transformer embeddings. Skip connections, introduced by He et al. (2016), provides a shortcut to gradient flow and preserve the context between layers.

$$f = [p_{mean}, p_{max}, h_{mean}, h_{max}]$$

$$f' = T_r + F_c([T_r, f])$$

Here, F_c is a two-layer neural network with dropout and ReLU activation. Finally, f' is passed through a classification layer to obtain the inference class.

3 Experiment and Analysis

Our experiments study the following questions.

RQ1: Is our proposed model competent in using external knowledge sources effectively to enhance performance across INFOTABS evaluations sets?

RQ2: How effective is our approach in settings with little supervision? How much supervision is necessary to outperform benchmark models?

RQ3: (a) Which reasoning types is our proposed model most effective at boosting? (b) Is our approach equally effective across all domains, that is, across all table categories? (c.f.§C)

RQ4: How does the model component choices impact performance? (a) To what extent are skip connections, (b) knowledge embeddings, (c) additional MNLI (Williams et al., 2018) pre-finetuning, and (d) a bigger pre-trained model beneficial?

3.1 Experimental setup

Here, we discuss the datasets, external knowledge sources, and the models used in the experiments.

Datasets. We use INFOTABS, a tabular Language inference dataset introduced by Gupta et al. (2020) for all our experiments. The dataset is diverse in categories and keys and requires background knowledge and semantic understanding of the text. Examples in INFOTABS are labeled with three types of inference: entailment, neutrality, and contradiction, based on their relation with premise tables. Along with the standard development set and test set (dubbed α_1), the dataset includes two adversarial test sets: a contrast set dubbed α_2 that is lexically similar to α_1 but contains fewer hypotheses, and a zero-shot set dubbed α_3 that contains long tables from various domains with little key overlap with the training set.

Table Representation. To represent tables, we utilize Neeraja et al. (2021) *Better Paragraph Representation* (BPR) technique in conjunction with *Distracting Row Removal* (DRR). The BPR technique turns its rows into sentences using a universal template, enabling it to be used as the input for a BERT-style model. We utilize the DRR approach to reduce the premise table by identifying the most relevant premise sentence. For finding the most relevant rows, we use cosine similarity over fastText embeddings (Bojanowski et al. (2017)) and word alignment with the specified hypothesis. We select the top four aligned table rows from each premise table with hypotheses.

Knowledge Sources. We utilize ConceptNet, as introduced by Speer et al. (2017) to extract external commonsense knowledge to create relational occurrences. We notice that 85% of premise-hypothesis pairings contain at least one relationship in the ConceptNet database. To supplement the coverage, we also use Wordnet (Miller, 1992), to extract additional lexical word relations, namely *Synonyms*, *Antonyms*, *Hypernyms*, *Hyponyms* and *Co-Hyponyms*. After combining the two knowledge databases and removing duplicates, the number of non-zero relational connection pairings increases to 90%. We create an English directional single word relations dataset by merging ConceptNet and Wordnet. The combined KG source contains 11.2 million relation triples. For example in the table 1, the relational occurrence { "coast" ← "California"} extracted from Conceptnet, provide the necessary world knowledge required for correct inference.

Word Embeddings. We utilize pre-learned word embeddings to initialize the BiLSTM encoders. The premise and hypothesis words are embedded in 300-dimensional vectors using Glove embeddings [3], introduced by Pennington et al. (2014). Glove is a collection of 400,000-word embeddings learned using the Wikipedia, Common crawl, and Twitter datasets. We realize that the GloVe vocabulary covers 85.6% of the terms in INFOTABS dataset.[4]

[3] We also investigate fastText embeddings for representation, but it has only 77.4 % coverage of all tokens. [4] Due to limited supervision, we found that freezing word embedding during the BiLSTM training is beneficial. For the remaining unseen tokens, we initialized with zero vectors.

Models. To evaluate we compare our model with INFOTABS (Gupta et al., 2020) and Knowledge-INFOTABS (Neeraja et al., 2021) baselines, specifically we employ the following methods:

- **RoBERTa**. The original RoBERTa baseline of INFOTABS . We append and encode premise-hypothesis pairs with BPR with DRR representation and generate an inference label with the RoBERTa classification head.
- **KG Explicit.** Knowledge-INFOTABS introduced this baseline. The baseline uses the same RoBERTa classifier as the INFOTABS , except that the premise end is augmented with extracted premise row key definitions from Wordnet and Wikipedia sources before encoding and classifying using RoBERTa. Additionally, prior to appending, the method employs key sense disambiguation to assure that only relevant hypothesis context-related definitions are added. For example, for a table with category *"Person"* and key *"Spouse"*, the definition of *"Spouse"* from Wikipedia, i.e., *"Spouse is defined as a spouse is a significant other in a marriage, civil union, or common-law marriage."* is appended as a suffix.
- **Tok-KTrans**. We utilize Wordnet to expand premise hypothesis pairs with word relations in Tokens added transformers before encoding and classifying using RoBERTa. We extend the tokenizer by including relational tokens and appending the relationships with the following format - {*<KNW> [premise_word$_1$: hypothesis_word$_1$; <relation$_1$>] [premise_word$_2$: hypothesis_word$_2$; <relation$_2$>]* ...}. For example, The table *Jallikattu* contains a key ***Mixed Gender*** with a value *NO*. The hypothesis, *Jallikattu is a single* ***sex*** *sport* contradicts the premise table. We append the relation {*<KNW> [gender : sex ; <SYN>]*} as suffix to input prior to the RoBERTa classification.
- **Trans-KBLSTM.** This is our proposed model as described in the §2. For details on model training and hyper-parameters, refer to Appendix §G.

3.2 Results and Analysis

This section summarizes our findings concerning the research questions.

Full Supervision Setting. To assess the effectiveness of our method Trans-KBLSTM (i.e. RQ1), we train baseline and our model Trans-KBLSTM with 100% of training data. Table 2 shows the performance (accuracy) for all models. We observe that Trans-KBLSTM outperform[5] all other baselines. On development, α_1 , and α_3 Trans-KBLSTM outperform 0.75 - 0.95 % with 100% training data.

Model	Dev	$\alpha 1$	$\alpha 2$	$\alpha 3$
w/o Knowledge	77.30	76.44	70.49	69.05
Tok-KTrans	78.17	76.19	70.75	69.77
KG Explicit	78.97	77.84	71.13	69.58
Trans-KBLSTM	**79.92**	**79.62**	**72.10**	**70.21**

Table 2: Performance in terms of accuracy with full supervision. **w/o Knoweldge** represent RoBERTa INFOTABS (Gupta et al., 2020) baseline, **KG Explicit** represent Knowledge-INFOTABS (Neeraja et al., 2021) baseline, **Tok-KTrans** is the token appended transformers and **Trans-KBLSTM** represent our proposed model. Reported number are average over three random seeds with standard deviation of 0.27 (w/o KG), 0.69 (Tok-KTrans), 0.23 (KG Explicit) and 0.36 (Trans-KBLSTM). All improvements are statistically significant with Student's t-test $p < 0.05$ except α_2 with KG Explicit.

Limited Supervision Setting. To ensure that our model works effectively in low-resource scenarios (i.e., RQ2), we analyze models trained under limited supervision. We randomly sampled {1, 2, 3, 5, 10, 15, 20, 25, 30, 50, and 100} data in an incremental method [6]. We experimented three times using random seeds for sampling/training to account for sample variability.

Figure 2 shows the accuracy for all models. We observe a huge performance improvement with Tran-KBLSTM over other baseline models for low data regimes. All improvements are statistically significant with Student's t-test $p < 0.05$ except dev results with 3% and 5%. For precise numbers and standard deviation plots, see Table refer Table 8 in the Appendix §D. Additionally, as the training supervision increases, the performance margin across models narrows. This improvement can be attributed to the fact that the model's reasoning ability increases when more training data is added, resulting in more accurate predictions without explicitly necessitating external knowledge addition. As a result, adding external knowledge may not be as beneficial if there is adequate supervision.

Reasoning Analysis To investigate the reasoning behind a model's prediction (i.e., RQ3(a)), INFOTABS adapted the set of reasoning categories from GLUE (Wang et al. (2018a)) for tabular premises. Thus, we also analyze performance across several reasoning types on the development set of INFOTABS . We utilized the reasoning annotated instances from INFOTABS for our analysis. Figure 3 show the performance across various reasoning types on the development set for 1% and 3% of INFOTABS development set. Trans-KBLSTM model shows improvements in several reasoning types including *"Lexical"*, *"Multi-Row"*, and *"KCS"*.

- *Lexical Reasoning* involves inferencing through words independent of context, where the word falls. Since we add relational connections between words which include synonyms, antonyms, etc. lexical reasoning ability of the model enhances. For example, in the table *"Chibuku Shake"*, the key *"Ingredients"* contains *"Sorghum"* and *"Maize"* while the hypothesis requires us to infer about *Corn* as an ingredient in the Chibuku shake. The relation {"corn" $\xleftarrow{Synonym}$ "Maize"} helps the model in making the correct prediction. For details refer to table 13 in Appendix §E.
- *Multi-Row Reasoning* involves making an inference using multiple rows of the table. When the reasoning involves multiple rows, the model needs to extract the relevant rows and rightly focus on selected related connected phrases. The relational connections that we propose between premise and hypothesis tokens establish these extractions and connections and thus enhancing the multi-row reasoning ability of the Trans-KBLSTM model. For example in a "Person" table relations such as { "born" $\xleftrightarrow{RelatedTo}$ "young" ; "born" $\xleftrightarrow{RelatedTo}$ "child" ; "child" $\xleftrightarrow{RelatedTo}$ "age" ; "year active" $\xleftrightarrow{Co-Hyponym}$ "child" } help in connected both the born, child and year active keys with the concern hypothesis. For details refer to table 12 in Appendix §E.
- *Knowledge and Common Sense Reasoning.* This reasoning is related to the World Knowledge and Common Sense category from GLUE-Benchmark (Wang et al., 2018b), which is quoted as "...the entailment rests not only on correct disambiguation of the sentences, but also, application of extra knowledge, whether factual knowledge about world affairs or more commonsense knowledge about word meanings or social or physical dynamics." Knowledge databases like ConceptNet contain many knowledge relations capable of enhancing these reasoning type. For example, in a "Country" table relations such

[5] reaches maximum in 6-7 epochs while Neeraja et al. (2021) takes 14-15 epochs [6] Higher % include all instances from lower %, i.e. a 20% includes all instances from a 10% samples.

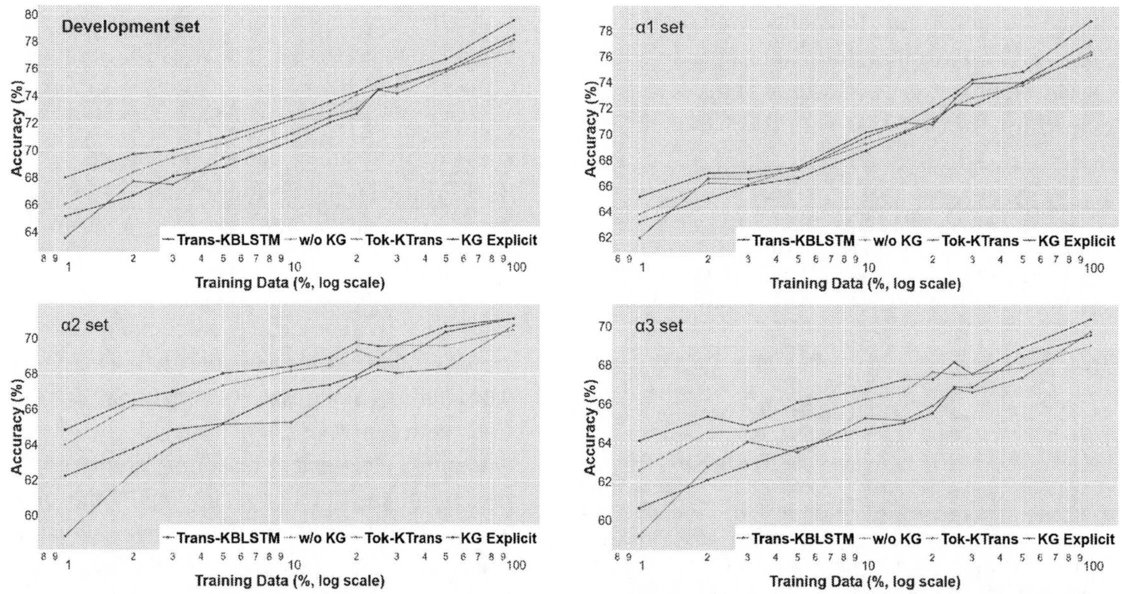

Figure 2: Performance in terms of accuracy in limited supervision setting. **w/o KG** represent RoBERTa INFOTABS (Gupta et al., 2020) baseline, **KG Explicit** represent Knowledge-INFOTABS (Neeraja et al., 2021) baseline, **Tok-KTrans** is the token appended transformers and **Trans-KBLSTM** represent our proposed model. Reported results are average over 3 random seed runs with average standard deviation of 0.233 (w/o KG), 0.49 (KG Explicit), 0.50 (Tok-KTrans) and 0.30 (Trans-KBLSTM). All the improvements are statistically significant with Student's t-test $p < 0.05$ of one-tailed Student t-test.

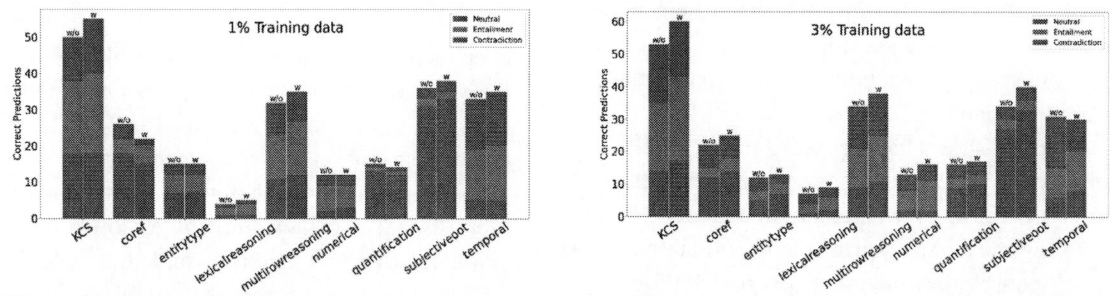

Figure 3: Number of correct model predictions across various reasoning types. **w/o** represents without knowledge (KG) i.e. original RoBERTa models and **w** represents Trans-KBLSTM model with explicitly added relational connection knowledge (KG).

as { "kingdom" $\xleftrightarrow{IsA}$ "monarchy" ; "democracy" $\xleftrightarrow{RelatedTo}$ "Government" } add additional information necessary for inference. For details refer to table 14 in Appendix §E.

Improvement across Inference Labels. In our analysis, we observe a performance improvement across the Entailment and Neutral labels, but only a negligible increase, for example, in instances labeled with the Contradiction label. Contradictory label prediction requires noise-free, contextually relevant knowledge to ascertain the negation. External knowledge addition with minimal noise can lead to the predicted Neutral or Entailment label. Additional ways for relational connection trimming may be explored in future studies.

3.3 Ablation Study

We perform ablation studies (i.e., RQ4) to understand the importance of individual model components further. The ablation study was conducted to ascertain the significance of (a) Trans-KBLSTM Skip Connection, (b) Knowledge Relations, (c) Implicit KG addition via. MNLI pre-training (Embeddings), and (d) Transformer Model Param Size. (e) Independent Component training.

Effect of Skip Connections. We study the significance of embedding skip connection and the knowledge relations (i.e., RQ4(a,b)). The knowledge relations are initialized with random vectors to examine model performance variations.

Table 3 shows the Trans-KBLSTM performance with several ablations. We observe that adding knowledge and the introduction of skip connection improve the model performance. The addition of knowledge to the model improves the performance on Dev, $\alpha 1$, and $\alpha 2$ sets. The inclusion of knowledge improves performance the most for Development, α_2 , and α_3 sets, whereas the addition of skip connection improves performance substantially in α_1 set. The performance improvement in α_3 set demonstrates that using external information benefits zero-shot settings (i.e., cross-domain transfer learning). The improved performance by the addition of skip connection demonstrates that effective knowledge integration significantly impacts model performance.

Ablations	Dev	α_1	α_2	α_3
Trans-KBLSTM	**67.55**	**65.16**	**64.00**	**63.38**
- Skip Connect	65.72	62.83	60.00	61.55
- KB	60.44	61.88	56.94	55.55
- (KB + Skip Connect)	60.11	61.50	55.94	57.38

Table 3: Ablation study performance on stratified 1% split of dataset. We systematically eliminate model components in order to evaluate the performance improvement.

Implicit Knowledge Addition. We examine the effect of implicit knowledge addition (i.e., RQ4(b)) in Trans-KGLSTM model. Thus, similar to the KG Implicit baseline of Knowledge-INFOTABS (Neeraja et al., 2021), we supplement implicit knowledge using the MNLI via data augmentation. To ensure a fair comparison, we compare the two Trans-KBLSTM RoBERTa-based classifiers, one with and the other without MNLI data pre-training.

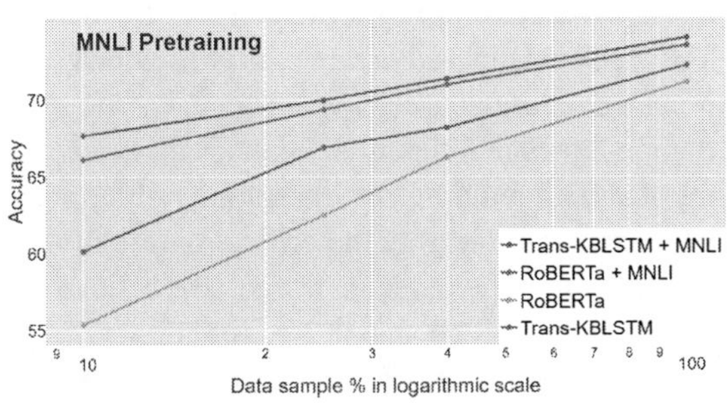

Figure 4: Performance improvement with MNLI pre-training across various models.

We observe an improvement in performance for all percentages of train data after pre-training using MNLI data. Pre-training enables the model to acquire domain-specific information, hence enhancing its performance. There is a more significant gain in performance for non-pre-trained than for MNLI pre-trained models, suggesting that external information addition is more beneficial for models without any implicit knowledge. In comparison, our approach uses relational connections to augment the model's knowledge in the phase, final training avoiding the computational, time, and economic cost of large MNLI pre-training.

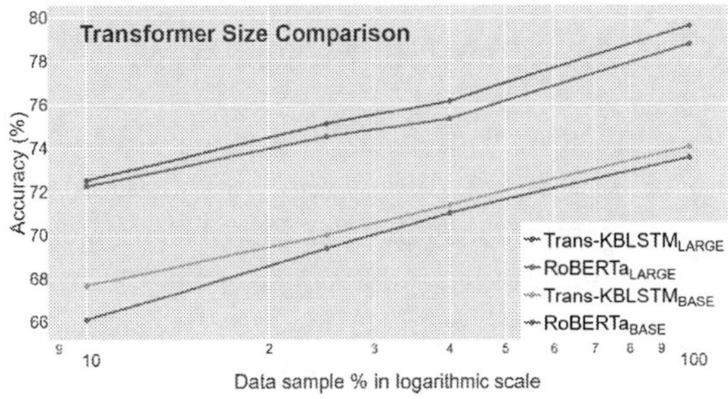

Figure 5: Improvement in model performance across varying models sizes.

Effect of Transformer Size. We substitute RoBERTa$_{LARGE}$ with RoBERTa$_{BASE}$ to study the effect of transformer size on performance (i.e. RQ4 (d)) of INFOTABS test sets. We pre-train both the transformers model using the MultiNLI dataset for all percentages. The performance is depicted in Figure 5. We see an increase in performance as the model's size increases, especially for external knowledge addition, i.e., Trans-KBLSTM model.

Independent Training. We examine the effect of training transformer and KBLSTM components independently. For independent training, we first train RoBERTa$_{LARGE}$ transformer model on INFOTABS . Then we utilize these weights to initialize the transformer component of Trans-KBLSTM. Finally, we trained the KBLSTM component of Trans-KBLSTM on INFOTABS while keeping these pre-trained transformer weights frozen (constant). Table 4 shows the results of training Trans-KBLSTM with different regimes. We observe that training the components together shows a more significant improvement in performance than training the KBLSTM component independently. Joint training of transformer and KBLSTM generates representations in the same embedding space, enhancing external knowledge integration.

Ablations	Dev	α_1	α_2	α_3
RoBERTa$_{LARGE}$	77.30	76.44	70.49	69.05
+ KBLSTM (Independent)	79.22	78.38	71.00	69.22
+ KBLSTM (Joint Train)	**79.92**	**79.62**	**72.10**	**70.21**

Table 4: Joint/Independent training performance on INFOTABS dataset. First row shows results of training only RoBERTa$_{LARGE}$ model without knowledge. Second row shows results of training KBLSTM independently after freezing RoBERTa$_{LARGE}$ parameters. Third row shows the results of our proposed approach i.e. Joint-training of RoBERTa$_{LARGE}$ and KBLSTM.

4 Comparison with Related Work

Recently, several papers have been published focusing on NLP tasks involving semi-structured Tabular data. Examples include tabular NLI (Gupta et al., 2020), and fact verification (Chen et al. (2020); Aly et al. (2021); Zhang and Balog (2019)). The use of external knowledge into Tabular data was first explored by Neeraja et al. (2021) through *KG-Explicit* model described in §3.1. We aim to improve on this benchmark through this extensive study.

Knowledge Integration. Traditional approaches to integrating external knowledge into deep learning models do not use contextual embeddings from pre-trained language models. The Knowledge-based Inference Model (KIM) (Chen et al., 2018) incorporates lexical relations (such as antonyms and synonyms) into the premise and hypothesis representations using attention and composition units. Lin et al. (2017) provides a method to mine and exploit commonsense knowledge by defining inference rules between elements under different kinds of commonsense relations, with an inference cost for each rule. KG-Augmented Entailment System (KES) (Kang et al., 2018) augments the NLI model with external knowledge encoded using graph convolutional networks. ConseqNet (Wang et al., 2019) concatenates the output of the text-based model and the graph-based model and then feeds it to a classifier. Lin et al. (2019) uses LSTMs and a novel knowledge-aware graph network module named KagNet to achieve state-of-the-art performance on CommonSenseQA. Bi-CAM (Gajbhiye et al., 2020) models incorporate knowledge from ConceptNet and AristoTuple KGs (Dalvi Mishra et al., 2017) by factorized bilinear pooling to improve performance on NLI Datasets.

Incorporating external knowledge into language models has been extensively explored in recent times. Approaches similar to the Tok-KTrans baseline described in §3.1 where external knowledge is added at input level were explored in Chen et al. (2021); Xu et al. (2021); Mitra et al. (2019). At the representational level, the model understands these external knowledge additions and interacts with these representations using multi-head attention modules (Chang et al., 2020). Other approaches include, pretraining on external knowledge corpus to inject knowledge (Wang et al., 2021; Peters et al., 2019; Umair and Ferraro, 2021), better knowledge representations (Bauer et al., 2021), modifications to multi-head attention in pre-trained language models (Li and Sethy, 2019; Haihong et al., 2019), designing relation-aware tasks (Xia et al., 2019) and integration of knowledge through multi-head attention (Gajbhiye et al., 2021).

Closely Related Work. Li et al. (2019) finds that when explicit knowledge is added in the form of word-pair information, models such as Chen et al. (2018) improve performance. However, such models necessitate the use of classic *seq2seq* architectures such as BiLSTM to integrate word-level knowledge. In our proposed approach, external knowledge is separately added to the premise and hypothesis using a multi-head attention dot product. To encode the contextual relationships between premise and hypothesis, we use a pre-trained language model, RoBERTa (Liu et al., 2019). We combine the LM embeddings (Gajbhiye et al., 2021) and BiLSTM embeddings using a skip connection which preserves the premise-hypothesis relational context and integrates knowledge effectively.

5 Conclusion and Future Work

In this paper, we introduce Trans-KBLSTM, a novel architecture to integrate external knowledge into tabular NLI models. Trans-KBLSTM is shown to improve reasoning on the INFOTABS dataset. The performance advantage is particularly pronounced in low-data regimes. The reasoning study demonstrates that the model enhances lexical, numerical, and multiple-row reasoning. Ablation experiments demonstrate the critical nature of each component in the model's design. We believe that our findings will be valuable to researchers working on the integration of external knowledge into deep learning architectures. Performance of the proposed architecture on more datasets can be explored in future studies. Looking forward, the application of this architecture to other NLP tasks that can benefit from external knowledge enhanced relational connections between sentence pairs, such as question answering and dialogue understanding.

Acknowledgement

We thank members of the Utah NLP group for their valuable insights and suggestions at various stages of the project; and reviewers their helpful comments. Additionally, we appreciate the inputs provided by Vivek Srikumar and Ellen Riloff. Vivek Gupta acknowledges support from Bloomberg's Data Science Ph.D. Fellowship.

References

Abien Fred Agarap. 2018. Deep learning using rectified linear units (relu). *arXiv preprint arXiv:1803.08375.*

Rami Aly, Zhijiang Guo, Michael Sejr Schlichtkrull, James Thorne, Andreas Vlachos, Christos Christodoulopoulos, Oana Cocarascu, and Arpit Mittal. 2021. The fact extraction and VERification over unstructured and structured information (FEVEROUS) shared task. In *Proceedings of the Fourth Workshop on Fact Extraction and VERification (FEVER)*, pages 1–13, Dominican Republic. Association for Computational Linguistics.

Lisa Bauer, Lingjia Deng, and Mohit Bansal. 2021. ERNIE-NLI: Analyzing the impact of domain-specific external knowledge on enhanced representations for NLI. In *Proceedings of Deep Learning Inside Out (DeeLIO): The 2nd Workshop on Knowledge Extraction and Integration for Deep Learning Architectures*, pages 58–69, Online. Association for Computational Linguistics.

Piotr Bojanowski, Edouard Grave, Armand Joulin, and Tomas Mikolov. 2017. Enriching word vectors with subword information. *Transactions of the Association for Computational Linguistics*, 5:135–146.

Samuel R. Bowman, Gabor Angeli, Christopher Potts, and Christopher D. Manning. 2015. A large annotated corpus for learning natural language inference. In *Proceedings of the 2015 Conference on Empirical Methods in Natural Language Processing*, pages 632–642, Lisbon, Portugal. Association for Computational Linguistics.

Ting-Yun Chang, Yang Liu, Karthik Gopalakrishnan, Behnam Hedayatnia, Pei Zhou, and Dilek Hakkani-Tur. 2020. Incorporating commonsense knowledge graph in pretrained models for social commonsense tasks. In *Proceedings of Deep Learning Inside Out (DeeLIO): The First Workshop on Knowledge Extraction and Integration for Deep Learning Architectures*, pages 74–79, Online. Association for Computational Linguistics.

Qian Chen, Xiaodan Zhu, Zhen-Hua Ling, Diana Inkpen, and Si Wei. 2018. Neural natural language inference models enhanced with external knowledge. In *Proceedings of the 56th Annual Meeting of the Association for Computational Linguistics (Volume 1: Long Papers)*, pages 2406–2417, Melbourne, Australia. Association for Computational Linguistics.

Wenhu Chen, Hongmin Wang, Jianshu Chen, Yunkai Zhang, Hong Wang, Shiyang Li, Xiyou Zhou, and William Yang Wang. 2020. Tabfact: A large-scale dataset for table-based fact verification. In *International Conference on Learning Representations*.

Xiang Chen, Ningyu Zhang, Xin Xie, Shumin Deng, Yunzhi Yao, Chuanqi Tan, Fei Huang, Luo Si, and Huajun Chen. 2021. Knowprompt: Knowledge-aware prompt-tuning with synergistic optimization for relation extraction. *arXiv preprint arXiv:2104.07650.*

Ido Dagan, Dan Roth, Mark Sammons, and Fabio Massimo Zanzotto. 2013. Recognizing Textual Entailment: Models and Applications. *Synthesis Lectures on Human Language Technologies*, 6(4):1–220.

Bhavana Dalvi Mishra, Niket Tandon, and Peter Clark. 2017. Domain-targeted, high precision knowledge extraction. *Transactions of the Association for Computational Linguistics*, 5:233–246.

Jacob Devlin, Ming-Wei Chang, Kenton Lee, and Kristina Toutanova. 2019. BERT: Pre-training of deep bidirectional transformers for language understanding. In *Proceedings of the 2019 Conference of the North American Chapter of the Association for Computational Linguistics: Human Language Technologies, Volume 1 (Long and Short Papers)*, pages 4171–4186, Minneapolis, Minnesota. Association for Computational Linguistics.

John Duchi, Elad Hazan, and Yoram Singer. 2011. Adaptive subgradient methods for online learning and stochastic optimization. *Journal of Machine Learning Research*, 12(61):2121–2159.

Amit Gajbhiye, Noura Al Moubayed, and Steven Bradley. 2021. Exbert: An external knowledge enhanced bert for natural language inference. In *Artificial Neural Networks and Machine Learning – ICANN 2021*, pages 460–472, Cham. Springer International Publishing.

Amit Gajbhiye, Thomas Winterbottom, Noura Al Moubayed, and Steven Bradley. 2020. Bilinear fusion of commonsense knowledge with attention-based nli models. In *International Conference on Artificial Neural Networks*, pages 633–646. Springer.

Yarin Gal and Zoubin Ghahramani. 2016. A theoretically grounded application of dropout in recurrent neural networks. In *Advances in Neural Information Processing Systems*, volume 29. Curran Associates, Inc.

Vivek Gupta, Maitrey Mehta, Pegah Nokhiz, and Vivek Srikumar. 2020. INFOTABS: Inference on tables as semi-structured data. In *Proceedings of the 58th Annual Meeting of the Association for Computational Linguistics*, pages 2309–2324, Online. Association for Computational Linguistics.

E Haihong, Wenjing Zhang, and Meina Song. 2019. Kb-transformer: Incorporating knowledge into end-to-end task-oriented dialog systems. In *2019 15th International Conference on Semantics, Knowledge and Grids (SKG)*, pages 44–48. IEEE.

Kaiming He, Xiangyu Zhang, Shaoqing Ren, and Jian Sun. 2016. Deep residual learning for image recognition. In *Proceedings of the IEEE conference on computer vision and pattern recognition*, pages 770–778.

Sepp Hochreiter and Jürgen Schmidhuber. 1997. Long short-term memory. *Neural computation*, 9(8):1735–1780.

Dongyeop Kang, Tushar Khot, Ashish Sabharwal, and Eduard Hovy. 2018. AdvEntuRe: Adversarial training for textual entailment with knowledge-guided examples. In *Proceedings of the 56th Annual Meeting of the Association for Computational Linguistics (Volume 1: Long Papers)*, pages 2418–2428, Melbourne, Australia. Association for Computational Linguistics.

Alexander Hanbo Li and Abhinav Sethy. 2019. Knowledge enhanced attention for robust natural language inference. *CoRR*, abs/1909.00102.

Tianda Li, Xiaodan Zhu, Quan Liu, Qian Chen, Zhigang Chen, and Si Wei. 2019. Several experiments on investigating pretraining and knowledge-enhanced models for natural language inference. *arXiv preprint arXiv:1904.12104*.

Bill Yuchen Lin, Xinyue Chen, Jamin Chen, and Xiang Ren. 2019. KagNet: Knowledge-aware graph networks for commonsense reasoning. In *Proceedings of the 2019 Conference on Empirical Methods in Natural Language Processing and the 9th International Joint Conference on Natural Language Processing (EMNLP-IJCNLP)*, pages 2829–2839, Hong Kong, China. Association for Computational Linguistics.

Hongyu Lin, Le Sun, and Xianpei Han. 2017. Reasoning with heterogeneous knowledge for commonsense machine comprehension. In *Proceedings of the 2017 Conference on Empirical Methods in Natural Language Processing*, pages 2032–2043, Copenhagen, Denmark. Association for Computational Linguistics.

Yinhan Liu, Myle Ott, Naman Goyal, Jingfei Du, Mandar Joshi, Danqi Chen, Omer Levy, Mike Lewis, Luke Zettlemoyer, and Veselin Stoyanov. 2019. RoBERTa: A Robustly Optimized BERT Pretraining Approach. *arXiv preprint arXiv:1907.11692. Version 1.*

George A. Miller. 1992. WordNet: A lexical database for English. In *Speech and Natural Language: Proceedings of a Workshop Held at Harriman, New York, February 23-26, 1992*.

Arindam Mitra, Pratyay Banerjee, Kuntal Kumar Pal, Swaroop Mishra, and Chitta Baral. 2019. How additional knowledge can improve natural language commonsense question answering? *arXiv preprint arXiv:1909.08855*.

J. Neeraja, Vivek Gupta, and Vivek Srikumar. 2021. Incorporating external knowledge to enhance tabular reasoning. In *Proceedings of the 2021 Conference of the North American Chapter of the Association for Computational Linguistics: Human Language Technologies*, pages 2799–2809, Online. Association for Computational Linguistics.

Adam Paszke, Sam Gross, Francisco Massa, Adam Lerer, James Bradbury, Gregory Chanan, Trevor Killeen, Zeming Lin, Natalia Gimelshein, Luca Antiga, Alban Desmaison, Andreas Kopf, Edward Yang, Zachary DeVito, Martin Raison, Alykhan Tejani, Sasank Chilamkurthy, Benoit Steiner, Lu Fang, Junjie Bai, and Soumith Chintala. 2019. Pytorch: An imperative style, high-performance deep learning library. In H. Wallach, H. Larochelle, A. Beygelzimer, F. d'Alché-Buc, E. Fox, and R. Garnett, editors, *Advances in Neural Information Processing Systems 32*, pages 8024–8035. Curran Associates, Inc.

Jeffrey Pennington, Richard Socher, and Christopher Manning. 2014. GloVe: Global vectors for word representation. In *Proceedings of the 2014 Conference on Empirical Methods in Natural Language Processing (EMNLP)*, pages 1532–1543, Doha, Qatar. Association for Computational Linguistics.

Matthew E. Peters, Mark Neumann, Robert Logan, Roy Schwartz, Vidur Joshi, Sameer Singh, and Noah A. Smith. 2019. Knowledge enhanced contextual word representations. pages 43–54.

Nils Reimers and Iryna Gurevych. 2019. Sentence-BERT: Sentence embeddings using Siamese BERT-networks. In *Proceedings of the 2019 Conference on Empirical Methods in Natural Language Processing and the 9th International Joint Conference on Natural Language Processing (EMNLP-IJCNLP)*, pages 3982–3992, Hong Kong, China. Association for Computational Linguistics.

Robyn Speer, Joshua Chin, and Catherine Havasi. 2017. Conceptnet 5.5: An open multilingual graph of general knowledge. In *Proceedings of the Thirty-First AAAI Conference on Artificial Intelligence*, AAAI'17, page 4444–4451. AAAI Press.

Mohammad Umair and Francis Ferraro. 2021. Transferring semantic knowledge into language encoders. *arXiv preprint arXiv:2110.07382*.

Ashish Vaswani, Noam Shazeer, Niki Parmar, Jakob Uszkoreit, Llion Jones, Aidan N Gomez, Łukasz Kaiser, and Illia Polosukhin. 2017. Attention is all you need. *Advances in neural information processing systems*, 30.

Alex Wang, Amanpreet Singh, Julian Michael, Felix Hill, Omer Levy, and Samuel Bowman. 2018a. GLUE: A multi-task benchmark and analysis platform for natural language understanding. In *Proceedings of the 2018 EMNLP Workshop BlackboxNLP: Analyzing and Interpreting Neural Networks for NLP*, pages 353–355, Brussels, Belgium. Association for Computational Linguistics.

Alex Wang, Amanpreet Singh, Julian Michael, Felix Hill, Omer Levy, and Samuel Bowman. 2018b. GLUE: A multi-task benchmark and analysis platform for natural language understanding. In *Proceedings of the 2018 EMNLP Workshop BlackboxNLP: Analyzing and Interpreting Neural Networks for NLP*, pages 353–355, Brussels, Belgium. Association for Computational Linguistics.

Xiaoyan Wang, Pavan Kapanipathi, Ryan Musa, Mo Yu, Kartik Talamadupula, Ibrahim Abdelaziz, Maria Chang, Achille Fokoue, Bassem Makni, Nicholas Mattei, and Michael Witbrock. 2019. Improving natural language inference using external knowledge in the science questions domain. *Proceedings of the AAAI Conference on Artificial Intelligence*, 33(01):7208–7215.

Xiaozhi Wang, Tianyu Gao, Zhaocheng Zhu, Zhengyan Zhang, Zhiyuan Liu, Juanzi Li, and Jian Tang. 2021. Kepler: A unified model for knowledge embedding and pre-trained language representation. *Transactions of the Association for Computational Linguistics*, 9:176–194.

Adina Williams, Nikita Nangia, and Samuel Bowman. 2018. A broad-coverage challenge corpus for sentence understanding through inference. In *Proceedings of the 2018 Conference of the North American Chapter of the Association for Computational Linguistics: Human Language Technologies, Volume 1 (Long Papers)*, pages 1112–1122, New Orleans, Louisiana. Association for Computational Linguistics.

Thomas Wolf, Lysandre Debut, Victor Sanh, Julien Chaumond, Clement Delangue, Anthony Moi, Pierric Cistac, Tim Rault, Rémi Louf, Morgan Funtowicz, Joe Davison, Sam Shleifer, Patrick von Platen, Clara Ma, Yacine Jernite, Julien Plu, Canwen Xu, Teven Le Scao, Sylvain Gugger, Mariama Drame, Quentin Lhoest, and Alexander M. Rush. 2020. Transformers: State-of-the-art natural language processing. In *Proceedings of the 2020 Conference on Empirical Methods in Natural Language Processing: System Demonstrations*, pages 38–45, Online. Association for Computational Linguistics.

Jiangnan Xia, Chen Wu, and Ming Yan. 2019. Incorporating relation knowledge into commonsense reading comprehension with multi-task learning. In *Proceedings of the 28th ACM International Conference on Information and Knowledge Management*, pages 2393–2396.

Yichong Xu, Chenguang Zhu, Ruochen Xu, Yang Liu, Michael Zeng, and Xuedong Huang. 2021. Fusing context into knowledge graph for commonsense question answering. In *Findings of the Association for Computational Linguistics: ACL-IJCNLP 2021*, pages 1201–1207, Online. Association for Computational Linguistics.

Wojciech Zaremba, Ilya Sutskever, and Oriol Vinyals. 2014. Recurrent neural network regularization. *arXiv preprint arXiv:1409.2329*.

Shuo Zhang and Krisztian Balog. 2019. Autocompletion for data cells in relational tables. In *Proceedings of the 28th ACM International Conference on Information and Knowledge Management*, CIKM '19, pages 761–770, New York, NY, USA. ACM.

A Hypothesis Attention Module

In Hypothesis attention module, we calculate hypothesis relation values by normalizing R_{ijk} with respect to row-axis(2), to generate $R_{ik}^{hyp} \in \mathbb{R}^{m \times k}$ which is the average hypothesis relation for every premise word.

$$R^{hyp}ik = \sum i = 1^{n} \frac{R_{ijk}}{n}$$

We reduce the dimension by applying the dot product attention.

$$R_{ik}^{r} = F_{H}^{r}(R_{ik}^{hyp}) \in \mathbb{R}^{m \times l_k}$$

F_{N}^{r} can again be a single layer neural network. We then use the Hypothesis attention head to highlight the importance of the hypothesis and its relations to the premise. The context-aware premise hidden state p^s is used as queries, the hypothesis hidden state is used as keys, and reduced hypothesis premise relation values are used. The attention function can be defined as follows:

$$\text{Attention}(p^s, h^s, R_{ik}^{r}) = \text{softmax}(\frac{p^s h^{sT}}{\sqrt{l}}) R_{ik}^{r}$$

Then the multi-head attention is as follows:

$$\begin{aligned} p_h^{att} &= \text{MH}(p^s, h^s, R_{ik}^{r}) \\ &= \text{Concat}(\text{head}_1, ..., \text{head}_h) W^o \end{aligned}$$

where, head$i$ = Attention$(p^s W_i^q, h^s W_i^k, R^r ik W_i^v)$ and W_i^q, W_i^k, and W_i^v are projection matrices and i is the number of attention heads. The output $p_h^{att} \in \mathbb{R}^{m \times l_k}$ is an attention-weighted context matrix measuring the importance of premise and relations to each of the hypothesis. We calculate $p_h^{att} \in \mathbb{R}^{m \times l_k}$, attention-weighted context matrix measuring the importance of premise and relations to each of the hypothesis. We also extract H^{att}, the attention weights of the hypothesis multi-head attention.

B Knowledge Relations to Sentence Conversion

We create templates to convert knowledge relations in ConceptNet & WordNet to natural language sentences. These templates resemble natural English text, which can be encoded using pretrained language models. The templates can be seen in table 5.

KB Relation	Natural Language
Antonym	is opposite of
AtLocation	is at location
CapableOf	is capable of
Causes	causes
CausesDesire	causes desire to
CreatedBy	is created by
DefinedAs	is defined as
DerivedFrom	is derived from
Desires	desires
DistinctFrom	is distinct from
Entails	entailes
EtymologicallyDerivedFrom	is etymologically derived from
EtymologicallyRelatedTo	is etymologically related to
ExternalURL	external url
FormOf	is a form of
HasA	has a
HasContext	has context
HasFirstSubevent	has first subevent
HasLastSubevent	has last subevent
HasPrerequisite	has prerequisite
HasProperty	has property
HasSubevent	has subevent
InstanceOf	is an instance of
IsA	is a
LocatedNear	is located near
MadeOf	is made of
MannerOf	is manner of
MotivatedByGoal	is motivated by goal
NotCapableOf	is not capable of
NotDesires	does not desire
NotHasProperty	does not have property
PartOf	is part of
ReceivesAction	receives action
RelatedTo	is related to
SimilarTo	is similar to
SymbolOf	is a symbol of
Synonym	is same as
UsedFor	is used for
dbpedia/capital	has capital
dbpedia/field	has field
dbpedia/genre	has genre
dbpedia/genus	has genus
dbpedia/influencedBy	is influenced by
dbpedia/knownFor	is known for
dbpedia/language	has language
dbpedia/leader	has leader
dbpedia/occupation	' has occupation
dbpedia/product	has product
Hypernym	is hypernym of
Hyponym	is hyponym of
Co-Hyponym	is co-hyponym of

Table 5: ConceptNet and Wordnet Relations with their Natural language templates

C Domain Analysis

To understand the models performance across tabular domains (i.e. RQ3(b)), we analyse domain-wise table category results. We evaluate the twelve major categories contained in the INFOTABS datasets. All remaining categories are grouped together in the *"Other"* category. Table summarizes the performance of models (trained with 2% and 5% INFOTABS train data)[7] on the INFOTABS development set across several categories.

Category	1%		3%		10%	
	w/o KG	w KG	w/o KG	w KG	w/o KG	w KG
Album	65.87	65.87	73.81	**76.98**	77.78	73.02
Animal	60.49	**66.67**	75.31	66.67	67.9	**72.84**
City	64.05	**64.71**	56.21	**61.44**	63.4	**64.71**
Country	56.48	54.63	56.48	55.56	60.19	**62.96**
Food & Drinks	69.44	**70.83**	72.22	**73.61**	83.33	79.17
Movie	61.11	**63.89**	63.89	63.89	70	**73.89**
Musician	62.57	**69.88**	73.1	**74.56**	75.73	**76.9**
Organization	61.11	58.33	55.56	**66.67**	69.44	**72.22**
Painting	80.25	80.25	75.31	**77.78**	77.78	**80.25**
Person	57	**62.96**	62.35	**67.28**	74.9	**75.72**
Sports	65.08	**73.02**	61.9	**71.43**	68.25	**69.84**
Others	63.89	**65.28**	66.67	**70.84**	63.89	61.11
TOTAL	62	**65.83**	65.88	**68.61**	72.27	**73.22**

Table 6: Accuracy (%) across different categories observed in the Development set (Others (<10%) includes the categories, University, Awards, Event, Book and Aircraft), trained on 1%, 3% and 5% samples of the data. **w/o KG** represents RoBERTa and **w KG** represents Trans-KBLSTM model.

As the supervision increases from 1% to 10%, we observe an increasing accurate prediction trend across the categories. Our proposed model shows significant improvements in *"Musician"* and *"Sports"* categories. We attribute these huge gains to two main reasons: (a) . Under minimal supervision, knowledge relations enable the model to concentrate on relevant context, thus helping in establishing premise rows and hypothesis tokens connections. For example refer to table 10 in Appendix §E. (b) and the acquisition of additional knowledge enhances the models' overall world knowledge and common sense reasoning capability. E.g. in the table 1, the understanding of the *California* is located at the *coast*.

Additionally, we observe that our proposed model performs poorly in a few categories. This part comprises instances from *"Album"*, *"Food & Drinks"*, and *"University"*. This can be attributed to the noisy addition of knowledge. Sometimes knowledge relations give out the relational context that might not be needed. For example refer to table 11 in Appendix §E. Additional knowledge filtering may be addressed in future studies. For domain analysis results of models trained on 2% and 5% training data, refer to table 7.

D Limited Supervision

We present detailed results on limited supervision experiments. All the reported numbers are aver-

[7] For details results on other percentages refer to Appendix §C Table 7.

Category	2%		5%	
	w/o KG	w KG	w/o KG	w KG
Album	68.25	67.46	72.22	**73.81**
Animal	65.43	64.20	72.84	69.14
City	55.56	**58.17**	60.13	**61.44**
Country	58.33	**62.96**	61.11	**68.52**
Food&Drinks	69.44	66.67	75.00	73.61
Movie	58.33	**65.00**	65.56	65.56
Musician	68.42	**71.64**	71.35	**76.32**
Organization	58.33	**61.11**	66.67	66.67
Painting	66.67	59.26	75.31	**76.54**
Person	61.32	60.49	68.72	67.08
Sports	66.67	**69.84**	61.90	**68.25**
Others	62.50	**66.67**	63.89	**65.28**
TOTAL	63.11	**64.44**	68.22	**69.50**

Table 7: Accuracy (%) across different categories observed in the Development set (Others (<10%) includes the categories, University, Awards, Event, Book and Aircraft), trained on 2% and 5% samples of the data. **w/o KG** represents RoBERTa baseline and **w KG** represents Trans-KBLSTM

age over three seed runs with a standard deviation of 0.233 (w/o KG), 0.49 (KG Explicit), 0.5 (Tok-KTrans), and 0.30 (Trans-KBLSTM). All the improvements are statistically significant with $p < 0.05$ of one-tailed Student t-test.

E Qualitative Examples

Table 10, 11, 12, 13, and 14 present examples to supplement the results presents in Section 3.

F Additional Results Reasoning Analysis

Table 15 detailed results of performance across reasoning keys for models trained on 1%, 3%, 5% and 10% data.

G Training and Hyperparameters Details

Trans-KBLSTM is implemented in PyTorch (Paszke et al., 2019) using Huggingface (Wolf et al., 2020) implementation of RoBERTa (Liu et al., 2019). We pretrain the transformer components on MultiNLI dataset (Williams et al., 2018) for fair comparison with the Knowledge-INFOTABS baseline of Neeraja et al. (2021). We use AdaGrad optimizer (Duchi et al., 2011) with an initial learning rate of 1e-4 for RoBERTa and 1e-3 for non-RoBERTa i.e. LSTM parameters with a scheduler. The batch size is slected from {3,4, 5}. All the hyper-parameters are fined tuned on the development set of INFOTABS .

% Train	Model	Dev	$\alpha 1$	$\alpha 2$	$\alpha 3$
1%	w/o KG	66.05	63.81	64.00	62.59
	KG Explicit	65.15	63.22	62.24	60.63
	Tok-KTrans	63.57	61.96	58.83	59.18
	Trans-KBLSTM	**68.03**	**65.18**	**64.83**	**64.12**
2%	w/o KG	68.42	66.24	66.22	64.55
	KG Explicit	66.70	65.07	63.77	62.11
	Tok-KTrans	67.74	66.59	62.46	62.78
	Trans-KBLSTM	**69.72**	**67.02**	**66.51**	**65.36**
3%	w/o KG	69.48	66.14	66.16	64.61
	KG Explicit	68.12	66.05	64.85	62.85
	Tok-KTrans	67.52	66.57	63.98	64.07
	Trans-KBLSTM	**70.00**	**67.09**	**67.00**	**64.90**
5%	w/o KG	70.50	67.44	67.33	65.18
	KG Explicit	68.78	66.65	65.20	63.74
	Tok-KTrans	69.44	67.31	65.14	63.53
	Trans-KBLSTM	**70.98**	**67.50**	**68.01**	**66.11**
10%	w/o KG	72.23	69.27	68.14	66.27
	KG Explicit	70.68	68.77	67.07	64.70
	Tok-KTrans	71.24	69.79	65.25	65.29
	Trans-KBLSTM	**72.51**	**70.18**	**68.40**	**66.77**
15%	w/o KG	72.92	70.27	68.46	66.66
	KG Explicit	72.05	70.16	67.37	65.05
	Tok-KTrans	72.47	70.94	66.68	65.20
	Trans-KBLSTM	**73.61**	**70.96**	**68.90**	**67.29**
20%	w/o KG	74.09	71.25	69.31	67.68
	KG Explicit	72.70	70.99	67.89	65.55
	Tok-KTrans	73.05	70.77	67.72	65.94
	Trans-KBLSTM	**74.29**	**72.16**	**69.77**	67.29
25%	w/o KG	74.50	72.25	68.90	67.53
	KG Explicit	74.46	72.32	68.61	66.91
	Tok-KTrans	74.44	72.79	68.22	66.83
	Trans-KBLSTM	**75.09**	**73.20**	**69.57**	**68.18**
30%	w/o KG	74.70	72.86	69.61	67.55
	KG Explicit	74.83	72.26	68.69	66.89
	Tok-KTrans	74.17	73.96	68.03	66.63
	Trans-KBLSTM	**75.57**	**74.25**	**69.62**	**67.57**
50%	w/o KG	75.93	73.79	69.59	67.90
	KG Explicit	75.99	74.05	70.36	68.51
	Tok-KTrans	78.44	76.38	70.66	70.38
	Trans-KBLSTM	**76.71**	**74.86**	**70.68**	**68.93**
100%	w/o KG	77.30	76.44	70.49	69.05
	KG Explicit	78.97	77.84	**71.13**	69.58
	Tok-KTrans	78.17	76.19	70.75	69.77
	Trans-KBLSTM	**79.73**	**78.92**	**71.62**	**70.21**

Table 8: Shows the results of of our experiments, where we train under limited supervision setting. **w/o KG** Original RoBERTa baseline, **KG Explicit** KG-Explicit knowledge addition, **Tok-KTrans** Token appended transformers, **Trans-KBLSTM** Proposed model. We train these models on data samples 1, 2, 3, 5, 10, 15, 20, 25, 30, 50, 100 %s. For full results, see appendix.

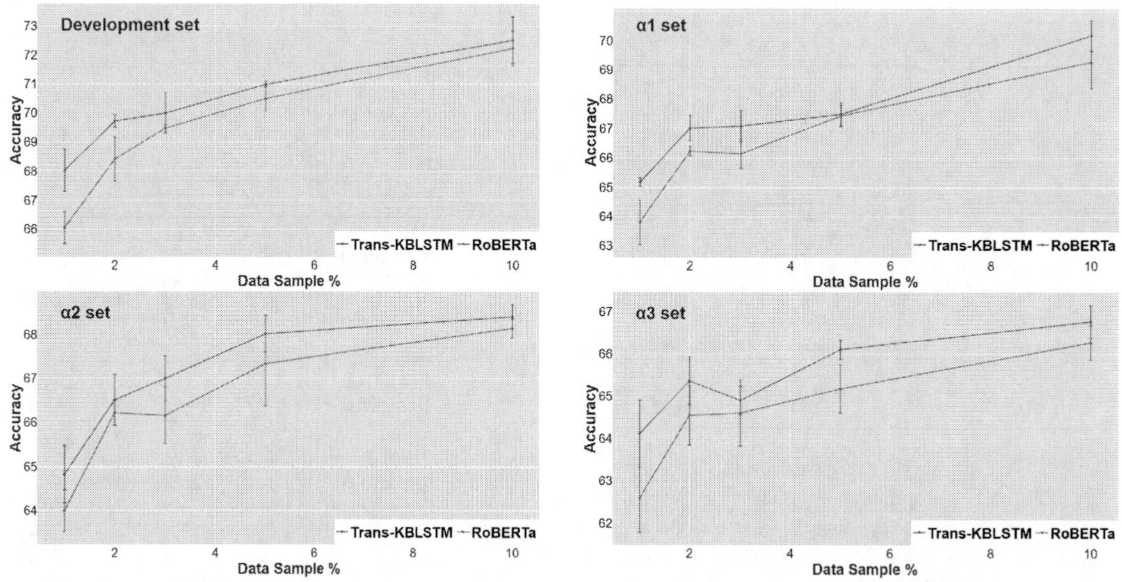

Figure 6: The figures show error bar plots of limited supervision training on 1,2,3,5,10 and 15% of data. for Trans-KBLSTM and RoBERTa baseline. We notice that the error overlap increases with increase in supervision. The improvements are higher under low-data regimes.

Hyperparameter	**Value**
LSTM Max Length	200
LSTM layers	2
LSTM learning rate	1e-3
LSTM Hidden state size	128
Word Embedding Dimension	300
RoBERTa Hidden state size	768
RoBERTa learning rate	1e-4
# Attention heads	4
Embedding Spatial Dropout	0.3
Dropout (Final classification)	0.2

Table 9: Enlists the hyperparameters used while training the baselines and proposed model on INFOTABS

Joe Budden Premise	
Premise	Joe Budden was Born on (1980-08-31) August 31, 1980 (age 38) in New York, New York. The Origin of Joe Budden are Jersey City, New Jersey. The Years active of Joe Budden are 1999-present. The Labels of Joe Budden are Mood Muzik, EMPIRE (current), Desert Storm, Def Jam, Amalgam Digital, and E1 (former)
Hypothesis	Joe Budden started his career in his twenties.
Focused Relation	age $\xleftrightarrow{Co-Hyponym}$ twenties
Gold Label	Contradiction
Prediction	
RoBERTa	Neutral
Trans-KBLSTM	Contradiction

Table 10: In the absence of knowledge, the model is unable to understand the word *twenties* and concludes that the information is not present in the text. However, addition of knowledge re-enforces the connection between *age* and *twenties* thereby producing correct label

Crooked Teeth Premise	
Premise	The Released of Crooked Teeth are May 19, 2017. The Studio of Crooked Teeth are Steakhouse Studios, North Hollywood, CA. The Genre of Crooked Teeth are Hard rock, nu metal, and rap rock. The Label of Crooked Teeth are Eleven Seven.
Hypothesis	The album Crooked Teeth took over a year to make.
Focused Relation	genre $\xleftrightarrow{Co-Hyponym}$ make ‖ metal $\xrightarrow{RelatedTo}$ make ‖ rap $\xrightarrow{Hypernym}$ make
Gold Label	Neutral
Prediction	
RoBERTa	Neutral
Trans-KBLSTM	Contradiction

Table 11: The baseline prediction correctly predicts the gold label. Our proposed model gets confused with semantically irrelevant relations and hence concludes the statement as contradiction.

Jeff Bridges Premise	
Premise	The Born of Jeff Bridges are December 4, 1949 (age 69) Los Angeles, California, U.S.. The Years active of Jeff Bridges are 1951-present. The Children of Jeff Bridges are 3. The Family of Jeff Bridges are Beau Bridges (brother), and Jordan Bridges (nephew).
Hypothesis	Jeff Bridges started his career as a young child.
Focused Relations	born $\xrightarrow{RelatedTo}$ young
	born $\xrightarrow{RelatedTo}$ child child $\xrightarrow{RelatedTo}$ age active $\xrightarrow{Co-Hyponym}$ child
Gold Label	Entailment
Prediction	
RoBERTa	Contradiction
Trans-KBLSTM	Entailment

Table 12: The inference of the hypothesis requires the model to focus on 1st and 2nd sentences at the same time. The original model gets confused due to mention of *age 69* and *young* and concludes contradiction. The focused relations develop appropriate connections to the first two sentences and enable better understanding to the model.

Chibuku Shake Premise	
Premise	The Type of Chibuku Shake shake are Opaque Beer. The Alcohol by volume of Chibuku Shake shake are 3.3% to 4.5%. The Colour of Chibuku Shake shake are Tan-pink to white. The Ingredients of Chibuku Shake shake are Sorghum, and Maize.
Hypothesis	Corn is an ingredient found in a Chibuku Shake.
Focused Relations	corn $\xleftrightarrow{Synonym}$ maize
Gold Label	Entailment
Prediction	
RoBERTa	Entailment
Trans-KBLSTM	Entailment

Table 13: The inference of the given hypothesis requires the knowledge of Synonymy between *Corn* and *Maize*

Hashemite Kingdom of Jordan Premise	
Premise	The Legislature of Hashemite Kingdom of Jordan are Parliament. The Religion of Hashemite Kingdom of Jordan are 95% Islam (official), 4% Christianity, and 1% Druze, Baha'i. The Government of Hashemite Kingdom of Jordan are Unitary parliamentary constitutional monarchy. The Monarch of Hashemite Kingdom of Jordan is Abdullah II.
Hypothesis	Hashemite Kingdom of Jordan does not have any democracy.
Focused Relation	Kingdom $\xleftrightarrow{IsA}$ Monarch
Gold Label	Contradiction
Prediction	
RoBERTa	Neutral
Trans-KBLSTM	Contradiction

Table 14: The focused external knowledge relation connects the *Monarchy* in premise to *Kingdom* in hypothesis.

Percent(%)	Reasoning keys	Entailment			Neutral			Contradiction		
		B.L	KtLSTM	.	B.L	KtLSTM	.	B.L	KtLSTM	.
1%	KCS	64.52	**70.97**	31	85.71	85.71	21	50.00	**62.50**	24
	coref	50.00	**62.50**	8	81.82	68.18	22	30.77	15.38	13
	entitytype	83.33	83.33	6	87.50	87.50	8	50.00	50.00	6
	lexicalreasoning	40.00	**60.00**	5	33.33	33.33	3	25.00	25.00	4
	multirowreasoning	60.00	**75.00**	20	68.75	**75.00**	16	52.94	47.06	17
	nameidentity	0.00	0.00	2	0.00	**100.00**	2	100.00	100.00	1
	negation	0.00	0.00	0	0.00	0.00	0	66.67	**83.33**	6
	numerical	63.64	54.55	11	66.67	**100.00**	3	42.86	42.86	7
	quantification	25.00	25.00	4	100.00	92.31	13	16.67	16.67	6
	subjectiveoot	33.33	33.33	6	75.61	**80.49**	41	50.00	50.00	6
	temporal	73.68	**78.95**	19	45.45	45.45	11	56.00	**60.00**	25
3%	KCS	67.74	**83.87**	31	66.67	**80.95**	21	75.00	70.83	24
	coref	37.50	**50.00**	8	54.55	**63.64**	22	53.85	53.85	13
	entitytype	50.00	50.00	6	62.50	**87.50**	8	66.67	50.00	6
	lexicalreasoning	60.00	**80.00**	5	33.33	**66.67**	3	75.00	75.00	4
	multirowreasoning	60.00	**70.00**	20	56.25	**68.75**	16	76.47	76.47	17
	nameidentity	50.00	**100.00**	2	100.00	100.00	2	100.00	100.00	1
	negation	0.00	0.00	0	0.00	0.00	0	100.00	100.00	6
	numerical	54.55	**81.82**	11	66.67	66.67	3	71.43	71.43	7
	quantification	75.00	75.00	4	69.23	**76.92**	13	66.67	66.67	6
	subjectiveoot	50.00	50.00	6	65.85	**80.49**	41	66.67	66.67	6
	temporal	47.37	**63.16**	19	54.55	**72.73**	11	64.00	40.00	25
5%	KCS	87.10	83.87	31	71.43	**90.48**	21	66.67	62.50	24
	coref	75.00	62.50	8	68.18	**81.82**	22	30.77	30.77	13
	entitytype	83.33	83.33	6	87.50	87.50	8	83.33	83.33	6
	lexicalreasoning	60.00	**80.00**	5	33.33	**66.67**	3	50.00	50.00	4
	multirowreasoning	85.00	85.00	20	68.75	**81.25**	16	58.82	**76.47**	17
	nameidentity	100.00	100.00	2	50.00	**100.00**	2	100.00	0.00	1
	negation	0.00	0.00	0	0.00	0.00	0	100.00	66.67	6
	numerical	72.73	**90.91**	11	100.00	100.00	3	71.43	**85.71**	7
	quantification	75.00	50.00	4	92.31	**100.00**	13	33.33	16.67	6
	subjectiveoot	66.67	33.33	6	73.17	**87.80**	41	50.00	50.00	6
	temporal	94.74	84.21	19	36.36	**63.64**	11	56.00	52.00	25
10%	KCS	74.19	**80.65**	31	95.24	90.48	21	70.83	70.83	24
	coref	50.00	**75.00**	8	77.27	77.27	22	46.15	23.08	13
	entitytype	66.67	**83.33**	6	87.50	87.50	8	100.00	83.33	6
	lexicalreasoning	80.00	80.00	5	66.67	66.67	3	25.00	**75.00**	4
	multirowreasoning	80.00	80.00	20	81.25	81.25	16	76.47	70.59	17
	nameidentity	50.00	50.00	2	100.00	100.00	2	100.00	100.00	1
	negation	0.00	0.00	0	0.00	0.00	0	83.33	**100.00**	6
	numerical	81.82	**100.00**	11	100.00	100.00	3	71.43	71.43	7
	quantification	50.00	50.00	4	84.62	**92.31**	13	33.33	33.33	6
	subjectiveoot	33.33	**50.00**	6	82.93	**87.80**	41	50.00	33.33	6
	temporal	78.95	**89.47**	19	63.64	63.64	11	68.00	68.00	25

Table 15: The above numbers represent accuracy on development dataset across different reasoning types with varying percentage of data. The third number indicates the number of examples corresponding to the reasoning type and label.

Fast Few-shot Debugging for NLU Test Suites

Christopher Malon and **Kai Li** and **Erik Kruus**
NEC Laboratories America
4 Independence Way
Princeton, NJ 08540
malon,kaili,kruus@nec-labs.com

Abstract

We study few-shot debugging of transformer based natural language understanding models, using recently popularized test suites to not just diagnose but correct a problem. Given a few debugging examples of a certain phenomenon, and a held-out test set of the same phenomenon, we aim to maximize accuracy on the phenomenon at a minimal cost of accuracy on the original test set. We examine several methods that are faster than full epoch retraining. We introduce a new fast method, which samples a few in-danger examples from the original training set. Compared to fast methods using parameter distance constraints or Kullback-Leibler divergence, we achieve superior original accuracy for comparable debugging accuracy.

1 Introduction

When deep transformer models make mistakes, ML engineers have had little recourse but to collect a better training set and hope the problem is fixed. Adversarial datasets have exposed a variety of phenomena under which models trained on common datasets fail, particularly for question answering and natural language inference (Jia and Liang, 2017; Gururangan et al., 2018; Kim et al., 2018; McCoy et al., 2019; Nie et al., 2020; Thorne et al., 2019). They have provided new test data to expose problems but not always new training data to correct them. Recently, the natural language processing community has adopted methodologies inspired by software development for probing and testing the capabilities of a model. Ribeiro et al. (2020) introduce CheckList, which helps users to develop test suites of examples, organized by capability.

Collecting hundreds or thousands of examples for each error phenomenon is slow, expensive, and not always feasible. In this paper, we investigate how just a few examples of a phenomenon ("debugging examples", which were not in the original dataset) can be utilized to correct a model. The goal is higher accuracy on the phenomenon ("debugging accuracy") while retaining accuracy on the original dataset ("original accuracy"). This problem differs from domain adaptation and few-shot learning because performance must be maintained on original examples, and no new classes are introduced.

We repurpose published test suites for several natural language understanding (NLU) tasks as debugging problems, not just diagnostics. We identify methods that can update a model using a few debugging examples without the expense of iterating over the whole original training set. We introduce a new fast method that samples in-danger examples from the original training set to obtain even better original accuracy for comparable debugging accuracy.

2 Related work

Two recent works (Zhu et al., 2020; De Cao et al., 2021) study how to modify transformer language models so that they store updated facts, testing their approaches on downstream tasks such as zero-shot relation extraction and closed-book fact checking. To apply these methods, one is given a modified fact as an example to train on, and one must predict the modified fact correctly (success rate) while achieving low performance deterioration on the original test set. Because success rate is measured on just one example which is available at training time, to determine whether the update really generalizes, De Cao et al. (2021) also measures *equivalence accuracy*, which reflects accuracy on paraphrases of the updated fact.

By contrast, our setting provides ten examples (not just one) for a phenomenon where the predictions are to be updated. The phenomenon being debugged may involve deeper semantics than a factoid update, which usually requires only a reassociation of particular words that appear in the example. We assume we are given a testing set for

Proceedings of Deep Learning Inside Out (DeeLIO 2022): The 3rd Workshop on Knowledge Extraction and Integration for Deep Learning Architectures, pages 79 - 86
May 27, 2022 ©2022 Association for Computational Linguistics

the phenomenon, so we can measure generalization by directly measuring accuracy on the testing examples instead of paraphrasing the training examples.

Despite these differences, ideas from these papers provide relevant ideas that can be used in our debugging setting as well. One baseline considered by Zhu et al. (2020), which we call *intensive fine-tuning*, simply takes the updated facts (for us, the debugging training set) and repeatedly performs gradient descent updates on them until they are classified correctly.

The proposed approach of Zhu et al. (2020) is to minimize loss on the updated facts (the debugging set) subject to either an L^∞ or L^2 constraint on the difference of the model parameters. We consider these as baselines.

As De Cao et al. (2021) observe, constraining the norm of the parameter update is only loosely tied to how a parameter change can affect the output of a model. For this reason they introduce an approach based on constraining the Kullback-Leibler divergence between the updated model and the original. Their proposed method trains a hyper-network to read a single updated example and make a change minimizing debugging loss subject to the Kullback-Leibler divergence constraint. That does not apply as well to our scenario of multiple debugging examples, but we borrow the idea of using Kullback-Leibler divergence to incentivize similar predictions in a more straightforward baseline.

Sinitsin et al. (2020) introduce a meta-learning method for making a model that will preserve original accuracy when performing a series of gradient descent steps to change the label of any particular example. We are interested in methods that can be applied to any model, and for real debugging it is not necessary that all examples be easily relabeled.

Contemporaneously to our work, Pasunuru et al. (2021) investigate few-shot debugging on error categories that are apparently too broad to be corrected with just a few examples. Although they report some success with feature matching methods such as prototypical networks (Snell et al., 2017), they either suppose that test examples are identified as needing a correction or not (i.e. debugging or original), more like domain adaptation, or else train the prototypical network on a combined training set, which is the slowness we are trying to avoid. Our setting requires a single model that can be applied to all examples without source information.

3 Method

We suppose we are given a model $p_\theta(x, y)$ trained on training set X. We are also given debugging training set X', and original test set X_{test} and debugging test set X'_{test}. These four sets are pairwise disjoint. We consider the cross-entropy loss

$$\mathcal{L}(x, y; \theta) = -p_\theta(x, y) \log p_\theta(x, y). \quad (1)$$

Our method initializes $\theta_0 = \theta$ and then performs *intensive fine-tuning* on the debugging set X', by performing Adam (Kingma and Ba, 2015) iterations $\theta_{t+1} = Adam(\mathcal{L}, X', \theta_t)$ where $Adam(\mathcal{L}, S, \theta)$ represents the parameter update achieved by training θ with respect to the loss $\mathcal{L}$ over a complete epoch on S. Intensive fine-tuning stops at the minimal step $t = t_{X'}$ such that $\text{argmax}_y p_{\theta_t}(x_i, y) = y_i$ for all $(x_i, y_i) \in X'$. We write $\theta_{X'} = \theta_{t_{X'}}$.

Next we collect random samples $W \subset X$ that are misclassified by $\theta_{X'}$ but not by θ. In our experiments we select $|W| = 2|X'|$ such examples. Collecting W is a fast process involving iterating through a random shuffle of X and stopping when the required number of examples is retrieved. The expected iteration time depends only on the error rates and correlation of the errors of the models and not on the size of the original training set $|X|$.

Finally we restart from the original parameters θ and intensively fine-tune using the set $X' \cup W$. We take $\theta'_0 = \theta$ and iterate Adam

$$\theta'_{t+1} = Adam(\mathcal{L}, X' \cup W, \theta'_t) \quad (2)$$

until we reach t' where $\text{argmax}_y p_{\theta'_{t'}}(x_i, y) = y_i$ for all $(x_i, y_i) \in X' \cup W$. The resulting $\theta' = \theta'_{t'}$ is the debugged model by our proposed method.

4 Experiments

We consider a BERT base model (Devlin et al., 2019) implemented in Pytorch (Paszke et al., 2019) by the HuggingFace Transformers library (Wolf et al., 2020) for all experiments, with batch size 16 per GPU on 3 or 4 GPU's, otherwise following default training parameters.

Our data sets are test suites from HANS (McCoy et al., 2019) debugging an MNLI model (Williams et al., 2018) and CheckList (Ribeiro et al., 2020) debugging models for SST-2 and QQP from GLUE (Wang et al., 2018). We take test cases with the worst accuracy before debugging, and select 10 examples from each suite for debugging (X') and use the rest (e.g. 990 examples for HANS) to test

Test suite	Dog	Or/And	Becoming	People	Passive
Before debugging	(.000, .913)	(.000, .913)	(.002, .913)	(.005, .913)	(.009, .913)
Fast					
Debug only	(.731, .909)	(1.000, .909)	(1.000, .910)	(.922, .910)	(.819, .910)
L^2 ($\delta = .1$)	(.704, .909)	(1.000, .909)	(1.000, .911)	(.880, .910)	(.876, .910)
L^∞ ($\delta = .1$)	(.704, .909)	(1.000, .909)	(1.000, .911)	(.880, .910)	(.876, .910)
K-L ($\lambda = 10$)	(1.000, .905)	(1.000, .908)	(1.000, .909)	(1.000, .908)	(1.000, .908)
Ours	(.731, .909)	(.994, .913)	(1.000, .913)	(.993, .911)	(.975, .912)
Slow					
Mixed in	(1.000, .913)	(.999, .912)	(1.000, .913)	(.933, .912)	(.859, .912)
Oversampling	(1.000, .911)	(1.000, .913)	(1.000, .912)	(.999, .914)	(1.000, .911)

Table 1: (Debugging accuracy, Original accuracy) on CheckList test suites for QQP.

Test suite	Used to but now	Negation with neutral	Opinion matters
Before debugging	(.793, .925)	(.448, .925)	(.616, .925)
Fast			
Debug only	(.860, .914)	(1.000, .917)	(.602, .915)
L^2 ($\delta = .1$)	(.860, .915)	(1.000, .919)	(.600, .915)
L^∞ ($\delta = .1$)	(.860, .915)	(1.000, .919)	(.600, .915)
K-L ($\lambda = 10$)	(.838, .915)	(1.000, .916)	(.538, .920)
Ours	(.877, .919)	(1.000, .913)	(.777, .885)
Slow			
Mixed in	(.909, .913)	(1.000, .925)	(.673, .923)
Oversampling	(.735, .931)	(1.000, .921)	(.512, .928)

Table 2: (Debugging accuracy, Original accuracy) on CheckList test suites for SST-2.

debugging (X'_{test}). See the appendix for details. Our data splits and our code for extracting examples from CheckList are available for download.[1] For HANS we use the BERT cased model and for CheckList we use the uncased model.

4.1 Fast baselines

The first of four fast baselines we consider, which is labeled "debug only," performs intensive fine-tuning on the debugging set X' only, returning the model $\theta_{X'}$. In every case we tested, $t_{X'} \leq 3$ epochs over ten examples, so this completed within a minute.

The next baselines from Zhu et al. (2020) are finding θ' to minimize $\mathcal{L}(X', \theta')$ subject to an L^∞ constraint $||\theta' - \theta||_\infty < \delta$ or an L^2 constraint $||\theta' - \theta||_2 < \delta$. Following Zhu et al. (2020) we use $\delta = 0.1$ and implement the optimization as projected gradient descent, *e.g.* for L^∞, taking a gradient descent step from θ_0 to θ and projecting the updated parameters back into the L^∞ ball as

$$\theta_0 + \min(\max(\theta - \theta_0, -\delta), \delta) \tag{3}$$

limiting the excursion in any coordinate to $\pm\delta$.

The fourth baseline we consider introduces a Kullback-Leibler divergence on randomly sampled examples from X into the loss:

$$\mathcal{L}'(\theta') = \mathcal{L}(X'; \theta') + \lambda \mathcal{L}_{KL}(X; \theta') \tag{4}$$

where

$$\mathcal{L}_{KL}(X; \theta') = \sum_{(x,y) \in X} \sum_{y'} p_\theta(x, y') \log \frac{p_\theta(x, y')}{p_{\theta'}(x, y')} \tag{5}$$

In practice, $\mathcal{L}_{KL}(X; \theta')$ is estimated on minibatches from X simultaneously with selecting a minibatch of the same size from X'.

Training on each of these baselines stops when we reach t' where $\text{argmax}_y p_{\theta'_{t'}}(x_i, y) = y_i$ for all $(x_i, y_i) \in X'$. In experiments, this always happens within three epochs over X' .

[1] https://github.com/necla-ml/debug-test-suites

Test suite	After If	P. Participle	Disjunction	Passive	NP/S
Before debugging	(.000, .838)	(.001, .838)	(.005, .838)	(.004, .838)	(.006, .838)
Fast					
Debug only	(1.000, .813)	(1.000, .804)	(1.000, .807)	(.929, .827)	(1.000, .811)
L^2 ($\delta = .1$)	(.999, .816)	(.999, .810)	(.999, .812)	(.933, .827)	(.999, .817)
L^∞ ($\delta = .1$)	(1.000, .812)	(1.000, .804)	(1.000, .807)	(.933, .827)	(1.000, .811)
K-L ($\lambda = 10$)	(1.000, .825)	(1.000, .820)	(1.000, .822)	(1.000, .824)	(1.000, .826)
Ours	(1.000, .841)	(.926, .835)	(1.000, .836)	(.994, .832)	(.939, .842)
Slow					
Mixed in	(.468, .835)	(.114, .833)	(.344, .837)	(.791, .835)	(.298, .837)
Oversampling	(.920, .836)	(.992, .837)	(1.000, .838)	(.869, .837)	(1.000, .833)

Table 3: (Debugging accuracy, Original accuracy) on HANS test suites for MNLI.

4.2 Slow baselines

Our first slow baseline is simply to train the model starting with the original BERT base parameters for three full epochs on randomly shuffled $X' \cup X$, without accounting for the difference in size $|X'| << |X|$. We call this "mixed in" training.

Our second baseline ("oversampling") equally weights X' and X in the training. It starts with original BERT base parameters and trains for three full epochs over X, each time taking a batch consisting half of examples from X and half of examples from X', interleaved. Although the X samples are sampled without replacement, the X' samples are replaced and are each seen many times.

4.3 Results

We consider the CheckList and HANS test suites for QQP, SST-2, and MNLI together (Tables 1, 2, and 3). Among fast methods, our method has the highest original accuracy in 11 out of 13 subcases and the highest debugging accuracy in 6 out of 13. This makes it a better choice for retaining original accuracy out of several fast, good methods for improving debugging accuracy. Kullback-Leibler divergence, which ranks first most often among fast methods in debugging accuracy, only ranks first in original accuracy once out of 13 subcases. Notably, both methods frequently outperform the debug only approach in debugging accuracy, showing that sampling non-debugging examples helps achieve an update that generalizes better even on the debugging phenomenon.

Considering slow methods, oversampling achieves maximal debugging accuracy on 8 of 13 subcases and best original accuracy on 8 of 13. On HANS, mixing the debugging examples into the full training set is not sufficient for them to be learned, though this method achieves reasonable debugging accuracy on the other datasets.

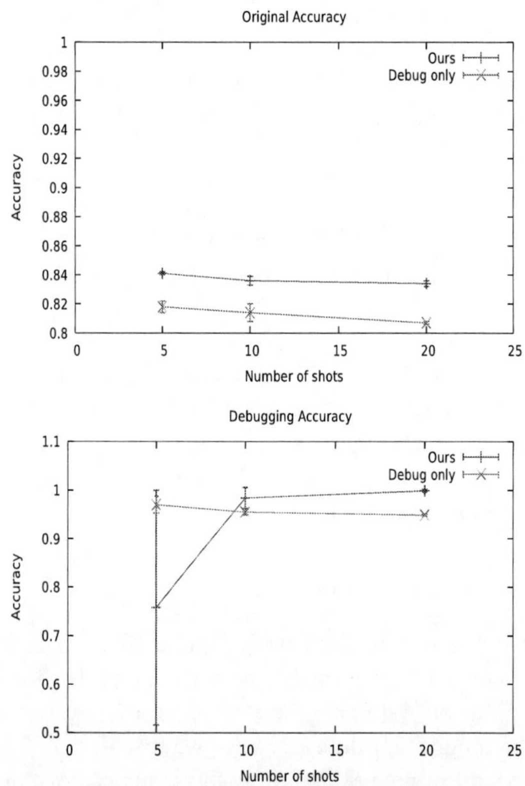

Figure 1: Comparing our method to debug-only intensive fine-tuning for different numbers of shots.

Number of shots and stability. Besides the 10 shot setting described above, we compare our method to "debug only" intensive fine-tuning for 5 shots and 20 shots. Results are shown for HANS's `cn_after_if_clause` test suite in Figure 1. Each experiment is repeated, sampling eight different sets of debugging and in-danger examples. The standard deviation in accuracy over the samples is indicated by the error bars around each mean result in the figure.

Five shots is too few to be sure of good debugging accuracy. Our method achieves significantly higher debugging accuracy and original accuracy, compared to intensive fine-tuning, with ten or twenty shots. With twenty shots the debug only method loses original accuracy, possibly due to the tightened constraints of classifying more debugging examples correctly.

Other base models. We repeat 10-shot experiments using Electra (Clark et al., 2020) instead of BERT. Using Electra, our method has the highest original accuracy among fast methods in 7 out of 13 subcases and the highest debugging accuracy in 8 out of 13.

Method	Seconds
Fast	
Debug only	10.89
L^2	14.74
L^∞	15.85
K-L	14.79
Ours - *total*	25.29
debug-only fine-tuning	10.89
finding new misclassifications W	2.86
final fine-tuning	11.54
Slow	
Mixed in	12663.14
Oversampling (*estimated*)	25326.28

Table 4: Model debugging time in seconds.

Time. Intensive fine-tuning usually finishes after a few small batches, but collecting the 20 misclassified examples potentially can require more evaluations. On QQP these can be found in 1/60 of an epoch (forward only) and at worst (on "negation with neutral" of SST-2) in 1/5, yielding roughly 720x and 60x speedups over oversampling (three epochs, forward and back, alternating with debugging examples), respectively.

In Table 4 we collect total timings for each debugging procedure on HANS's `cn_after_if_clause` test suite, including the time our method needs to collect the new misclassifications W from the original MNLI training set. Whereas the slow methods require hours to update the model, all the fast methods finish in a matter of seconds.

5 Conclusion

We study the new problem of few-shot debugging natural language understanding problems on narrowly defined test suites, addressing a real-life need not addressed by past benchmark datasets. Intensive fine-tuning on debugging examples with a few newly misclassified examples is substantially faster than full epoch retraining, and retains superior accuracy on the original dataset in more of our tests than any other fast method, for competitive debugging accuracy. Kullback-Leibler regularization may achieve better debugging accuracy, but its original accuracy is lagging, probably because it samples randomly rather than focusing on the newly misclassified examples that the debugging examples are opposed to. Our results suggest a way for practitioners to quickly address problems in deployed systems and inspire the search for more refined ways of using debugging information.

To further this research, there is a need for test suites that are not constructed by templates, so that the debugging phenomena are less easily learned, and yet not too broad to be taught in the few-shot setting. This limitation forced us to focus on relatively small differences in accuracy. Because our method requires only a few debugging examples, it should be practical to construct test suites by hand or by manually organizing existing misclassifications.

References

Kevin Clark, Minh-Thang Luong, Quoc V. Le, and Christopher D. Manning. 2020. Electra: Pre-training text encoders as discriminators rather than generators. In *International Conference on Learning Representations*.

Nicola De Cao, Wilker Aziz, and Ivan Titov. 2021. Editing factual knowledge in language models. In *Proceedings of the 2021 Conference on Empirical Methods in Natural Language Processing*, pages 6491–6506, Online and Punta Cana, Dominican Republic. Association for Computational Linguistics.

Jacob Devlin, Ming-Wei Chang, Kenton Lee, and Kristina Toutanova. 2019. BERT: Pre-training of deep bidirectional transformers for language understanding. In *Proceedings of the 2019 Conference of the North American Chapter of the Association for Computational Linguistics: Human Language Technologies, Volume 1 (Long and Short Papers)*, pages 4171–4186, Minneapolis, Minnesota. Association for Computational Linguistics.

Suchin Gururangan, Swabha Swayamdipta, Omer Levy, Roy Schwartz, Samuel Bowman, and Noah A.

Smith. 2018. Annotation artifacts in natural language inference data. In *Proceedings of the 2018 Conference of the North American Chapter of the Association for Computational Linguistics: Human Language Technologies, Volume 2 (Short Papers)*, pages 107–112, New Orleans, Louisiana. Association for Computational Linguistics.

Robin Jia and Percy Liang. 2017. Adversarial examples for evaluating reading comprehension systems. In *Proceedings of the 2017 Conference on Empirical Methods in Natural Language Processing*, pages 2021–2031, Copenhagen, Denmark. Association for Computational Linguistics.

Juho Kim, Christopher Malon, and Asim Kadav. 2018. Teaching syntax by adversarial distraction. In *Proceedings of the First Workshop on Fact Extraction and VERification (FEVER)*, pages 79–84, Brussels, Belgium. Association for Computational Linguistics.

Diederik P. Kingma and Jimmy Ba. 2015. Adam: A method for stochastic optimization. In *3rd International Conference on Learning Representations, ICLR 2015, San Diego, CA, USA, May 7-9, 2015, Conference Track Proceedings*.

Tom McCoy, Ellie Pavlick, and Tal Linzen. 2019. Right for the wrong reasons: Diagnosing syntactic heuristics in natural language inference. In *Proceedings of the 57th Annual Meeting of the Association for Computational Linguistics*, pages 3428–3448, Florence, Italy. Association for Computational Linguistics.

Yixin Nie, Adina Williams, Emily Dinan, Mohit Bansal, Jason Weston, and Douwe Kiela. 2020. Adversarial NLI: A new benchmark for natural language understanding. In *Proceedings of the 58th Annual Meeting of the Association for Computational Linguistics*, pages 4885–4901, Online. Association for Computational Linguistics.

Ramakanth Pasunuru, Veselin Stoyanov, and Mohit Bansal. 2021. Continual few-shot learning for text classification. In *Proceedings of the 2021 Conference on Empirical Methods in Natural Language Processing*, pages 5688–5702, Online and Punta Cana, Dominican Republic. Association for Computational Linguistics.

Adam Paszke, Sam Gross, Francisco Massa, Adam Lerer, James Bradbury, Gregory Chanan, Trevor Killeen, Zeming Lin, Natalia Gimelshein, Luca Antiga, Alban Desmaison, Andreas Kopf, Edward Yang, Zachary DeVito, Martin Raison, Alykhan Tejani, Sasank Chilamkurthy, Benoit Steiner, Lu Fang, Junjie Bai, and Soumith Chintala. 2019. Pytorch: An imperative style, high-performance deep learning library. In *Advances in Neural Information Processing Systems*, volume 32. Curran Associates, Inc.

Marco Tulio Ribeiro, Tongshuang Wu, Carlos Guestrin, and Sameer Singh. 2020. Beyond accuracy: Behavioral testing of NLP models with CheckList. In *Proceedings of the 58th Annual Meeting of the Association for Computational Linguistics*, pages 4902–4912, Online. Association for Computational Linguistics.

Anton Sinitsin, Vsevolod Plokhotnyuk, Dmitry Pyrkin, Sergei Popov, and Artem Babenko. 2020. Editable neural networks. In *International Conference on Learning Representations*.

Jake Snell, Kevin Swersky, and Richard Zemel. 2017. Prototypical networks for few-shot learning. In *Advances in Neural Information Processing Systems*, volume 30. Curran Associates, Inc.

Richard Socher, Alex Perelygin, Jean Wu, Jason Chuang, Christopher D. Manning, Andrew Ng, and Christopher Potts. 2013. Recursive deep models for semantic compositionality over a sentiment treebank. In *Proceedings of the 2013 Conference on Empirical Methods in Natural Language Processing*, pages 1631–1642, Seattle, Washington, USA. Association for Computational Linguistics.

James Thorne, Andreas Vlachos, Oana Cocarascu, Christos Christodoulopoulos, and Arpit Mittal. 2019. The FEVER2.0 shared task. In *Proceedings of the Second Workshop on Fact Extraction and VERification (FEVER)*, pages 1–6, Hong Kong, China. Association for Computational Linguistics.

Alex Wang, Amanpreet Singh, Julian Michael, Felix Hill, Omer Levy, and Samuel Bowman. 2018. GLUE: A multi-task benchmark and analysis platform for natural language understanding. In *Proceedings of the 2018 EMNLP Workshop BlackboxNLP: Analyzing and Interpreting Neural Networks for NLP*, pages 353–355, Brussels, Belgium. Association for Computational Linguistics.

Adina Williams, Nikita Nangia, and Samuel Bowman. 2018. A broad-coverage challenge corpus for sentence understanding through inference. In *Proceedings of the 2018 Conference of the North American Chapter of the Association for Computational Linguistics: Human Language Technologies, Volume 1 (Long Papers)*, pages 1112–1122, New Orleans, Louisiana. Association for Computational Linguistics.

Thomas Wolf, Lysandre Debut, Victor Sanh, Julien Chaumond, Clement Delangue, Anthony Moi, Pierric Cistac, Tim Rault, Remi Louf, Morgan Funtowicz, Joe Davison, Sam Shleifer, Patrick von Platen, Clara Ma, Yacine Jernite, Julien Plu, Canwen Xu, Teven Le Scao, Sylvain Gugger, Mariama Drame, Quentin Lhoest, and Alexander Rush. 2020. Transformers: State-of-the-art natural language processing. In *Proceedings of the 2020 Conference on Empirical Methods in Natural Language Processing: System Demonstrations*, pages 38–45, Online. Association for Computational Linguistics.

Chen Zhu, Ankit Singh Rawat, Manzil Zaheer, Srinadh Bhojanapalli, Daliang Li, Felix X. Yu, and Sanjiv

Kumar. 2020. Modifying memories in transformer models. *CoRR*, abs/2012.00363.

A Test suites

HANS. The Multi-Genre Natural Language Inference (MNLI) dataset (Williams et al., 2018) tests natural language inference in multiple domains, such as fiction, letters, telephone speech, and government reports. It is framed as a three-class classification problem of pairs of sentences, as entailment, neutral, or contradiction. MNLI provides matched and mismatched development and test sets, in which the mismatched setting tests domains not present in the training data. Here we consider a model trained on MNLI and take its accuracy on the matched development set as a measure of its original performance.

HANS (McCoy et al., 2019) is a dataset that compiles phenomena that may not be adequately learned from the MNLI training set. Three heuristics (lexical overlap, sequence, or constituent) for generating challenging examples are considered, each with ten subcases, for a total of thirty subcases. Templates are used to generate one thousand training and one thousand test examples for each. For our experiments, we individually consider the five subcases on which the MNLI model attains the lowest accuracy before debugging. Since we are interested in few-shot debugging, we randomly take ten of the HANS training examples for a subcase as our debugging set X' but use the rest (990) as X'_{test} for testing debugging performance.

HANS examples are labeled only as entailment or non-entailment, without specifying whether the non-entailments should be contradiction or neutral classifications. When training on a non-entailment example, we backpropogate through a logit representing the total non-entailment probability specified by the three-class model

$$p_\theta(x, nonent) = p_\theta(x, n) + p_\theta(x, c) \quad (6)$$

$$\log p_\theta(x, nonent) = \log \frac{e^{l_n} + e^{l_c}}{e^{l_e} + e^{l_n} + e^{l_c}} \quad (7)$$

where $l_y = \log e^{p_\theta(x,y)}$ and y ranges over the entailment (e), neutral (n), and contradiction (c) classes.

CheckList. CheckList (Ribeiro et al., 2020) compiles test suites for sentiment analysis (SST-2) and duplicate question detection (QQP), two datasets which can be found in the GLUE benchmark (Wang et al., 2018).

SST-2 binarizes classifications from Stanford Sentiment Treebank (Socher et al., 2013) into positive or negative, but some test suites of CheckList utilize a neutral target label. We eliminate such test suites. Some test suites of CheckList test invariance or directional properties of classifications (*e.g.* whether two examples are classified with the same label, without specifying what that label should be) and we eliminate those as well, focusing only on suites with given labels for each example. We are left with three suites on which accuracy of the base SST-2 model before debugging is worse than the overall SST-2 accuracy.

Quora Question Pairs (QQP) is already a binary classification task and no adjustments to the test suites are needed. Again, we consider only test suites consisting of individually labeled examples. We take the five suites where the base QQP model achieves lowest accuracy before debugging. For each suite, we randomly pick 10 examples for X' and put the rest (usually about 1000) in X'_{test}.

The full names of the tests utilized are as follows.

For HANS: `cn_after_if_clause`, `sn_past_participle`, `cn_disjunction`, `ln_passive`, and `sn_NP/S`.

For SST-2: Used to but now, Hard negation of positive with neutral stuff in the middle should be negative, and My opinion is what matters.

For QQP: Do you have to X your dog before Y it, A or B is not the same as A and B, What was person's life before becoming X / What was person's life after becoming X, Traditional SRL wrong active passive swap, and Traditional SRL wrong active passive swap with people.

On Masked Language Models for Contextual Link Prediction

Angus Brayne **Maciej Wiatrak** **Dane Corneil**
BenevolentAI
4-8 Maple St, London
{angus.brayne, maciej.wiatrak, dane.corneil}@benevolent.ai

Abstract

In the real world, many relational facts require context; for instance, a politician holds a given elected position only for a particular timespan. This context (the timespan) is typically ignored in knowledge graph link prediction tasks, or is leveraged by models designed specifically to make use of it (i.e. *n-ary* link prediction models). Here, we show that the task of n-ary link prediction is easily performed using language models, applied with a basic method for constructing cloze-style query sentences. We introduce a pre-training methodology based around an auxiliary entity-linked corpus that outperforms other popular pre-trained models like BERT, even with a smaller model. This methodology also enables n-ary link prediction without access to any n-ary training set, which can be invaluable in circumstances where expensive and time-consuming curation of n-ary knowledge graphs is not feasible. We achieve state-of-the-art performance on the primary n-ary link prediction dataset WD50K and on WikiPeople facts that include literals - typically ignored by knowledge graph embedding methods.

1 Introduction

Large-scale knowledge graphs (KGs) have gained prominence over the past several decades as a means for representing complex structured data at scale, leading to the development of machine learning models designed to predict new or unknown information from a KG (Ji et al., 2021). A subclass of such models deals with *link prediction*, i.e. inferring new facts from a given KG consisting of (*subject*, *relation*, *object*) *triples*. For instance, a link prediction model might reason from a KG containing the triple (*USA*, *ElectedPresident*, *JFK*) to infer that the triple (*JFK*, *BornInCountry*, *USA*) also likely exists (i.e. *JFK was born in the country USA*).

The triple format is often too restrictive to represent a query effectively. For instance, the query

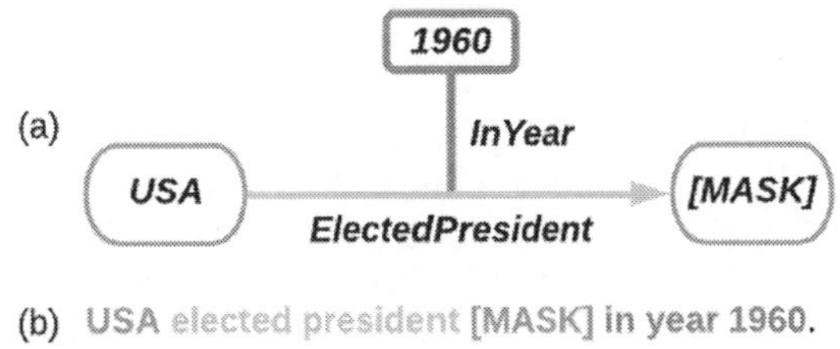

Figure 1: N-ary query representation in KG vs. natural language frameworks. (a) In a knowledge graph, the primary triple query (*USA*, *ElectedPresident*, [MASK]) is augmented with an auxiliary link for qualifer information (*InYear*, *1960*). Each entity or relationship is represented by a unique identifier. Qualifiers require the use of specialised encoder architectures; literal qualifiers like *1960* typically cannot be used at all. (b) We instead represent the query in a templated language model, where the qualifier detail can be directly appended.

Who was elected President of the United States in 1960? permits multiple correct answers when simplified to the triple format (*USA*, *ElectedPresident*, [MASK]), in the absence of the context *1960* (also referred to as a *qualifier* (Vrandečić and Krötzsch, 2014)). Recently, several KG completion models have been developed aimed specifically at link prediction in the presence of qualifiers, collectively referred to as hyper-relational or *n-ary* link prediction models (Wen et al., 2016; Zhang et al., 2018; Guan et al., 2019; Liu et al., 2020; Rosso et al., 2020; Galkin et al., 2020; Yu and Yang, 2021; Wang et al., 2021b). Usage of qualifiers becomes particularly difficult when they include literals, i.e. values that cannot be efficiently represented as discrete graph entities. Examples of literals include years (like *1960*), times, or numerals. Existing KG completion algorithms typically remove literals (Rosso et al., 2020; Galkin et al., 2020) or use specialised techniques to leverage them (Kristiadi et al., 2019).

The need for new models to leverage qualifiers and literals reveals some fundamental weaknesses in discrete, triple-based knowledge graph represen-

Proceedings of Deep Learning Inside Out (DeeLIO 2022):
The 3rd Workshop on Knowledge Extraction and Integration for Deep Learning Architectures, pages 87 - 99
May 27, 2022 ©2022 Association for Computational Linguistics

tations. Unlike graphs, written languages clearly permit the use of qualifiers and literals to represent facts and queries. Pre-trained language models like BERT (Devlin et al., 2019) have already shown competitive performance compared to existing KG link prediction approaches on triple-based KGs (Clouâtre et al., 2021; Yao et al., 2019). As such, it is natural to ask whether Language Models (LMs) present a better alternative for inferring facts with qualifiers and literals compared to n-ary KG inference models.

Apart from their ability to represent qualifiers and literals, using LMs with novel pre-training methodologies on vast corpora also presents opportunities to enable n-ary link prediction without access to any n-ary training set. The need to construct large, partially complete n-ary knowledge graphs in new domains is an expensive and time-consuming requirement of link prediction (Nicholson and Greene, 2020).

Here, we present Hyper Relational Link Prediction using an auxiliary Entity Linked Corpus (Hyper-ELC), the first fully natural-language-based approach applied to KG link prediction benchmarks containing qualifiers and literals. We make use of model pre-training to leverage the large corpora directly available to language models, applying a simple entity-linking approach to prime the model for later inference on named KG entities and to enable link prediction without access to any n-ary training set. To our knowledge, this is the first approach to link prediction without KG supervision. We also use fine-tuning to specifically focus Hyper-ELC on the types of queries represented in the training set. By using KG link prediction datasets, we can directly compare language models to KG models specifically designed to take advantage of additional context in form of qualifiers and literals. Our results show competitive performance compared to these link prediction models, suggesting that language models provide a performant and practical alternative to KG models for link prediction beyond triple-based datasets.

2 Related Work

2.1 N-Ary Link Prediction

Several models have been developed over the past decade to learn from and infer on n-ary relationships. This has been driven by the recognition that knowledge bases like Freebase (Bollacker et al., 2008) contain a sizeable number of relationships involving more than two named entities. Wen et al. (2016) generalized the triple-based translational embedding model *TransH* (Wang et al., 2014) to hyper-relational facts. Zhang et al. (2018) extended this approach using a binary loss learned from the probability that any two entities participate in the same n-ary fact.

Unlike these earlier embedding-based models, **NaLP** (Guan et al., 2019) addressed the n-ary link prediction problem with a neural network, representing n-ary facts as permutation-invariant sets of role-value pairs. Liu et al. (2020) developed the first tensor decomposition-based approach to the problem, adapting earlier tensor decomposition methods applied to link prediction in triple-based KGs. **HINGE** (Rosso et al., 2020) applied a convolutional network to the underlying triples and qualifiers in an n-ary fact.

More recently, several specialised n-ary prediction models have been developed by combining knowledge graph embeddings with attention-based transformer architectures (Vaswani et al., 2017); namely **StarE** (Galkin et al., 2020), **Hy-Transformer** (Yu and Yang, 2021) and **GRAN** (Wang et al., 2021b). In the StarE model, embeddings are fed through a graph neural network before entering the transformer layer. Hy-Transformer and GRAN instead feed the processed embeddings into the transformer directly. Hy-Transformer also adds a qualifier prediction-based auxiliary task, while GRAN modifies the transformer attention model to represent the link structure of the n-ary input. Together, these three transformer-based models have achieved state-of-the-art performance on the n-ary link prediction task.

Hyper-ELC differs from other n-ary link prediction models in that it represents facts in natural language, eliminating the need for specialised encoders or graph-based methods and introducing the ability to pre-train on massive natural language corpora. By representing facts as token sequences, earlier modelling constraints can be avoided; e.g. multiple arities can be supported with the same model (unlike Liu et al. (2020)), and structural information can be retained in token positional encodings, unlike Wen et al. (2016) and Guan et al. (2019). The pre-training introduced here also enables prediction on the downstream task without access to any n-ary training set. Nonetheless, like the most recent approaches, we also use a transformer architecture. In particular, Hyper-ELC is most similar to Hy-Transformer and GRAN, with named graph entities exchanged for word tokens with positional embeddings.

2.2 Literals in Link Prediction

Parallel to research on incorporating qualifiers, several groups have investigated leveraging numerical attributes of entities in triple-based KG completion tasks (García-Durán and Niepert, 2017; Tay et al., 2017; Wu and Wang, 2018; Kristiadi et al., 2019). In these models, the numerical literals are general attributes associated with one of the entities involved in the triple (e.g. the latitude of a city entity); conversely, in the tasks we consider here, literals directly participate in n-ary facts. Nonetheless, we note that our approach could be straightforwardly applied to numerical attributes as well, by inserting them into the textual templates.

Hyper-ELC also differs from previous models by using a standard word-piece tokenisation approach to efficiently parse the literal data. While some literals, like *1962*, are single tokens in the BERT base uncased vocabulary, less commonly discussed dates are split into multiple tokens - for example *1706* becomes *170* and *##6*. Additionally, pre-training gives the model additional context to learn the relationships between dates - e.g. that similar people and events are discussed in sentences containing *1961* and sentences containing *1962*, revealing a similarity.

Notably, literal attributes composed of textual descriptions have also been investigated in KG completion, e.g. Xie et al. (2016); Xu et al. (2016). While we focus on numerical literals here, our natural language-based approach could also be extended to general textual attributes.

2.3 Language Models for Link Prediction

The success of large pre-trained language models has motivated multiple investigations into whether they can be used as knowledge bases. Petroni et al. (2019) proposed a benchmark for evaluating factual knowledge present in LMs with cloze-style queries. Their work has been further extended to probing areas including semantic (Ettinger, 2020; Wallace et al., 2019), commonsense (Tamborrino et al., 2020; Forbes et al., 2019; Roberts et al., 2020), and linguistic (Lin et al., 2019; Tenney et al., 2019) knowledge. Furthermore, in order to improve the performance of LMs in extracting factual knowledge, Jiang et al. (2020) and Shin et al. (2020) proposed methods for automatic discovery and creation of cloze-style queries. This body of work focuses mainly on predicting tokens for filling in blanks, rather than ranking unique entity IDs, as we do here, and therefore requires an entity disambiguation post-processing step. It also focuses on comparison to open-domain question answering or relation extraction approaches rather than link prediction.

Several groups have proposed using LMs for triple-based link prediction. Yao et al. (2019) proposed KG-BERT, which encodes a triple as a sequence, where the entities and relation are separated by a [SEP] token and represented by their textual descriptions. They train to classify whether an individual triplet is correct or not, scoring every (h, r, ?) and (?, r, t) triplet to be ranked. This approach can involve millions of inference steps for a single completion. This work was extended for improved efficiency and performance in Kim et al. (2020); Wang et al. (2021a). This methodology, including entity separation and precise entity descriptions, diverges from plain masked text and is therefore incompatible with our simple pre-training approach that enables n-ary link prediction without access to a training knowledge graph.

An alternative approach to triple-based link prediction is MLMLM (Clouâtre et al., 2021), which also improves on KG-BERT's inference complexity with respect to the number of entities in the KG. They instead use the MLM setup to generate the logits for the tokens required to rebuild all of the entities. These logits are used alongside mean likelihood sampling to rank all entities. The head entity prediction input includes the head entity mask, relation, tail entity and tail entity definition. The tail entity prediction input is analogous. Unlike KG-BERT and its extensions, this method shares the MLM setup with our approach, however they predict tokens rather than unique entity ids. The maximum number of tokens of all of the entities is predicted for each example - predicting the pad token if necessary. This has the benefit that they can predict previously unseen entities (as long as they have fewer than the maximum number of tokens). However, again, this work requires entity disambiguation to go from tokens to a unique entity.

Finally, none of the language model approaches discussed above have been adapted to higher order link prediction with qualifiers and literals. Hyper-ELC additionally extends upon these approaches with a task-specific pre-training approach that en-

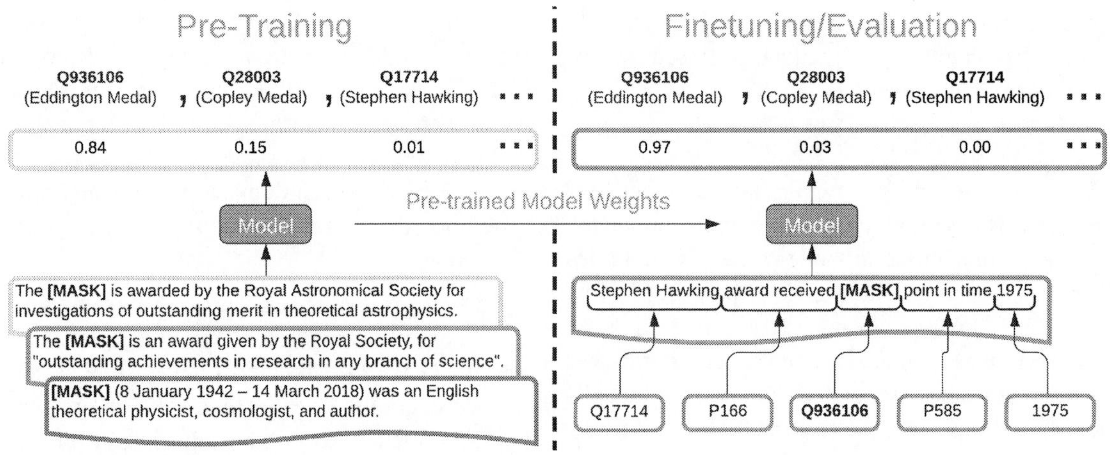

Figure 2: Overview of the training procedure. The names in brackets below the labels are purely informative; as in the typical link prediction setup, we rank the unique identifiers. [Left] Entities of interest in the pre-training corpus are linked and replaced with mask tokens; the model is trained to predict the corresponding named entity of interest. [Right] The finetuning task is the same, but performed on automatically generated sentences from the train set. Surface forms are used for the other entities in each fact.

ables us to perform this task without access to a training knowledge graph.

3 Definitions

A hyper-relational (n-ary) graph, made up of hyper-relational facts, can be defined as $\mathcal{G} = (\mathcal{V}, \mathcal{R}, \mathcal{E})$, where $\mathcal{V}$ is the set of vertices (entities), $\mathcal{R}$ is the set of relations, and $\mathcal{E}$ is a set $(e_1, \ldots, e_n)$ of edges with $e_j \in \mathcal{V} \times \mathcal{R} \times \mathcal{V} \times \mathcal{P}(\mathcal{R} \times \mathcal{V})$ for $1 \leq j \leq n$. Here, $\mathcal{P}$ denotes the power set.

A hyper-relational fact $e_j \in \mathcal{E}$ is written as a tuple $(s, r, o, \mathcal{Q})$, with $s, o \in \mathcal{V}$ and $r \in \mathcal{R}$. Here, $\mathcal{Q}$ is the set of qualifier pairs (qr_i, qv_i) with qualifier relations $qr_i \in \mathcal{R}$ and qualifier values $qv_i \in \mathcal{V}$. An example of a fact in this representation would be (*StephenHawking* (s), *AwardReceived* (r), *EddingtonMedal* (o), (*PointInTime* (qr_1), *1975* (qv_1))).

4 Methods

Our approach consists of three stages:

1. **Pre-training** to predict the unique identifier of a masked entity in the sentences of an auxiliary *entity linked corpus*.

2. **Finetuning** on sentence-like natural language templates created from the training set of the *n-ary link prediction dataset*.

3. **Evaluation** on the test set of the n-ary link prediction dataset using the same format of natural language templates.

For a visual representation of the process, see Figure 2.

4.1 Pre-Training

Our method may use any corpus that references the entities of interest and any entity linking methodology for recognising them within the corpus. As we use the entity linked corpus only in pre-training and not for evaluation, we do not require it to be gold standard. However, increased coverage and precision of the linking may result in better downstream performance.

Each pre-training example is a tuple consisting of a unique entity ID and a masked sentence in which that entity occurs. In the sentence, the span of every occurrence of the entity of interest is replaced by a "[MASK]" token. A single unique entity is masked in each example while all other entities are left as plain text. For example, the label for the entity *StephenHawking* is Q17714 and a masked sentence would be: "[MASK] (8 January 1942 – 14 March 2018) was an English theoretical physicist, cosmologist, and author."

4.2 Finetuning and Evaluation

In order to use our pre-trained language model for the n-ary link prediction task, we must format the query in natural language as a cloze-style sentence. This may be done in any way that represents the query, but linguistic alignment with the pre-training corpus may benefit performance (Jiang et al., 2020; Shin et al., 2020).

Dataset	Statements		Statements w/ Qualifiers (%)		Statements w/ Literals (%)		Entities
	Train	Test	Train	Test	Train	Test	
WikiPeople Pre	37.4M	380,396	—	—	—	—	29,720
WikiPeople	294,439	37,712	2.6	2.6	0	0	34,839
WikiPeople Lit	294,439	3,906	12.1	100	10.9	100	34,839
WD50K Pre	48.6M	494,881	—	—	—	—	42,800
WD50K	166,435	46,159	13.8	13.1	0	0	47,155
WD50K (100)	22,738	5,297	100	100	0	0	18,791

Table 1: Statistics of the datasets used in the experiments. The "Pre" and "Lit" labels on the datasets indicate pre-training and literal datasets, respectively. "M" indicates million. Validation set statistics have been left out for brevity, but they follow a similar pattern to the test set statistics. In the original WikiPeople source data, 10.9% of statements have literals in the qualifiers. The source data also includes 12,363 (3.3%) statements with a literal in the tail position, which are removed from all datasets.

One simple approach is to space separate the entities, relationships and roles in the $(s, r, o, \mathcal{Q})$ order (Figure 2) described in Section 3. This requires that each of the entities have associated textual names, which is usually the case in knowledge graphs.

4.3 Model

Our models are all based on the Transformer architecture (Vaswani et al., 2017), more specifically BERT (Devlin et al., 2019). However, we found a smaller version of the BERT architecture to be more stable during pre-training, which enabled a higher learning rate and larger batch size (see Table 5 in the Appendix). We use the BERT base uncased word-piece tokenisation for all text-based models.

We use a single linear layer as a decoder, followed by a softmax. For optimisation, we leverage a standard categorical cross-entropy loss. All of our models are trained with the Adam optimiser, and are regularised via dropout and gradient clipping. We follow the same setup during pre-training and finetuning. We believe that this alignment between pre-training and the downstream task is part of what makes this approach so powerful. Note that the pre-trained model can also be applied on the downstream task even without additional finetuning on a training graph (Section 6.3).

5 Datasets

5.1 WikiPeople and WD50K

For finetuning and evaluation we use two n-ary link prediction datasets: WikiPeople[1] (Guan et al., 2019) and WD50K[2] (Galkin et al., 2020). Both WikiPeople and WD50K are extracted from Wikidata and contain a mixture of binary and higher-order facts. WikiPeople is a commonly used benchmark containing facts related to entities representing humans.

WD50K was created by Galkin et al. (2020) from the 2019/08/01 Wikidata dump[3]. It was developed with the goal of containing a higher proportion of non-literal higher-order relationships. It is based on the entities from FB15K-237 (Bordes et al., 2013) that have a direct mapping in Wikidata.

In order to transform the facts in these datasets into natural language queries, we use the English Wikidata names for each of the entity and relationship/role IDs[4]. We then create templates in the simple manner described in Section 4.2. We find that while the queries are not particularly natural in their structure and vocabulary, their meaning remains largely the same (an example template is shown in Figure 2, right).

5.2 Non-Named Entity Qualifiers

Galkin et al. (2020) noted that most of the qualifier values in WikiPeople are literals, in this case date-time instances. Literals appear in approximately 13% of the statements in the WikiPeople dataset, but they are typically ignored in knowledge graph embedding approaches (Rosso et al., 2020). If the literals are ignored, only 2.6% of statements in WikiPeople are higher-order. None of the previous approaches to this dataset encode literals.

Note that, for evaluation purposes, alternative correct entities are filtered from the ranking at evaluation time when assessing a given potential answer (Bordes et al., 2013). This has implications

[1]Downloaded from: `https://github.com/gsp2014/NaLP/tree/master/data/WikiPeople`

[2]Downloaded from: `https://zenodo.org/record/4036498`

[3]https://dumps.wikimedia.org/wikidatawiki/20190801/

[4]https://www.wikidata.org/wiki/Special:EntityData

for treating literals. Consider the case where literals are ignored: when evaluating whether the model correctly predicted *EddingtonMedal* as a completion for the fact (*StephenHawking*, *AwardReceived*, [MASK], (*PointInTime*, *1975*)), the entity *CopleyMedal* would be filtered out of the ranking if the fact (*StephenHawking*, *AwardReceived*, *CopleyMedal*, (*PointInTime*, *2006*)) also exists in the dataset. This occurs because the *PointInTime* qualifier is ignored, so that the subject and relation of the facts are identical (and both medals are equally valid completions). When literal-containing qualifiers are not ignored, the facts are distinct, with only one correct answer for each.

The primary WikiPeople dataset used here was adapted by Rosso et al. (2020) from the original WikiPeople (Guan et al., 2019). To investigate whether this literal data can be leveraged by our model, we generated a new dataset from a subset of WikiPeople that we call *WikiPeople Literal*. Unlike in Rosso et al. (2020) and Galkin et al. (2020), where literal qualifier terms are ignored when filtering the rankings for evaluation, we include the literal terms during filtering in *WikiPeople Literal*. Additionally, we evaluate only on facts that include at least one literal. This focus enables us to probe the model's ability to interpret literal qualifiers.

Following Rosso et al. (2020), we drop all statements that contain literals in the main triple.

5.3 Entity Linked Corpus

For pre-training we create an entity linked corpus based on the 2019/08/01 English Wikipedia[5] dump used in BLINK (Ledell Wu, 2020). We process the XML with Gensim[6], which we adapt to leave article hyperlinks in the text.

For simplicity, we use a regex to find occurrences of the entities of interest in the large hyperlinked Wikipedia corpus. For each article we extract the title entity and all of the hyperlinked entities, along with their surface forms in the text and their title name in the hyperlink. We find the wikidata IDs for each of these entities[7] and we retain those entities that are in our downstream n-ary dataset. We then split the article into sentences and run a case insensitive regex over each sentence to find the spans of these entities and link them to their Wikidata IDs, using the ID to surface form/title name dictionaries. Given this collection of entity linked sentences, we create the pre-training examples as described in Section 4.1.

6 Experiments

Throughout this section we compare to the following external baselines developed for n-ary link prediction: (i) NaLP-Fix (Rosso et al., 2020), (ii) HINGE (Rosso et al., 2020), (iii) StarE (Galkin et al., 2020), (iv) Hy-Transformer (Yu and Yang, 2021), and (v) GRAN (Wang et al., 2021b). NaLP-Fix is an improved version of the original NaLP model (Guan et al., 2019). None of these methods make predictions over natural language and none of them encode literals.

The metrics that we use are based on predicting only the subject and object of the hyper-relational facts. We follow the *filtered* setting introduced by Bordes et al. (2013) as discussed in Section 5.2 to ensure that corrupted facts are not valid facts from the rest of the dataset. For each test example, we filter from the model's predicted ranking all of the entities that appear in the same position in otherwise identical examples in either the training, validation or test set (except the test entity of interest). We consider mean reciprocal rank (MRR) and hits at 1 and 10 (H@1 and H@10 respectively).

6.1 Link Prediction with Literals

In order to showcase the expressive power of natural language as a representation, we employ an experiment that involves making predictions with non-named entity qualifier terms (i.e. literals). We use an evaluation dataset (described in Section 5.2) that contains only the examples in the WikiPeople dataset that have at least one literal qualifier. Additionally, we consider these qualifiers when filtering the ranking at evaluation time, unlike the typical WikiPeople evaluation.

To the best of our knowledge, no existing works leverage literals in qualifiers, so no strong baselines exist. We therefore use two baselines that cannot leverage literals as comparison points. The first, **Hyper-ELC [UNK]**, is an ablated version of our model that replaces any literal entity with the [UNK] token. We also used the publicly-available StarE repository [8] to reproduce StarE performance

[5] http://dl.fbaipublicfiles.com/BLINK/enwiki-pages-articles.xml.bz2

[6] https://github.com/RaRe-Technologies/gensim/blob/develop/gensim/corpora/wikicorpus.py

[7] https://dumps.wikimedia.org/wikidatawiki/latest/wikidatawiki-latest-wb_items_per_site.sql.gz

[8] Hy-Transformer did not have a published codebase, and we were unable to successfully run the published GRAN code.

Method	WikiPeople Literal			WikiPeople		
	MRR	H@1	H@10	MRR	H@1	H@10
NaLP-Fix	—	—	—	0.420	0.343	0.556
HINGE	—	—	—	0.476	0.415	0.585
StarE	0.246	0.161	0.424	0.491	0.398	**0.648**
Hy-Transformer	—	—	—	**0.501**	0.426	0.634
GRAN	—	—	—	**0.503**	**0.438**	0.620
Hyper-ELC [UNK]	0.211	0.141	0.347	0.415	0.325	0.566
Hyper-ELC	**0.322**	**0.226**	**0.519**	0.440	0.348	0.592

Table 2: Performance comparison on the two WikiPeople-derived datasets. WikiPeople Literal evaluates only on examples with literal qualifiers (about 10.9% of the full test set) and filters ranking for evaluation with literals included. Methods above the line can encode literal terms, while methods below can't.

on literal-containing qualifiers after adding them back into the dataset (note that StarE achieves state-of-the-art on the full dataset on Hits@10).

On the WikiPeople Literal dataset, Hyper-ELC significantly outperformed both StarE and Hyper-ELC [UNK] (Table 2, first three columns). In particular, the performance boost over the [UNK] ablation illustrates that our model specifically makes use of the information represented in literal qualifiers.

Hyper-ELC also performed reasonably well on the standard WikiPeople dataset (Table 2, last three columns), outperforming NaLP-Fix, but with lower overall performance than the most recent baselines (StarE, Hy-Transformer and GRAN).

To investigate the differences between Hyper-ELC and the other state-of-the-art baselines on WikiPeople, we examined the MRR performance ratio of StarE compared to Hyper-ELC for the relationship-entity position (i.e. head or tail) pairs that occur more than 500 times in the evaluation set (see Appendix, Table 6 in the appendix). Notably, Hyper-ELC displayed the most pronounced performance deficit compared to StarE on inferring correct entities in one-to-many relationships with many possible answers. In Section 7, we discuss potential reasons for this deficit and possible future improvements.

6.2 Link Prediction with Named Entities Only

Next, we evaluated Hyper-ELC on the WD50K datasets (Table 3), which do not contain any literal entities. WD50K (100) has been created by filtering WD50K to have 100% higher order relationships.

In order to understand the value of the pre-training and finetuning steps, we consider multiple ablation models:

Hyper-ELC (only P): a pre-trained version of Hyper-ELC without any exposure to the templated finetuning data (the train set).

Hyper-ELC (only F): a randomly initialised (i.e. only finetuned) version of Hyper-ELC.

BERT (only F): a BERT model (base uncased) with its own initialisation followed by a randomly initialised classification layer, finetuned.

On the full WD50K dataset, Hyper-ELC achieved an MRR of 0.354, nearly identical to the state-of-the-art Hy-Transformer with 0.356. While Hy-Transformer achieved the best performance on Hits@1, Hyper-ELC achieved state-of-the-art on Hits@10.

On the smaller, purely hyper-relational WD50K (100) dataset, Hyper-ELC performed comparably to StarE but was outperformed by Hy-Transformer (see discussion in Section 7).

6.3 Link Prediction without a Training Graph

Finally, we focus specifically on hyper-relational link prediction with the ablated version of Hyper-ELC exposed only to the pre-training data (Table 3, last row, and Table 4). Hyper-ELC (only P) has some ability to perform inference, without any access to the training knowledge graph; it achieves an MRR of 0.087 and 0.207 on WD50K and WD50K (100) respectively, compared to 0.0003 and 0.0006 for the random model and 0.356 and 0.699 for the state-of-the-art Hy-Transformer. This approach could be very powerful in domains where expensive and time consuming curation of hyper-relational knowledge graphs is not feasible.

The significant performance difference between Hyper-ELC and Hyper-ELC (only P) can likely be partially attributed to the distributional shift in the language from pre-training to the templated format used in finetuning and evaluation on the "Ba-

Method	WD50K			WD50K (100)		
	MRR	H@1	H@10	MRR	H@1	H@10
NaLP-Fix	0.177	0.131	0.264	0.458	0.398	0.563
HINGE	0.243	0.176	0.377	0.492	0.417	0.636
StarE	0.349	0.271	0.496	0.654	0.588	0.777
Hy-Transformer	**0.356**	**0.281**	0.498	**0.699**	**0.637**	**0.812**
Hyper-ELC	**0.354**	0.273	**0.508**	0.642	0.564	0.789
Hyper-ELC (only F)	0.283	0.214	0.415	0.549	0.475	0.688
BERT (only F)	0.29	0.22	0.43	0.609	0.536	0.748
Random	< 0.001	< 0.0001	< 0.001	< 0.001	0.00	< 0.001
Hyper-ELC (only P)	0.087	0.051	0.157	0.207	0.129	0.360

Table 3: Performance comparison on the WD50K datasets. We train and test on the dataset indicated following the approach used by the baselines. Model names "only P" and "only F" indicate that only pre-training or finetuning was performed respectively. Methods above the line use the n-ary training graph, while those below do not.

Method	Dataset	WD50K (100)
		MRR
Random	—	< 0.001
Hyper-ELC (only P)	Basic	0.207
Hyper-ELC (only P)	Cleaned	**0.232**
Hyper-ELC	Basic	0.642
Hyper-ELC	Cleaned	0.645

Table 4: With some minor adjustments to the wording of some of the most frequent relationships/roles, to move from the "Basic" to the "Clean" dataset, we can boost performance for the model that doesn't have access to graph based training data. Here, "only P" indicates only pre-training, without finetuning.

sic" dataset, where the templates are often stilted and ungrammatical. To test the hypothesis that improved templates could drive improved performance, we considered 37 of the roles/relationships that occur most frequently in the WD50K (100) training dataset and altered some to make the templates for the "Clean" dataset to be more similar to the natural language occurring in the Wikipedia pre-training corpus; for instance, we improved the grammar with stop words like "the". Table 7 in the appendix shows the 37 roles/relationships that we considered and the changes that we made. In Table 4 we can see a performance increase from 0.207 MRR to 0.232 for Hyper-ELC (only P) with these simple template changes. However, we saw only a minimal improvement when finetuning was introduced, from 0.642 MRR to 0.645, suggesting that the model adapts effectively to the templated linguistic style with finetuning.

7 Discussion and Future Work

Here, we presented Hyper-ELC, the first purely natural language-based approach to n-ary link prediction and the first model to leverage literals in n-ary qualifiers. The natural language-based approach allows us to take advantage of pre-training on massive entity-linked corpora and easily leverage the detail present in hyper-relational facts.

Hyper-ELC matched state-of-the-art performance on WD50K and established state-of-the-art on a version of WikiPeople containing only literal qualifiers. However, it did not reach the performance of existing KG models on the full WikiPeople dataset. As shown in Table 6, Hyper-ELC tends to perform significantly worse than StarE on one-to-many relationships; e.g. ([MASK], *SexOrGender*, *Male*). One hypothesis for this result is that the softmax loss function used in training the model assumes a single correct answer out of all entities for a given masked template; for each unique training example, all competing entities (including valid ones) are treated as false. The objective function and negative sampling approach are therefore potential areas for investigation in future work.

In addition, we expect performance improvements by increasing coverage of relevant information for the entities of interest in the pre-training dataset. The WD50K and WikiPeople pre-training datasets only have 88.2% and 85.3% coverage of the WD50K and WikiPeoople entities, respectively. This could be achieved by improving the quality of the entity linking methodology used. Simple improvements could be made to our regex method, such as including the WikiData surface forms in the regex dictionaries. Even greater improvements could likely be made with feature based or neural entity linking methodologies.

Finally, we found that Hy-Transformer had the best performance on WD50K (100), though Hyper-ELC performed similarly to or better than the other KG baselines. Yu and Yang (2021) propose that Hy-Transformer's auxiliary masked qualifier prediction task allows it to better leverage the train set, which could explain why Hy-Transformer performs well on the smaller train set in WD50K (100). A similar qualifier prediction task could also be investigated in the context of a language model, which we leave for future work.

Overall, our results show how a language model can leverage weakly relevant data (an entity-linked corpus) to reach strong performance on a complex link prediction task. In particular, we note that many practical relational inference problems do not exist in isolated domains where only a structured KG model is available; rather, they are loosely informed by massive, readily available unstructured natural language datasets. In these cases, the sheer quantity and variety of data available to language models, combined with their inherent flexibility in representing context, may swing the balance in their favour.

References

Kurt Bollacker, Colin Evans, Praveen Paritosh, Tim Sturge, and Jamie Taylor. 2008. Freebase: a collaboratively created graph database for structuring human knowledge. In *Proceedings of the 2008 ACM SIGMOD international conference on Management of data*, pages 1247–1250.

Antoine Bordes, Nicolas Usunier, Alberto Garcia-Duran, Jason Weston, and Oksana Yakhnenko. 2013. Translating embeddings for modeling multi-relational data. In *Advances in Neural Information Processing Systems*, volume 26. Curran Associates, Inc.

Louis Clouâtre, Philippe Trempe, Amal Zouaq, and A. P. Sarath Chandar. 2021. Mlmlm: Link prediction with mean likelihood masked language model. In *FINDINGS*.

Jacob Devlin, Ming-Wei Chang, Kenton Lee, and Kristina Toutanova. 2019. BERT: Pre-training of deep bidirectional transformers for language understanding. In *Proceedings of the 2019 Conference of the North American Chapter of the Association for Computational Linguistics: Human Language Technologies, Volume 1 (Long and Short Papers)*, pages 4171–4186, Minneapolis, Minnesota. Association for Computational Linguistics.

Allyson Ettinger. 2020. What BERT Is Not: Lessons from a New Suite of Psycholinguistic Diagnostics for Language Models. *Transactions of the Association for Computational Linguistics*, 8:34–48.

Maxwell Forbes, Ari Holtzman, and Yejin Choi. 2019. Do neural language representations learn physical commonsense? *CoRR*, abs/1908.02899.

Mikhail Galkin, Priyansh Trivedi, Gaurav Maheshwari, Ricardo Usbeck, and Jens Lehmann. 2020. Message passing for hyper-relational knowledge graphs. *arXiv preprint arXiv:2009.10847*.

Alberto García-Durán and Mathias Niepert. 2017. Kblrn: End-to-end learning of knowledge base representations with latent, relational, and numerical features. *arXiv preprint arXiv:1709.04676*.

Saiping Guan, Xiaolong Jin, Yuanzhuo Wang, and Xueqi Cheng. 2019. Link prediction on n-ary relational data. In *The World Wide Web Conference*, pages 583–593.

Shaoxiong Ji, Shirui Pan, Erik Cambria, Pekka Marttinen, and S Yu Philip. 2021. A survey on knowledge graphs: Representation, acquisition, and applications. *IEEE Transactions on Neural Networks and Learning Systems*.

Zhengbao Jiang, Frank F. Xu, Jun Araki, and Graham Neubig. 2020. How can we know what language models know? *Transactions of the Association for Computational Linguistics*, 8:423–438.

Bosung Kim, Taesuk Hong, Youngjoong Ko, and Jungyun Seo. 2020. Multi-task learning for knowledge graph completion with pre-trained language models. In *Proceedings of the 28th International Conference on Computational Linguistics*, pages 1737–1743, Barcelona, Spain (Online). International Committee on Computational Linguistics.

Agustinus Kristiadi, Mohammad Asif Khan, Denis Lukovnikov, Jens Lehmann, and Asja Fischer. 2019. Incorporating literals into knowledge graph embeddings. In *International Semantic Web Conference*, pages 347–363. Springer.

Martin Josifoski Sebastian Riedel Luke Zettlemoyer Ledell Wu, Fabio Petroni. 2020. Zero-shot entity linking with dense entity retrieval. In *EMNLP*.

Yongjie Lin, Yi Chern Tan, and Roberta Frank. 2019. Open sesame: Getting inside bert's linguistic knowledge. *ArXiv*, abs/1906.01698.

Yu Liu, Quanming Yao, and Yong Li. 2020. Generalizing tensor decomposition for n-ary relational knowledge bases. In *Proceedings of The Web Conference 2020*, pages 1104–1114.

David N. Nicholson and Casey S. Greene. 2020. Constructing knowledge graphs and their biomedical applications. *Computational and Structural Biotechnology Journal*, 18:1414–1428.

Fabio Petroni, Tim Rocktäschel, Patrick Lewis, Anton Bakhtin, Yuxiang Wu, Alexander H Miller, and Sebastian Riedel. 2019. Language models as knowledge bases? *arXiv preprint arXiv:1909.01066*.

Adam Roberts, Colin Raffel, and Noam Shazeer. 2020. How much knowledge can you pack into the parameters of a language model? In *Proceedings of the 2020 Conference on Empirical Methods in Natural Language Processing (EMNLP)*, pages 5418–5426, Online. Association for Computational Linguistics.

Paolo Rosso, Dingqi Yang, and Philippe Cudré-Mauroux. 2020. Beyond triplets: hyper-relational knowledge graph embedding for link prediction. In *Proceedings of The Web Conference 2020*, pages 1885–1896.

Taylor Shin, Yasaman Razeghi, Robert L. Logan IV, Eric Wallace, and Sameer Singh. 2020. AutoPrompt: Eliciting Knowledge from Language Models with Automatically Generated Prompts. In *Proceedings of the 2020 Conference on Empirical Methods in Natural Language Processing (EMNLP)*, pages 4222–4235, Online. Association for Computational Linguistics.

Alexandre Tamborrino, Nicola Pellicanò, Baptiste Pannier, Pascal Voitot, and Louise Naudin. 2020. Pre-training is (almost) all you need: An application to commonsense reasoning. *ArXiv*, abs/2004.14074.

Yi Tay, Luu Anh Tuan, Minh C Phan, and Siu Cheung Hui. 2017. Multi-task neural network for non-discrete attribute prediction in knowledge graphs. In *Proceedings of the 2017 ACM on Conference on Information and Knowledge Management*, pages 1029–1038.

Ian Tenney, Patrick Xia, Berlin Chen, Alex Wang, Adam Poliak, R. Thomas McCoy, Najoung Kim, Benjamin Van Durme, Samuel R. Bowman, Dipanjan Das, and Ellie Pavlick. 2019. What do you learn from context? probing for sentence structure in contextualized word representations. *ArXiv*, abs/1905.06316.

Ashish Vaswani, Noam Shazeer, Niki Parmar, Jakob Uszkoreit, Llion Jones, Aidan N Gomez, Ł ukasz Kaiser, and Illia Polosukhin. 2017. Attention is all you need. In *Advances in Neural Information Processing Systems*, volume 30. Curran Associates, Inc.

Denny Vrandečić and Markus Krötzsch. 2014. Wikidata: a free collaborative knowledgebase. *Communications of the ACM*, 57(10):78–85.

Eric Wallace, Yizhong Wang, Sujian Li, Sameer Singh, and Matt Gardner. 2019. Do NLP models know numbers? probing numeracy in embeddings. In *Proceedings of the 2019 Conference on Empirical Methods in Natural Language Processing and the 9th International Joint Conference on Natural Language Processing (EMNLP-IJCNLP)*, pages 5307–5315, Hong Kong, China. Association for Computational Linguistics.

Bo Wang, Tao Shen, Guodong Long, Tianyi Zhou, Ying Wang, and Yi Chang. 2021a. Structure-augmented text representation learning for efficient knowledge graph completion. In *Proceedings of the Web Conference 2021*, WWW '21, page 1737–1748, New York, NY, USA. Association for Computing Machinery.

Quan Wang, Haifeng Wang, Yajuan Lyu, and Yong Zhu. 2021b. Link prediction on n-ary relational facts: A graph-based approach. *arXiv preprint arXiv:2105.08476*.

Zhen Wang, Jianwen Zhang, Jianlin Feng, and Zheng Chen. 2014. Knowledge graph embedding by translating on hyperplanes. In *Proceedings of the AAAI Conference on Artificial Intelligence*, volume 28.

Jianfeng Wen, Jianxin Li, Yongyi Mao, Shini Chen, and Richong Zhang. 2016. On the representation and embedding of knowledge bases beyond binary relations. *arXiv preprint arXiv:1604.08642*.

Yanrong Wu and Zhichun Wang. 2018. Knowledge graph embedding with numeric attributes of entities. In *Proceedings of The Third Workshop on Representation Learning for NLP*, pages 132–136.

Ruobing Xie, Zhiyuan Liu, Jia Jia, Huanbo Luan, and Maosong Sun. 2016. Representation learning of knowledge graphs with entity descriptions. In *Proceedings of the AAAI Conference on Artificial Intelligence*, volume 30.

Jiacheng Xu, Kan Chen, Xipeng Qiu, and Xuanjing Huang. 2016. Knowledge graph representation with jointly structural and textual encoding. *arXiv preprint arXiv:1611.08661*.

Liang Yao, Chengsheng Mao, and Yuan Luo. 2019. Kg-bert: Bert for knowledge graph completion. *ArXiv*, abs/1909.03193.

Donghan Yu and Yiming Yang. 2021. Improving hyper-relational knowledge graph completion. *arXiv preprint arXiv:2104.08167*.

Richong Zhang, Junpeng Li, Jiajie Mei, and Yongyi Mao. 2018. Scalable instance reconstruction in knowledge bases via relatedness affiliated embedding. In *Proceedings of the 2018 World Wide Web Conference*, pages 1185–1194.

A Appendices

Hyperparameter	Hyper-ELC	BERT
lr	0.0001	0.00001
gradient clip	1	1
pre-FF dropout	0.2	0.2
max sentence length	100	100
batch size	512	128
ES patience	3	3
ES monitor quantity	val mrr	val mrr
max pretrain epochs	20	—
hidden size	256	768
intermediate size	512	3072
# attention heads	4	12
# hidden layers	4	12
# encoder parameters	10M	109M
# decoder parameters WD50K	12M	37M
# decoder parameters WikiPeople	9M	27M

Table 5: Hyperparameters used for pre-training and finetuning models. During pre-training the model was trained with early stopping and a maximum number of epochs, but for finetuning only early stopping was used. Only learning rate (lr) was tuned. [0.00001, 0.0001, 0.001] were experimented with and the maximum learning rate that led to convergence was used. FF indicates the feed-foward layer and ES indicates early stopping.

MRR Ratio (StarE/Hyper-ELC)	Count	Relationship (head/tail)
0.23	1205	given name (t)
0.69	691	nominated for (h)
0.93	1038	educated at (h)
0.96	1175	member of sports team (h)
0.98	586	described by source (t)
0.99	1982	sex or gender (t)
0.99	542	family (t)
0.99	691	nominated for (t)
1.01	1688	country of citizenship (t)
1.02	1075	languages spoken, written or signed (t)
1.05	1019	place of birth (t)
1.05	596	work location (t)
1.05	606	position held (t)
1.08	695	father (t)
1.08	883	place of death (t)
1.09	606	position held (h)
1.1	1205	given name (h)
1.11	6657	sibling (t)
1.15	3892	occupation (t)
1.17	1038	educated at (t)
1.17	1492	bmember of (t)
1.17	6657	sibling (h)
1.18	4018	award received (t)
1.19	875	child (t)
1.19	875	child (h)
1.19	695	father (h)
1.24	4018	award received (h)
1.44	542	family (h)
1.47	3892	occupation (h)
1.47	883	place of death (h)
1.47	1019	place of birth (h)
1.5	1492	member of (h)
1.58	586	described by source (h)
1.63	1175	member of sports team (t)
2.09	1075	languages spoken, written or signed (h)
2.18	1688	country of citizenship (h)
2.23	596	work location (h)
6.77	1982	sex or gender (h)

Table 6: MRR ratio between Hyper-Elc and StarE for relationship head/tail prediction combinations on WikiPeople. Limited to the relationship head/tail pairs that occur more than 500 times in the evaluation set.

ID	Train Count	Original Name	Clean Name
P805	9204	statement is the subject of	is the subject of
P1686	9204	for work	for their work on
P1411	5590	nominated for	was nominated for the
P1346	4867	winner	winner was
P530	3515	diplomatic relation	diplomatic relations with
P166	3432	award received	received the award of
P2453	3011	nominee	the nominee was
P3831	1856	object has role	had the role of
P459	1755	determination method	which was determined by
P518	999	applies to part	for the part of
P453	989	character role	played the character
P17	879	country	in the country of
P2293	859	genetic association	is genetically associated with
P6942	736	animator	(movie) animator
P3092	682	film crew member	(movie) film crew member
P161	537	cast member	(movie) cast member
P750	477	distributed by	is distributed by
P421	414	located in time zone	is located in the time zone
P725	409	voice actor	—
P1264	400	valid in period	during the period of
P366	297	use	used for
P2852	259	emergency telephone number	emergency telephone number is
P159	241	headquarters location	is located in
P1552	237	has quality	has the quality
P642	221	of	—
P131	204	located in the administrative territorial entity	in
P39	202	position held	held the position of
P69	200	educated at	was educated at
P812	199	academic major	with academic major
P156	187	followed by	is followed by
P5800	178	narrative role	had the narrative role of
P31	175	instance of	is an instance of
P1365	167	replaces	—
P674	166	characters	character
P155	166	follows	—
P1366	157	replaced by	was replaced by
P19	153	place of birth	place of birth is

Table 7: 37 of the roles/relationships that occur most frequently in the WD50K (100) train dataset were considered and some were altered to make templates more similar to natural language - for example improving grammar.

What Makes Good In-Context Examples for GPT-3?

Jiachang Liu[1]*, Dinghan Shen[2], Yizhe Zhang[3], Bill Dolan[4], Lawrence Carin[1], Weizhu Chen[2]
[1]Duke University [2]Microsoft Dynamics 365 AI [3]Meta AI [4]Microsoft Research
[1]{jiachang.liu, lcarin}@duke.edu
[3]yizhe.zhang@hotmail.com
[2,4]{dishen, billdol, wzchen}@microsoft.com

Abstract

GPT-3 has attracted lots of attention due to its superior performance across a wide range of NLP tasks, especially with its in-context learning abilities. Despite its success, we found that the empirical results of GPT-3 depend heavily on the choice of in-context examples. In this work, we investigate whether there are more effective strategies for judiciously selecting in-context examples (relative to random sampling) that better leverage GPT-3's in-context learning capabilities. Inspired by the recent success of leveraging a retrieval module to augment neural networks, we propose to retrieve examples that are semantically-similar to a test query sample to formulate its corresponding prompt. Intuitively, the examples selected with such a strategy may serve as more informative inputs to unleash GPT-3's power of text generation. We evaluate the proposed approach on several natural language understanding and generation benchmarks, where the retrieval-based prompt selection approach consistently outperforms the random selection baseline. Moreover, it is observed that the sentence encoders fine-tuned on task-related datasets yield even more helpful retrieval results. Notably, significant gains are observed on tasks such as table-to-text generation (44.3% on the ToTTo dataset) and open-domain question answering (45.5% on the NQ dataset).

1 Introduction

GPT-3 (Brown et al., 2020) is a new breakthrough in NLP research. Previously, NLP models are firstly pre-trained and then fine-tuned on a specific task. What sets GPT-3 apart from other models is its impressive "in-context" learning ability. Provided with a few in-context examples, GPT-3 can generalize to unseen cases without further fine-tuning. This opens up many new technological possibilities that are previously considered unique

Trial	1	2	3	4	5
Accuracy	94.6	95.0	95.8	93.9	86.9

Table 1: Results of GPT-3 on the SST-2 sentiment analysis dataset. Five different examples are randomly selected from the training set for each trial. Different contexts induce different accuracies on the test set.

to human. Future NLP systems can be developed to expand emails, extract entities from text, generate code based on natural language instructions with a few demonstration examples.

Despite its powerful and versatile in-context learning ability, GPT-3 has some practical challenges. The original paper utilizes task-relevant examples that are randomly sampled from the training set. However, we observe that the performance of GPT-3 tends to fluctuate with different choices of in-context examples. As shown in Table 1, the variance with distinct in-context examples can be significant. Our work aims to carefully examine this issue to gain a deeper understanding on how to better select in-context examples to improve GPT-3's performance without fine-tuning. Note that our approach requires a training set to select examples. With such a training dataset, it is possible to fine-tune GPT-3 to take full advantage of the model's strength. However, currently GPT-3 has not been released to public for fine-tuning. Even if it is available, fine-tuning GPT-3 requires hundreds of GPUs to load the 175B model, which is prohibitively expensive and time-consuming for ordinary research labs. Another issue is that storing large fine-tuned model checkpoints require huge storage space. Consequently, we resort to prompt/example engineering strategy. Nevertheless, the fine-tuning results using T5 are provided for reference.

A brute-force approach for selecting the optimal in-context instances would be to perform combinatorial search over the entire dataset. Unfortunately, this strategy is computationally impractical. To this

*Work was done when Jiachang (intern) and Yizhe were at Microsoft.

Proceedings of Deep Learning Inside Out (DeeLIO 2022):
The 3rd Workshop on Knowledge Extraction and Integration for Deep Learning Architectures, pages 100 - 114

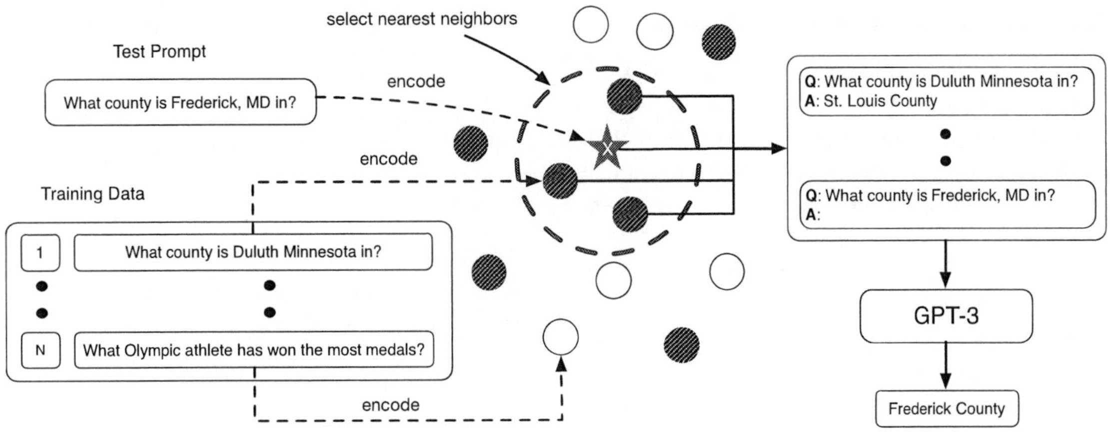

Figure 1: In-context example selection for GPT-3. White dots: unused training samples; grey dots: randomly sampled training samples; red dots: training samples selected by the k-nearest neighbors algorithm in the embedding space of a sentence encoder.

end, we empirically investigate the influences of employing different in-context examples. Interestingly, we find that the in-context examples that are closer to the test sample in the embedding space consistently give rise to stronger performance (relative to the farther ones). Inspired by this observation and the recent success of retrieval-augmented models (Hashimoto et al., 2018), we propose to utilize nearest neighbors of a given test sample (among all the training instances available) as the in-context examples.

To verify the effectiveness of the proposed method, we evaluate it on several natural language understanding and generation tasks, including sentiment analysis, table-to-text generation and open-domain question answering. It is observed that the retrieval-based in-context examples unleash the in-context learning capabilities of GPT-3 much more effectively than the random sampling baseline, even when the number of examples is small. Moreover, we find that the specific sentence encoders employed for the retrieval procedure play a critical role. Thus, an extensive exploration is conducted and shows that encoders fine-tuned on natural language matching tasks serve as more effective in-context examples selector on the QA task. In summary, our contributions are as follows:

i) to the best of our knowledge, we take a first step towards understanding the sensitivity of GPT-3's in-context learning ability with respect to the choice of in-context examples;

ii) to alleviate the sensitivity issue, an additional retrieval module is introduced to find semantically-similar in-context examples of a test instance, which greatly outperforms the baseline based on randomly sampled in-context examples;

iii) empirically, the better selected examples lead GPT-3 to achieve comparable performance to a fine-tuned T5 model on the table-to-text task and *outperforms* the T5 model on the QA tasks;

iv) fine-tuning the retrieval model on task-related dataset(s) leads to stronger empirical results;

v) the performance of GPT-3 improves as the number of examples for retrieval increases.

2 Method

2.1 GPT-3 for In-Context Learning

The in-context learning scenario of GPT-3 can be regarded as a conditional text generation problem. Concretely, the probability of generating a target y is conditioned on the context C, which includes k examples, and the source x. Therefore, the probability can be expressed as:

$$p_{\text{LM}}(y|C, x) = \prod_{t=1}^{T} p(y_t|C, x, y_{<t}) \quad (1)$$

where LM denotes the parameters of the language model, and $C = \{x_1, y_1, x_2, y_2, ..., x_k, y_k\}$ is a context string concatenating k training instances with the special character "\n". A concrete illustration can be found in the Appendix.

For GPT-3, this generation process is implemented through a giant transformer-based architecture (Vaswani et al., 2017). Due to the computational burden of fine-tuning, GPT-3 is leveraged in an in-context learning manner as described above. Unfortunately, as shown in Table 1, the results of GPT-3 tend to fluctuate significantly with different in-context examples. We aim to alleviate this issue via judicious in-context example selection.

2.2 The Impact of In-Context Examples

We start the investigation by looking at the role of in-context examples from an empirical perspective. Previous retrieve-and-edit literature usually retrieve prototypes that are close to the test source x in some embedding space. These examples and the test source x often share semantic or lexical similarities. This hints on how we may select in-context examples for GPT-3.

To this end, we examine the impact of the distance between the in-context example and the test sample on GPT-3's performance. Concretely, a comparison is made on the the Natural Questions (NQ) dataset between two selection strategies. Given a test example, the first method utilizes the 10 farthest training instances as the in-context examples, while the second employs the 10 closest neighbors. We use the CLS embeddings of a pre-trained RoBERTa-large model as sentence representations to measure the proximity of two sentences (using the Euclidean distance).

For evaluation, 100 test questions are randomly sampled and the average Exact Match (EM) scores with the two distinct strategies are reported in Table 2. It can be observed that the nearest neighbors, used as the in-context examples, give rise to much better results relative to the farthest ones. Moreover, the pre-trained RoBERTa model serves as effective sentence embeddings for the retrieval procedure.

Method	Closest	Farthest
Accuracy	**46.0**	31.0

Table 2: Comparison of the EM score on the closest 10 neighbors and farthest 10 neighbors on a subset of 100 test samples of the NQ dataset.

Algorithm 1 kNN In-context Example Selection

Given: test prompt $\boldsymbol{x}_{\text{test}}$, training set $\mathcal{D}_T = \{\boldsymbol{x}_i, \boldsymbol{y}_i\}_{i=1}^N$, sentence encoder $\mu_\theta(\cdot)$, and number of in-context examples k (hyperparameter).

$\boldsymbol{v}_{\text{test}} = \mu_\theta(\boldsymbol{x}_{\text{test}})$

for $\boldsymbol{x}_i \in \mathcal{D}_T$ **do**

$\quad \boldsymbol{v}_i = \mu_\theta(\boldsymbol{x}_i)$

$\quad \boldsymbol{s}_i = -\|\boldsymbol{v}_{\text{test}} - \boldsymbol{v}_i\|_2 \quad (\text{or } \frac{\boldsymbol{v}_{\text{test}} \cdot \boldsymbol{v}_i}{\|\boldsymbol{v}_{\text{test}}\|_2 \|\boldsymbol{v}_i\|_2})$

end for

Select largest k similarities $\boldsymbol{s}_i$'s (in descending order) with indices $\{\sigma(1), ..., \sigma(k)\}$

$C = [\boldsymbol{x}_{\sigma(1)}; \boldsymbol{y}_{\sigma(1)}; ...; \boldsymbol{x}_{\sigma(k)}; \boldsymbol{y}_{\sigma(k)}]$

$\hat{\boldsymbol{y}}_{\text{test}} = \text{GPT-3}([C; \boldsymbol{x}_{\text{test}}])$

2.3 kNN-augmented Example Selection

Based on the findings above, we propose KATE[1], a strategy to select good examples for in-context learning. The process is visualized in Figure 1. Specifically, we first use a sentence encoder to convert sources in both the training set and test set to vector representations. For online prediction, we can convert the training set first and encode each test source on the fly. Then, for each test source x, we retrieve its nearest k neighbors $x_1, x_2, ..., x_k$ from the training set (according to the distances in the embedding space). Given some pre-defined similarity measure s such as the negative Euclidean distance or the cosine similarity, the neighbors are ordered so that $s(x_i, x) \geq s(x_j, x)$ when $i < j$.

The k sources are concatenated with their targets to form the context $C = \{x_1, y_1, x_2, y_2, ..., x_k, y_k\}$, which is sent to GPT-3 along with the test input. The algorithm is presented in Algorithm 1. Note that different numbers of examples can be employed, and we conduct study on its impact in a later section.

Choices of Retrieval Module A core step for our context selection approach is mapping sentences into a latent semantic space, leaving a question as what sentence encoders we should choose. We compared among existing pre-trained text encoders and found them sufficient to retrieve semantically similar sentences. The sentence encoders can be divided into two categories.

The first category includes generally pre-trained sentence encoders such as the BERT, RoBERTa, and XLNet models. These models have been trained on large quantities of unsupervised tasks and achieved good performance on many natural language tasks. The corresponding embeddings contain rich semantic information from the original sentences.

The second category includes sentence encoders fine-tuned on specific tasks or datasets. For example, a sentence encoder trained on the STS dataset should be able to assess similarities among different questions better than a generally pre-trained sentence encoder. Sentence-BERT (Wolf et al., 2019; Reimers and Gurevych, 2019, 2020) shows that these fine-tuned encoders have achieved great performance on tasks such as sentence clustering, paraphrase mining, and information retrieval.

[1]KATE: **K**nn-**A**ugmented in-con**T**ext **E**xample selection

3 Experimental Setup

We apply our proposed method to the following three tasks: sentiment analysis, table-to-text generation, and question answering. Dataset split setups and prompt templates are shown in Table 9 and 11 in the Appendix. For the hyper-parameters in the GPT-3 API, we set the temperature to 0.

3.1 Sentence Embeddings for Retrieval

To retrieve semantically-similar training instances, we consider two types of sentence embeddings.

- The original RoBERTa-large model (Liu et al., 2019), which is abbreviated as $\text{KATE}_{\text{roberta}}$;
- The RoBERTa-large models which are: *i)* fine-tuned on the SNLI and MultiNLI datasets (KATE_{nli}) (Bowman et al., 2015; Williams et al., 2017); *ii)* first fine-tuned on the SNLI and MultiNLI dataset and then on the STS-B datasets ($\text{KATE}_{\text{nli+sts-b}}$) (Cer et al., 2017).

All sentence encoders share the same architecture. The only differences are the specific datasets used for fine-tuning. The negative Euclidean distance is used for $\text{KATE}_{\text{roberta}}$, while the cosine similarity is employed for KATE_{nli} and $\text{KATE}_{\text{nli+sts-b}}$.

Sentiment Analysis For this task, we conduct experiments under the dataset-transfer setting. In-context examples are selected from one dataset, and the evaluation is made on another dataset. This setting is designed to simulate a real-world scenario where we want to leverage an existing labeled dataset for a unlabeled one (of a similar task).

Specifically, we select examples from the SST-2 training set (Socher et al., 2013; Wang et al., 2018) and ask GPT-3 to predict on the IMDB test set (Maas et al., 2011). To explore whether a sentence encoder fine-tuned on a similar task would benefit KATE, we also employ a pre-trained RoBERTa-large model fine-tuned on the SST-2 training set (dubbed as $\text{KATE}_{\text{sst-2}}$). The number of examples is chosen to be 3 since adding more examples does not further improve the performance.

Table-to-Text Generation Given a Wikipedia table and a set of highlighted cells, this task focuses on producing human-readable texts as descriptions. ToTTo (Parikh et al., 2020)[2] is utilized for evaluation due to its popularity. We use BLEU (Papineni et al., 2002) and PARENT (Dhingra et al., 2019) metrics for evaluation. Because the token length limit of GPT-3 is 2048, we add a preprocessing step by deleting the closing angle brackets such as </cell> and </table> to save space. The number of in-context examples is set as 2 so that the input length is within the token limit.

Question Answering We conduct experiments on three QA benchmarks: Natural Questions (NQ) (Kwiatkowski et al., 2019), Web Questions (WQ) (Berant et al., 2013), and TriviaQA (Joshi et al., 2017). For evaluation, we use the Exact Match (EM) score, which is defined as the proportion of the number of predicted answers being exactly one of the ground-truth answers. The matching is performed after string normalization, which includes article and punctuation removal. The number of examples is set to be 64 for NQ and WQ and 10 for TriviaQA (The retrieved 64 examples exceed the token limit). We evaluate on the test sets of NQ and WQ and the dev set of TriviaQA.

3.2 Baseline Methods

Random Sampling For each test sentence, we randomly select in-context examples from the training set. We refer to this method as *Random* in the experimental results. On the test set, the random baseline is repeated for five times to obtain the average score and corresponding standard deviation.

k-Nearest Neighbor Additionally, to investigate whether the retrieval module is complementary to GPT-3's in-context learning ability, we further consider a k-nearest neighbor baseline. Specifically, the target y_1 associated with the first retrieved example is considered as the predicted target for the test sample. For the sentiment analysis and QA tasks, the top k retrieved examples $\{y_1, ..., y_k\}$ are utilized, where the final prediction is determined by majority voting among the k examples' targets. If there is a tie case, we use the target of the example most similar to the test sentence. To ensure fair comparison, we compare the baseline kNN and KATE under the same embedding space of a pre-trained RoBERTa-large model. This baseline is abbreviated as $k\text{NN}_{\text{roberta}}$.

Fine-tuned T5 Although this work aims at improving the in-context learning abilities of GPT-3, we include a fine-tuned T5 (3B) model as a baseline. This comparison informs us where GPT-3 performs comparably or surpasses a fine-tuned model.

[2] The ToTTo code base and evaluation scripts can be found at `https://github.com/google-research/language/tree/master/language/totto`

Method	Accuracy
T5 (fine-tuned)	95.2
Ours	
Random	87.95 ± 2.74
kNN$_{\text{roberta}}$	50.20
KATE$_{\text{roberta}}$	91.99
KATE$_{\text{nli}}$	90.40
KATE$_{\text{nli+sts-b}}$	90.20
KATE$_{\text{sst-2}}$	**93.43**

Table 3: Results on the IMDB dataset. In-context examples are from the SST-2 dataset.

4 Experimental Results

4.1 Sentiment Analysis

We first evaluate KATE on the sentiment analysis task. The results are in Table 3. KATE consistently produces better performance relative to the random selection baseline. Notably, there is no variance with the obtained results since the fixed retrieved in-context examples are employed. For KATE, when the pre-trained sentence encoder is fine-tuned on NLI or NLI+STS-B datasets, the performance slightly decreases. Since the objectives of the IMDB and the NLI+STS-B datasets are different, this shows that fine-tuning on a dissimilar task hurts KATE's performance. In contrast, KATE$_{\text{sst-2}}$ obtains the best accuracy, showing that fine-tuning on a similar task improves KATE's performance. To verify that the gains are not merely from the retrieval step, we further compare KATE$_{\text{roberta}}$ with the kNN$_{\text{roberta}}$. It turns out that the performance of kNN$_{\text{roberta}}$ is close to random guessing. This observation is consistent when one neighbor or three neighbors are retrieved. Notably, with the sentence encoder fine-tuned on the SST-2 dataset, the accuracy of kNN$_{\text{sst-2}}$ is 92.46, which is lower than that of KATE$_{\text{sst-2}}$. These results suggest that GPT-3 is critical to the final results, and the retrieval module is complementary to GPT-3.

The fine-tuned T5 model works better since its parameters has been adapted to this specific task. However, fine-tuning requires access to model parameters, lots of memory storage, and time. The fine-tuning result here is just for reference. Through KATE, the performance of GPT-3 has increased significantly without fine-tuning.

4.2 Table-to-text Generation

We next evaluate KATE on the ToTTo dataset and present results in Table 4. KATE gives rise to considerable gains over the random baseline, according to both the BLEU and PARENT scores. Notably, KATE enables GPT-3 to achieve performance comparable to a fine-tuned T5 model. On a finer scale, the evaluation can be done on the overlap subset and the nonoverlap subset. The overlap dev subset shares a significant number of header names with the training set, while the nonoverlap one does not. KATE improves results on both subsets, meaning that the retrieval module is helpful even when the dev set is out of distribution of the training set. Similar to sentiment analysis, there is a slight drop in performance from KATE$_{\text{roberta}}$ to KATE$_{\text{nli}}$ and KATE$_{\text{nli+sts-b}}$. This is due to the difference between the objectives of the ToTTo dataset and NLI+STS-B datasets. The drop from KATE$_{\text{nli}}$ to KATE$_{\text{nli+sts-b}}$ further validates the idea that fine-tuning on a dissimilar task can hurt KATE's performance. For the kNN baseline, it performs much worse than the random selection method and KATE, suggesting that the retrieval process and GPT-3 work collaboratively to achieve better results.

To understand how the retrieval mechanism helps GPT-3, we conduct a case study on the retrieved examples (see Table 5). By retrieving relevant examples from the training set, KATE provides useful detailed information within the table, *e.g.*, the number of points, rebounds, and assists, to GPT-3 for more accurate description. On the other hand, the random selection method has the issue of hallucination, where the generated sequences contain information (*i.e.*, "senior year" and "University of Texas") not present in the table.

4.3 Questing Answering

Lastly, we evaluate KATE on the open-domain QA tasks, as shown in Table 6. We compare with some state-of-the-art fine-tuned methods such as RAG (Lewis et al., 2020) and T5 (Raffel et al., 2019). The T5 results were reported in (Brown et al., 2020) using the 11B model, which needs specialized TPUs to do fine-tuning. KATE again improves GPT-3's performance substantially across various benchmarks. Moreover, KATE helps GPT-3 to even outperform the fine-tuned T5 model. It is worth noting that this time both KATE$_{\text{nli}}$ and KATE$_{\text{nli+sts-b}}$ improve upon KATE$_{\text{roberta}}$ because fine-tuning on NLI or STS-B datasets is helpful for retrieving semantically similar questions from the QA datasets. Moreover, on the NQ and TriviaQA datasets, further fine-tuning on the STS-B dataset improves KATE's results. We evaluate the baseline kNN$_{\text{roberta}}$ by using the top-1 nearest neighbor. The kNN baseline results again suggest that

Method	Overall		Overlap Subset		Nonoverlap Subset	
	BLEU	PARENT	BLEU	PARENT	BLEU	PARENT
T5 (fine-tuned)	41.2	53.0	46.7	56.1	35.8	50.0
Ours						
Random	28.4 ± 2.1	39.3 ± 2.6	31.2 ± 2.5	41.8 ± 3.0	25.6 ± 1.8	37.0 ± 2.3
kNN$_{roberta}$	14.1	12.6	20.1	17.9	8.0	7.52
KATE$_{roberta}$	**41.0**	**50.6**	**48.4**	**55.9**	**33.6**	**45.5**
KATE$_{nli}$	39.9	49.5	47.4	54.6	32.5	44.5
KATE$_{nli+sts\text{-}b}$	38.8	48.2	46.2	53.1	31.5	43.4

Table 4: Table-to-text generation results on the ToTTo dev dataset.

Test Table	**Table**: <page_title >Trey Johnson <section_title >College <table ><cell >32 <col_header > GP <cell >4.8 <col_header >RPG <cell >2.3 <col_header >APG <cell >23.5 <col_header >PPG
Retrieved Examples	**Table**: <page_title >Dedric Lawson <section_title >College <table ><cell >9.9 <col_header > RPG <cell >3.3 <col_header >APG <cell >19.2 <col_header >PPG **Sentence**: Dedric Lawson averaged 19.2 points, 9.9 rebounds and 3.3 assists per game. **Table**: <page_title >Carsen Edwards <section_title >College <table ><cell >3.8 <col_header > RPG <cell >2.8 <col_header >APG <cell >18.5 <col_header >PPG **Sentence**: Edwards averaged 18.5 points, 3.8 rebounds and 2.8 assists per game.
Predictions	**Ground-truth**: Trey Johnson averaged 23.5 points, 4.8 rebounds, and 2.3 assists in 32 games. **Random**: Trey Johnson averaged 23.5 points per game in his senior year at the University of Texas. **KATE**: Johnson averaged 23.5 points, 4.8 rebounds and 2.3 assists per game.

Table 5: A sample of retrieved in-context examples from the ToTTo dataset. For the KATE method, GPT-3 pays more attention to detailed information such as the number of points, rebounds, and assists. In contrast, the random selection method leads GPT-3 to generate details which do not exist in the original table.

Method	NQ	WQ	TriviaQA*
RAG (Open-Domain)	44.5	45.5	68.0
T5+SSM (Closed-Book)	36.6	44.7	60.5
T5 (Closed-Book)	34.5	37.4	50.1
GPT-3 (64 examples)	29.9	41.5	-
Ours			
Random	28.6 ± 0.3	41.0 ± 0.5	59.2 ± 0.4
kNN$_{roberta}$	24.0	23.9	26.2
KATE$_{roberta}$	40.0	47.7	57.5
KATE$_{nli}$	40.8	**50.6**	60.9
KATE$_{nli+sts\text{-}b}$	**41.6**	50.2	**62.4**

Table 6: Results on QA datasets. (*) We used 10 examples for TriviaQA and 64 examples for NQ and WQ.

the retrieval module and GPT-3 work together to achieve better performance. We also explore using 64 nearest neighbors (10 for TriviaQA) to determine the answer (by majority voting explained in Section 3.2). The EM score are similar to retrieving the top-1 nearest neighbor.

To investigate why the retrieved examples are helpful, we present a case study. Concretely, the retrieval examples from the NQ dataset are shown in Table 7. For the first and second cases, the random baseline provides wrong answers because GPT-3 is unable to recall the exact detail. However, the in-context examples selected by KATE contain the correct details, which facilitate GPT-3 to answer questions. For the third case, the random baseline leads GPT-3 to misinterpret the question as asking for a specific location. In contrast, KATE selects similar types of questions asking for the origins of objects. Using these in-context examples, GPT-3 is able to interpret and answer the question correctly.

5 Analysis of Different Factors

5.1 Number of In-context Examples

We first investigate the impact of the number of examples on KATE's performance. Concretely, on the NQ dataset, we choose the number of examples to be 5, 10, 20, 35, and 64, and KATE$_{nli+sts\text{-}b}$ is compared with the random baseline and KATE$_{roberta}$ across different settings. As shown in the left plot of Figure 2, both KATE and the random baseline benefit from utilizing more examples. However, KATE consistently outperforms the random selection method, even when the number of in-context examples is as few as 5. This result is interesting because in practice, employing less examples leads to more efficient inference with GPT-3.

5.2 Size of Training Set for Retrieval

We further examine how the size of the training set may influence the KATE method. On the NQ dataset, we create new subsets from the original training set, with sizes of 1k, 2k, 5k, 10k, 30k, and

In-Context Examples	Predictions
Question: The Mughal Gardens of Rashtrapati Bhavan is modelled on which garden?	
The Mughal Garden of Rashtrapati Bhavan is modelled on? The Persian style of architecture Who built the first Mughal Garden in India? Babur The landscape design of the Gardens of Versailles is known as which style? French garden	**Ground-truth**: Persian garden **KATE**: The Persian gardens **Random Baseline**: Shalimar gardens
Question: What city was Zeus the patron god of?	
What is the symbol of Zeus the Greek God? Bull Where did Zeus spend most of his time? Mount Olympus Where was the statue of Zeus at Olympia located? In the Temple of Zeus	**Ground-truth**: Olympia **KATE**: Olympia **Random Baseline** Athens
Question: Where did the Dewey decimal system come from?	
Where did the formula for area of a circle come from? Archimedes Where did the name jack russell come from? Reverend John Russell Where did the letters of the alphabet come from? The Phoenician alphabet	**Ground-truth**: Melvil Dewey **KATE**: Melvil Dewey **Random Baseline**: the library of Congress

Table 7: Three samples of retrieved in-context examples from the NQ dataset. Three retrieved Q-A pairs are shown on the left. Predictions by the KATE method and useful details from in-context examples are shown in Green. Gold-standard references are shown in Blue. Predictions by the random baseline are shown in Red.

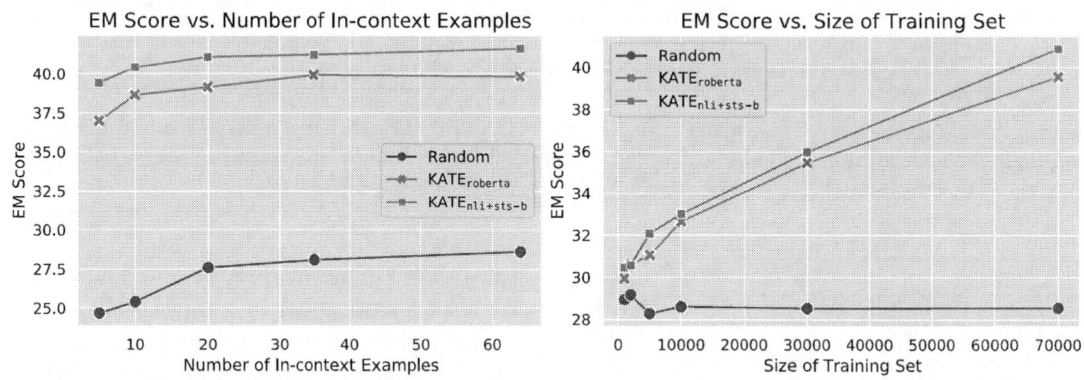

Figure 2: Left: Effect of number of in-context examples for different selection methods. Right: Effect of the size of training set for retrieval on KATE. Two representative sentence encoders are used in these studies.

70k, respectively. In-context examples are retrieved from these subsets instead of the original training set. The number of nearest neighbors is set to 64. We compare KATE$_{\text{nli+sts-b}}$ with the random selection method and KATE$_{\text{roberta}}$, and the results are shown in the right plot of Figure 2. For KATE$_{\text{roberta}}$ and KATE$_{\text{nli+sts-b}}$, as the size of the training set increases, the EM scores also increase. In contrast, the result of the random sampling baseline does not change much. Intuitively, as the training size gets larger, it is more likely for KATE to retrieve relevant in-context examples to help GPT-3 answer a question correctly. As we have shown previously in Table 7, the retrieved in-context examples could provide critical detailed information to GPT-3, thus helping GPT-3 to better answer the questions.

5.3 Order of In-context Examples

Moreover, we explore how the order of in-context examples may affect KATE's results. As mentioned in Section 2.3, under the standard setting, the retrieved in-context examples are ordered such that $s(x_i, x) \geq s(x_j, x)$ whenever $i < j$. Here, we randomly permute the order of in-context examples in the NQ dataset for the proposed KATE$_{\text{nli+sts-b}}$ method, and conduct the experiments for 3 different orders. Additionally, we explore the reverse order where $s(x_i, x) \leq s(x_j, x)$ whenever $i < j$. The results are presented in Table 8. On this particular NQ dataset, the reverse order performs the best. However, we also did the experiments on the WQ and TriviaQA and find that the default order performs slightly better than the reverse order. Hence,

Trial	1	2	3	Default	Reverse
EM Score	42.0	42.5	42.0	41.6	42.8

Table 8: Analysis on the effect of orders of in-context example on the NQ dataset using KATE$_{\text{nli+sts-b}}$. The default order puts the most similar example in the front, and the reverse order does the opposite.

the choice of orders is data-dependent. Additionally, it can be observed that the variation among the NQ results tends to be quite small (compared with the difference between the random baseline and KATE), indicating that the example order does not have a significant impact on KATE's performance.

6 Related Work

Pre-trained Language Models NLP systems have made tremendous progress by pre-training models on unlabeled text (Devlin et al., 2018; Liu et al., 2019; Yang et al., 2019; Lewis et al., 2019; Raffel et al., 2019; Xue et al., 2020; Lample and Conneau, 2019; Radford et al., 2018, 2019). These models can be fine-tuned for a wide range of downstream tasks. GPT-3 (Brown et al., 2020), however, can perform in-context learning without fine-tuning. People have just started trying to understand GPT-3 from different perspectives. (Hendrycks et al., 2020) studies which categories of questions GPT-3 is more capable of answering. (Zhao et al., 2021) proposes to improve the model by contextual calibration. However, their method is limited to predicting very few tokens because for long sequence generation, the contextual calibration step needs to be repeatedly performed after each newly generated token. In contrast, our work, KATE, only calls the API once and is suitable for both text classification and generation tasks. Another related work is LM-BFF (Gao et al., 2020), which uses a smaller language model (RoBERTa-large) to demonstrate that prompt-based fine-tuning can outperform standard fine-tuning on text classification tasks. Our work differs by showing that, without fine-tuning, relevant examples can still substantially improve the performance of GPT-3 for both text classification and generation tasks. Finally, AutoPrompt (Shin et al., 2020) explores adding some additional tokens to smaller language models to improve performance on classification tasks.

Retrieval-based Text Generation There is a long history of applying information retrieval to text generation (Sumita and Hitoshi, 1991). It is very related to the exemplar-based learning (Jäkel et al., 2008; Ziyadi et al., 2020). Some representative applications in the field of deep learning include machine translation (Gu et al., 2018), sentiment transfer (Li et al., 2018; Guu et al., 2018), QA (Karpukhin et al., 2020; Mao et al., 2020), dialogue generation (Yan et al., 2016; Cai et al., 2018; Song et al., 2016; Pandey et al., 2018; Weston et al., 2018; Wu et al., 2019), text summarization (Cao et al., 2017; Peng et al., 2019), data-to-text generation (Peng et al., 2019), and text-to-code generation (Hashimoto et al., 2018). All these retrieve-and-edit frameworks require their editors to be trained or fine-tuned on specific tasks. In contrast, our work uniquely examines how to better use GPT-3 as a universal editor without fine-tuning. We find that the more semantically similar context we provide to GPT-3, the better results the model can generate.

Improve NLP Systems with kNN Some recent works try to incorporate non-parametric methods to improve a given model's performance. For example, the newly introduced kNN-LM (Khandelwal et al., 2019), kNN-MT (Khandelwal et al., 2020), and BERT-kNN (Kassner and Schütze, 2020) generate the next token by retrieving the nearest k neighbors from the datastore. Another related work kNN classification model (Rajani et al., 2020) uses kNN as backoff when the confidence is low from the classification model. There are two key differences between our work and other approaches. First, we retrieve the nearest k neighbors to modify the conditional context instead of the prediction. Second, we do not have access to the parameters of GPT-3. Instead, we rely on some independently pre-trained models to get the sentence embeddings to retrieve the nearest k neighbors.

7 Conclusion

This work presented a first step towards investigating the sensitivity of GPT-3 to in-context examples. To this end, we proposed KATE, a non-parametric selection approach that retrieves in-context examples according to their semantic similarity to the test samples. On several natural language understanding and generation tasks, the proposed method improves GPT-3's performance, over the random sampling baseline, by a significant margin. Particularly, KATE enables GPT-3 to achieve performance comparable to a fine-tuned T5 model on the table-to-text generation task and *outperforms* T5 on the QA task. Moreover, we found that fine-tuning the sentence embeddings for retrieval on task-related datasets gave rise to further empirical gains. Detailed analysis was conducted to explore the robustness of KATE to different hyperprameters, such as the number of in-context examples, examples' order, *etc.* One limitation we notice is that despite the improved performance on sentiment analysis,

GPT-3 still lags behind the fine-tuned T5 model by a small margin. This suggests that our proposed method is more suitable and effective on long text generation tasks. We hope this work could provide insights for better understanding the behaviors of GPT-3 and represents a helpful step towards further improving its in-context learning capabilities.

8 Ethical and Broader Impacts

Risk Our proposed KATE method significantly improves the in-context learning ability of GPT-3 and makes long-text generation more easily without fine-tuning the pre-trained model. However, one risk implication is that our proposed method will benefit the research groups which are financially capable of using such huge models. For individual or small-group researchers, they cannot apply our proposed method to their specific applications since they don't have access to the model. Our work has suggested researchers should focus more on investigating the in-context learning of pre-trained models. One potential future direction is for researchers to scale-down the sizes of pre-trained models to find a balance between model performance and model size. Once a smaller model is obtained with comparable performance (enhanced by KATE), our proposed method can become more widely accessible to individual researchers.

Potential Bias During the experiment on table-to-text generation, we have pointed out that large pre-trained language models could be susceptible to hallucination (case study in Table 5). This problem is more pronounced when we use randomly sampled examples. This happens because the language model is biased toward the training dataset. As shown in Table 5, when random examples are used, the sentence generated by GPT-3 is grammatically correct, but some details never exist in the given table. In contrast, our proposed method, KATE, can significantly alleviate this problem by guiding GPT-3 to look for and generate the correct information. For similar reasons, large pre-trained models could be potentially susceptible to gender and racial bias. Since our KATE method shows that in-context examples are crucial for high-quality long-text generations, one way to alleviate the racial and gender bias is to incorporate an additional module to filter out offensive in-context examples. Since racial and gender bias are not our main research focus, a full investigation goes beyond the scope of our work. However, we believe this is an exciting opportunity for future work.

Code Availability

Implementations of the proposed KATE method discussed in this paper are available at `https://github.com/jiachangliu/KATEGPT3`.

References

Jonathan Berant, Andrew Chou, Roy Frostig, and Percy Liang. 2013. Semantic parsing on freebase from question-answer pairs. In *Proceedings of the 2013 conference on empirical methods in natural language processing*, pages 1533–1544.

Samuel R Bowman, Gabor Angeli, Christopher Potts, and Christopher D Manning. 2015. A large annotated corpus for learning natural language inference. *arXiv preprint arXiv:1508.05326*.

Tom B Brown, Benjamin Mann, Nick Ryder, Melanie Subbiah, Jared Kaplan, Prafulla Dhariwal, Arvind Neelakantan, Pranav Shyam, Girish Sastry, Amanda Askell, et al. 2020. Language models are few-shot learners. *arXiv preprint arXiv:2005.14165*.

Deng Cai, Yan Wang, Wei Bi, Zhaopeng Tu, Xiaojiang Liu, Wai Lam, and Shuming Shi. 2018. Skeleton-to-response: Dialogue generation guided by retrieval memory. *arXiv preprint arXiv:1809.05296*.

Ziqiang Cao, Furu Wei, Wenjie Li, and Sujian Li. 2017. Faithful to the original: Fact aware neural abstractive summarization. *arXiv preprint arXiv:1711.04434*.

Daniel Cer, Mona Diab, Eneko Agirre, Inigo Lopez-Gazpio, and Lucia Specia. 2017. Semeval-2017 task 1: Semantic textual similarity-multilingual and cross-lingual focused evaluation. *arXiv preprint arXiv:1708.00055*.

Jacob Devlin, Ming-Wei Chang, Kenton Lee, and Kristina Toutanova. 2018. Bert: Pre-training of deep bidirectional transformers for language understanding. *arXiv preprint arXiv:1810.04805*.

Bhuwan Dhingra, Manaal Faruqui, Ankur Parikh, Ming-Wei Chang, Dipanjan Das, and William W Cohen. 2019. Handling divergent reference texts when evaluating table-to-text generation. *arXiv preprint arXiv:1906.01081*.

Tianyu Gao, Adam Fisch, and Danqi Chen. 2020. Making pre-trained language models better few-shot learners. *arXiv preprint arXiv:2012.15723*.

Jiatao Gu, Yong Wang, Kyunghyun Cho, and Victor OK Li. 2018. Search engine guided neural machine translation. In *AAAI*, pages 5133–5140.

Kelvin Guu, Tatsunori B Hashimoto, Yonatan Oren, and Percy Liang. 2018. Generating sentences by editing prototypes. *Transactions of the Association for Computational Linguistics*, 6:437–450.

Tatsunori B Hashimoto, Kelvin Guu, Yonatan Oren, and Percy S Liang. 2018. A retrieve-and-edit framework for predicting structured outputs. In *Advances in Neural Information Processing Systems*, pages 10052–10062.

Dan Hendrycks, Collin Burns, Steven Basart, Andy Zou, Mantas Mazeika, Dawn Song, and Jacob Steinhardt. 2020. Measuring massive multitask language understanding. *arXiv preprint arXiv:2009.03300*.

Frank Jäkel, Bernhard Schölkopf, and Felix A Wichmann. 2008. Generalization and similarity in exemplar models of categorization: Insights from machine learning. *Psychonomic Bulletin & Review*, 15(2):256–271.

Mandar Joshi, Eunsol Choi, Daniel S Weld, and Luke Zettlemoyer. 2017. Triviaqa: A large scale distantly supervised challenge dataset for reading comprehension. *arXiv preprint arXiv:1705.03551*.

Vladimir Karpukhin, Barlas Oğuz, Sewon Min, Ledell Wu, Sergey Edunov, Danqi Chen, and Wen-tau Yih. 2020. Dense passage retrieval for open-domain question answering. *arXiv preprint arXiv:2004.04906*.

Nora Kassner and Hinrich Schütze. 2020. Bert-knn: Adding a knn search component to pretrained language models for better qa. *arXiv preprint arXiv:2005.00766*.

Urvashi Khandelwal, Angela Fan, Dan Jurafsky, Luke Zettlemoyer, and Mike Lewis. 2020. Nearest neighbor machine translation. *arXiv preprint arXiv:2010.00710*.

Urvashi Khandelwal, Omer Levy, Dan Jurafsky, Luke Zettlemoyer, and Mike Lewis. 2019. Generalization through memorization: Nearest neighbor language models. *arXiv preprint arXiv:1911.00172*.

Tom Kwiatkowski, Jennimaria Palomaki, Olivia Redfield, Michael Collins, Ankur Parikh, Chris Alberti, Danielle Epstein, Illia Polosukhin, Jacob Devlin, Kenton Lee, et al. 2019. Natural questions: a benchmark for question answering research. *Transactions of the Association for Computational Linguistics*, 7:453–466.

Guillaume Lample and Alexis Conneau. 2019. Cross-lingual language model pretraining. *arXiv preprint arXiv:1901.07291*.

Mike Lewis, Yinhan Liu, Naman Goyal, Marjan Ghazvininejad, Abdelrahman Mohamed, Omer Levy, Ves Stoyanov, and Luke Zettlemoyer. 2019. Bart: Denoising sequence-to-sequence pre-training for natural language generation, translation, and comprehension. *arXiv preprint arXiv:1910.13461*.

Patrick Lewis, Ethan Perez, Aleksandara Piktus, Fabio Petroni, Vladimir Karpukhin, Naman Goyal, Heinrich Küttler, Mike Lewis, Wen-tau Yih, Tim Rocktäschel, et al. 2020. Retrieval-augmented generation for knowledge-intensive nlp tasks. *arXiv preprint arXiv:2005.11401*.

Juncen Li, Robin Jia, He He, and Percy Liang. 2018. Delete, retrieve, generate: A simple approach to sentiment and style transfer. *arXiv preprint arXiv:1804.06437*.

Yinhan Liu, Myle Ott, Naman Goyal, Jingfei Du, Mandar Joshi, Danqi Chen, Omer Levy, Mike Lewis, Luke Zettlemoyer, and Veselin Stoyanov. 2019. Roberta: A robustly optimized bert pretraining approach. *arXiv preprint arXiv:1907.11692*.

Andrew Maas, Raymond E Daly, Peter T Pham, Dan Huang, Andrew Y Ng, and Christopher Potts. 2011. Learning word vectors for sentiment analysis. In *Proceedings of the 49th annual meeting of the association for computational linguistics: Human language technologies*, pages 142–150.

Yuning Mao, Pengcheng He, Xiaodong Liu, Yelong Shen, Jianfeng Gao, Jiawei Han, and Weizhu Chen. 2020. Generation-augmented retrieval for open-domain question answering. *arXiv preprint arXiv:2009.08553*.

Gaurav Pandey, Danish Contractor, Vineet Kumar, and Sachindra Joshi. 2018. Exemplar encoder-decoder for neural conversation generation. In *Proceedings of the 56th Annual Meeting of the Association for Computational Linguistics (Volume 1: Long Papers)*, pages 1329–1338.

Kishore Papineni, Salim Roukos, Todd Ward, and Wei-Jing Zhu. 2002. Bleu: a method for automatic evaluation of machine translation. In *Proceedings of the 40th annual meeting of the Association for Computational Linguistics*, pages 311–318.

Ankur P Parikh, Xuezhi Wang, Sebastian Gehrmann, Manaal Faruqui, Bhuwan Dhingra, Diyi Yang, and Dipanjan Das. 2020. ToTTo: A controlled table-to-text generation dataset. In *Proceedings of EMNLP*.

Hao Peng, Ankur P Parikh, Manaal Faruqui, Bhuwan Dhingra, and Dipanjan Das. 2019. Text generation with exemplar-based adaptive decoding. *arXiv preprint arXiv:1904.04428*.

Alec Radford, Karthik Narasimhan, Tim Salimans, and Ilya Sutskever. 2018. Improving language understanding by generative pre-training.

Alec Radford, Jeffrey Wu, Rewon Child, David Luan, Dario Amodei, and Ilya Sutskever. 2019. Language models are unsupervised multitask learners. *OpenAI blog*, 1(8):9.

Colin Raffel, Noam Shazeer, Adam Roberts, Katherine Lee, Sharan Narang, Michael Matena, Yanqi Zhou, Wei Li, and Peter J Liu. 2019. Exploring the limits of transfer learning with a unified text-to-text transformer. *arXiv preprint arXiv:1910.10683*.

Nazneen Fatema Rajani, Ben Krause, Wengpeng Yin, Tong Niu, Richard Socher, and Caiming Xiong. 2020. Explaining and improving model behavior with k nearest neighbor representations. *arXiv preprint arXiv:2010.09030*.

Nils Reimers and Iryna Gurevych. 2019. Sentence-bert: Sentence embeddings using siamese bert-networks. *arXiv preprint arXiv:1908.10084*.

Nils Reimers and Iryna Gurevych. 2020. Making monolingual sentence embeddings multilingual using knowledge distillation. *arXiv preprint arXiv:2004.09813*.

Taylor Shin, Yasaman Razeghi, Robert L Logan IV, Eric Wallace, and Sameer Singh. 2020. Autoprompt: Eliciting knowledge from language models with automatically generated prompts. *arXiv preprint arXiv:2010.15980*.

Richard Socher, Alex Perelygin, Jean Wu, Jason Chuang, Christopher D Manning, Andrew Y Ng, and Christopher Potts. 2013. Recursive deep models for semantic compositionality over a sentiment treebank. In *Proceedings of the 2013 conference on empirical methods in natural language processing*, pages 1631–1642.

Yiping Song, Rui Yan, Xiang Li, Dongyan Zhao, and Ming Zhang. 2016. Two are better than one: An ensemble of retrieval-and generation-based dialog systems. *arXiv preprint arXiv:1610.07149*.

Eiichiro Sumita and HDA Hitoshi. 1991. Experiments and prospects of example-based machine translation. In *29th Annual Meeting of the Association for Computational Linguistics*, pages 185–192.

Ashish Vaswani, Noam Shazeer, Niki Parmar, Jakob Uszkoreit, Llion Jones, Aidan N Gomez, Łukasz Kaiser, and Illia Polosukhin. 2017. Attention is all you need. *Advances in neural information processing systems*, 30:5998–6008.

Alex Wang, Amanpreet Singh, Julian Michael, Felix Hill, Omer Levy, and Samuel R Bowman. 2018. Glue: A multi-task benchmark and analysis platform for natural language understanding. *arXiv preprint arXiv:1804.07461*.

Jason Weston, Emily Dinan, and Alexander H Miller. 2018. Retrieve and refine: Improved sequence generation models for dialogue. *arXiv preprint arXiv:1808.04776*.

Adina Williams, Nikita Nangia, and Samuel R Bowman. 2017. A broad-coverage challenge corpus for sentence understanding through inference. *arXiv preprint arXiv:1704.05426*.

Thomas Wolf, Lysandre Debut, Victor Sanh, Julien Chaumond, Clement Delangue, Anthony Moi, Pierric Cistac, Tim Rault, Rémi Louf, Morgan Funtowicz, et al. 2019. Huggingface's transformers: State-of-the-art natural language processing. *arXiv preprint arXiv:1910.03771*.

Yu Wu, Furu Wei, Shaohan Huang, Yunli Wang, Zhoujun Li, and Ming Zhou. 2019. Response generation by context-aware prototype editing. In *Proceedings of the AAAI Conference on Artificial Intelligence*, volume 33, pages 7281–7288.

Linting Xue, Noah Constant, Adam Roberts, Mihir Kale, Rami Al-Rfou, Aditya Siddhant, Aditya Barua, and Colin Raffel. 2020. mt5: A massively multilingual pre-trained text-to-text transformer. *arXiv preprint arXiv:2010.11934*.

Rui Yan, Yiping Song, and Hua Wu. 2016. Learning to respond with deep neural networks for retrieval-based human-computer conversation system. In *Proceedings of the 39th International ACM SIGIR conference on Research and Development in Information Retrieval*, pages 55–64.

Zhilin Yang, Zihang Dai, Yiming Yang, Jaime Carbonell, Russ R Salakhutdinov, and Quoc V Le. 2019. Xlnet: Generalized autoregressive pretraining for language understanding. In *Advances in neural information processing systems*, pages 5753–5763.

Tony Z Zhao, Eric Wallace, Shi Feng, Dan Klein, and Sameer Singh. 2021. Calibrate before use: Improving few-shot performance of language models. *arXiv preprint arXiv:2102.09690*.

Morteza Ziyadi, Yuting Sun, Abhishek Goswami, Jade Huang, and Weizhu Chen. 2020. Example-based named entity recognition. *arXiv preprint arXiv:2008.10570*.

A An Example of In-context Learning

As shown in the illustration of Figure 3, GPT-3 is asked to translate "mountain" to its German version based on the three examples given as part of the input.

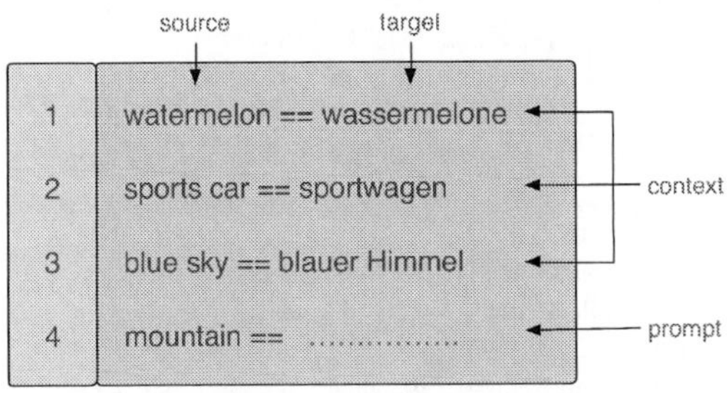

Figure 3: The figure above shows how to perform in-context learning with a language model. Three in-context examples and the test prompt are concatenated as a single string input for GPT-3, with a special character "\n" inserted between two adjacent examples. GPT-3 keeps generating tokens until there is a special character "\n".

B Data Split

Dataset	Train	Dev	Test
SST-2	67k	872	1.8k
IMDB	25k	-	25k
ToTTo	120k	7.7k	7.7k
NQ	79k	8.8k	3.6k
WQ	3.4k	361	2k
TriviaQA	78.8k	8.8k	11.3k

Table 9: Data split for different datasets. In-context examples are selected from the training set. Because ToTTo and TriviaQA require submitting to their leaderboards, the evaluation is done on the dev sets. For all other datasets, the evaluation is done on the test sets.

C Complete ToTTo Case Study

Due to the length limit of the main paper, we present in the appendix the full ToTTo case study comparing the random sampling baseline and our proposed KATE method. We present the case study in Table 10.

As we have discussed in the main paper, the in-context examples retrieved by KATE facilitates GPT-3 to effectively extract key information from the given table. Detailed numbers such as the number of points, rebounds, and assists have all been included in the sentence.

In contrast, the sentence generated by GPT-3 using randomly sampled in-context examples only extract partial information from the table. Only the number of points is included while the numbers of rebounds and assists are ignored. Moreover, the random sampling baseline could lead to the issue of hallucination. Both "senior year" and "University of Texas" are not present in the given table. One may wonder whether these wrong phrases were present in the randomly sampled in-context examples, which might have caused this issue. However, if we look at the randomly sampled in-context examples in the second block of the table, such information do not exist. This suggests such hallucinated phrases are generated by the language model itself.

This comparison provides some key insights on why KATE works better than the random sampling baseline. By retrieving semantically/syntactically similar in-context examples, KATE provides GPT-3 with a much more accurate template/structure to do text generation. Without such structure, GPT-3 can generate sentences that are fluent but do not meet the goal of a particular task.

D On Prompt Engineering vs. Fine-tuning

As we mentioned in the main paper, given a training dataset, we could take the full advantage of the GPT-3's model strength through fine-tuning. However, there are several advantages of prompt engineering over fine-tuning. First, fine-tuning requires access to the model parameters and gradients. It is impossible to access this information via the current GPT-3's API. Second, fine-tuning large models are time-consuming and costly. Ordinary research labs and individual developers do not have resources to accomplish such tasks. Third, storing large fine-tuned model checkpoints requires large storage space. Even if GPT-3 is fine-tuned and stored for many specific tasks/datasets, many fine-tuned checkpoints may not be frequently called. This is not energy efficient. Our proposed KATE method does not require costly fine-tuning and improves the random baseline on both text classification and generation tasks, sometimes by a significant margin. This makes it more practical to deploy the same GPT-3 model across all tasks.

E T5 Baseline

Although our primary goal is to improve GPT-3's in-context learning ability, we also include the fine-tuned T5 results as a reference (3B T5 on SST-2 and

Test Table	**Table**: <page_title >Trey Johnson <section_title >College <table ><cell >32 <col_header > GP <cell >4.8 <col_header >RPG <cell >2.3 <col_header >APG <cell >23.5 <col_header >PPG
Randomly Sampled Examples	**Table**: <page_title >List of RAGBRAI overnight stops <section_title >By year <table ><cell > 1986 <col_header ><col_header >Year <cell >Audubon (1) <col_header >Route - start to finish (number indicates occurrence) <col_header >Monday <cell >2006 <col_header ><col_header > Year <cell >Audubon (2) <col_header >Route - start to finish (number indicates occurrence) <col_header >Monday **Sentence**: Audubon has been an RAGBRAI overnight stop in 1986 and 2006. **Table**: <page_title >List of Administrators of British Brunei <section_title >British Brunei administrators <table ><cell >Malcolm Stewart Hannibal McArthur <col_header >Consul Generals to Brunei <col_header >British Consuls in Brunei <col_header >British Residents in Brunei **Sentence**: Malcolm Stewart Hannibal McArthur was the first British resident in Brunei.
KATE-Retrieved Examples	**Table**: <page_title >Dedric Lawson <section_title >College <table ><cell >9.9 <col_header > RPG <cell >3.3 <col_header >APG <cell >19.2 <col_header >PPG **Sentence**: Dedric Lawson averaged 19.2 points, 9.9 rebounds and 3.3 assists per game. **Table**: <page_title >Carsen Edwards <section_title >College <table ><cell >3.8 <col_header > RPG <cell >2.8 <col_header >APG <cell >18.5 <col_header >PPG **Sentence**: Edwards averaged 18.5 points, 3.8 rebounds and 2.8 assists per game.
Predictions	**Ground-truth**: Trey Johnson averaged 23.5 points, 4.8 rebounds, and 2.3 assists in 32 games. **Random**: Trey Johnson averaged 23.5 points per game in his senior year at the University of Texas. **KATE**: Johnson averaged 23.5 points, 4.8 rebounds and 2.3 assists per game.

Table 10: A sample of retrieved in-context examples from the ToTTo dataset. For the KATE method, GPT-3 pays more attention to detailed information such as the number of points, rebounds, and assists. In contrast, the random selection method leads GPT-3 to generate details which do not exist in the original table. Information such as "senior year" and "University of Texas" also do not exist in the randomly sampled in-context examples. This suggests that the wrong information was generated by the language model itself. Although the sentence by the random sampling baseline is fluent, it does meet the goal of the table-to-text task.

ToTTo datasets, and 11B T5 on the QA datasets). The reason for reporting the 3B T5 results on the SST-2 and ToTTo datasets is that this is the largest T5 model we can use. For the 3B T5 model, Google Colab [3] provides a free V2-8 TPU to fine-tune the 3B model. We used the Colab tutorial notebook to fine-tune the 3B T5 model on the SST-2 and ToTTo training sets. We couldn't fine-tune the 11B T5 model because the model size is too large. Fine-tuning such a large model requires a V3-8 TPU, which is not free of charge. Fortunately, the original GPT-3 paper (Brown et al., 2020) has already reported the finet-tuned 11B T5 results on the three QA datasets, so we reuse these results in our main paper for the QA task. Our proposed KATE method significantly improves GPT-3, performing comparably to the fine-tuned T5 model on the table-to-text task and outperforming the fine-tuned T5 model on the QA task.

F Details on Retrieval Modules

As we mention in the main paper, we use the pre-trained RoBERTa-large model (Liu et al., 2019) as the first retrieval module, which has 355M parameters and is pre-trained with the MLM (masked language modeling) objective. The result given by this module is denoted as $\text{KATE}_{\text{roberta}}$. We directly download this model from the HuggingFace Model Zoo (MIT license) [4]. All other retrieval modules share the same architecture as the RoBERTa-large module but are fine-tuned on specific datasets.

For the fine-tuned retrieval modules, the first we use is the RoBERTa-large model fine-tuned on the SNLI and MultiNLI datasets (KATE_{nli}) (Bowman et al., 2015; Williams et al., 2017); the next we use is the RoBERTa-large model fine-tuned on the SNLI and MultiNLI dataset and then on the STS-B datasets ($\text{KATE}_{\text{nli+sts-b}}$) (Cer et al., 2017). These fine-tuned models have already been accomplished and included by the Sentence-BERT family and are publicly available, so we directly download from the Sentence-BERT Model Zoo [5].

Lastly, specifically for the sentiment analysis task, we include a RoBERTa-large model fine-tuned on the SST-2 dataset ($\text{KATE}_{\text{sst-2}}$) (Socher et al., 2013; Wang et al., 2018). At the time of our

[3] The Colab notebook on how to fine-tune the 3B T5 model can be found at https://github.com/google-research/text-to-text-transfer-transformer.

[4] The HuggingFace Model Zoo can be found at https://huggingface.co/models.

[5] The Sentence-BERT Model Zoo can be found at https://huggingface.co/sentence-transformers.

research, we didn't find a good publicly available fine-tuned model, so we fine-tune the pre-trained RoBERTa-large model on SST-2 by ourselves. The exact fine-tuning procedure, including the hyperparameters and learning rate, can be found at the HuggingFace website [6]. We fine-tune the RoBERTa-large model using a single V100 GPU.

G Prompt Templates Used

For reproducibility, we show the prompt templates used for all tasks in Tables 11 .

[6]The fine-tuning script we use can be found at `https://huggingface.co/transformers/v2.7.0/examples.html#glue`.

Task	Prompt Template
SST-2 & IMDB	Sentence: comes from the brave , uninhibited performances. Label: Positive Sentence: This tearful movie about a sister and her battle to save as many souls as she can is very moving. The film does well in picking up the characters and showing how Sister Helen deals with each. A wonderful journey from life to death. Label:
ToTTo	Table: <page_title>Dedric Lawson <section_title>College <table><cell>9.9 <col_header>RPG <cell>3.3 <col_header>APG <cell>19.2 <col_header>PPG Sentence: Dedric Lawson averaged 19.2 points, 9.9 rebounds and 3.3 assists per game. Table: <page_title>Trey Johnson <section_title>College <table><cell>32 <col_header>GP <cell>4.8 <col_header>RPG <cell>2.3 <col_header>APG <cell>23.5 <col_header>PPG Sentence:
QA	Q: The landscape design of the Gardens of Versailles is known as which style? A: The Persian style of architecture. Q: The Mughal Gardens of Rashtrapati Bhavan is modelled on which garden? A:

Table 11: The prompt templates used for all tasks discussed in the paper. We show only one in-context example per task for illustration purposes.

Author Index

Association for Computational Linguistics
209 N. Eighth Street
Stroudsburg, Pennsylvania 18360

ISBN 978-1-7138-6733-3

9 781713 867333

CURRAN ASSOCIATES INC.
proceedings.com